Mark Foley   Diane Hall

ELEMENTARY

Total English

Students' Book

PEARSON
Longman

Contents

LESSON 3	COMMUNICATION	FILM BANK
Grammar: *a/an;* negative forms of *to be* **Vocabulary:** jobs **Can do:** understand and complete a simple form	**Can do:** start and finish a basic conversation	Meeting people page 131
Grammar: *this, that, these, those,* noun plurals **Vocabulary:** everyday objects; colours; some adjectives **Can do:** identify everyday objects	**Can do:** ask simple questions for information and understand simple answers	Unreal City page 132
Functions: making suggestions; using the phone **Vocabulary:** large numbers **Can do:** understand and leave a simple phone message	**Can do:** talk about other people's abilities	Deborah's day page 133
Grammar: object pronouns; *I'd like* **Vocabulary:** menus, prices **Can do:** order food in a fast food restaurant	**Can do:** shop for food at a market	Two soups page 134
Grammar: modifiers *(very, quite, really)* **Vocabulary:** adjectives to describe places **Can do:** write an informal email about your country	**Can do:** talk about furnishing an apartment	ResidenSea page 135
Grammar: Past Simple: negative **Vocabulary:** transport **Can do:** describe your last holiday	**Can do:** understand a store guide and ask for things in shops	Amazing buildings page 136
Grammar: Past Simple: irregular verbs **Vocabulary:** phrasal verbs **Can do:** understand an article	**Can do:** identify a person from a simple description	Great Expectations page 137
Grammar: Present Simple and Present Continuous **Vocabulary:** the weather; health **Can do:** take part in a factual conversation on a simple topic	**Can do:** make a complaint in a shop, write a simple letter of complaint	The Notting Hill Carnival page 138
Grammar: *prefer* + noun/*-ing* form; *will* for spontaneous decisions and offers **Vocabulary:** art **Can do:** talk about personal preferences	**Can do:** discuss and plan activities	Spirit of the city page 139
Grammar: *-ing* form as a noun (subject only) **Vocabulary:** types of transport **Can do:** book a travel ticket	**Can do:** understand basic hotel information, book a hotel room	Commuting page 140
Grammar: Present Continuous for future **Vocabulary:** education **Can do:** talk about future arrangements	**Can do:** make future arrangements and appointments	Rock climbing page 141
Grammar: verbs + infinitive/*-ing* form (*want, would like, like,* etc.) **Vocabulary:** leisure activities **Can do:** talk about likes, dislikes and ambitions	**Can do:** plan study objectives	Ten great adventures page 142

Do you know...?

1 **a** `0.1` Do you know the alphabet? Listen and repeat the alphabet.

**a b c d e f g h i
j k l m n o p q r
s t u v w x y z**

b Listen to the alphabet again. Write the letters in the correct place.

sounds	letters
/eɪ/	a h __ __
/iː/	b c d __ __ __ __ __
/e/	f l m __ __ __ __
/aɪ/	i __
/əʊ/	o
/uː/	q __ __
/ɑː/	r

c `0.2` Listen and check your answers.

d Write six consonants and three vowels. Read them to your partner. Write your partner's list.

Consonants: _____

Vowels: _____

2 **a** `0.3` Do you know numbers? Match the numbers to the words. Then listen, check and repeat.

0 1 2 3 4 5 6 7 8 9 10

eight   five   nine   oh/zero   one
         four   seven   six   ten   three   two

b `0.4` Complete the sequence with numbers from the box. Then listen, check and repeat.

> eighty   fifty   fourteen   nineteen   ninety   seventeen   seventy   sixteen   thirty   twenty-two

11 eleven	21 twenty-one
12 twelve	22 _____
13 thirteen	30 _____
14 _____	40 forty
15 fifteen	50 _____
16 _____	60 sixty
17 _____	70 _____
18 eighteen	80 _____
19 _____	90 _____
20 twenty	100 a hundred

3 **a** Do you know classroom instructions? Match the instructions to the pictures.

> Complete.   Ask and answer.   Correct.   Match.
> Look at page...   Check your answers.   Write.
> Repeat.   Listen.   Read.

b `0.5` Listen and check your answers.

4 **a** Do you know English words? Look at the photos. Write the things you see in the table.

FOOD / DRINK	
FAMILY	
EQUIPMENT	
SPORT	
TRANSPORT	
COLOURS	

b Work in groups. Do you know other English words? Write them in the table.

1 Your life

Lead-in

1 a **1.1** Complete the dialogues. Use expressions from the box. Then listen and check.

> My name's   Hello   Hi   What's your name   I'm   It's   meet

1 A: Hi _____ Jana. _____ _____ _____?
  B: _____, Jana. _____ _____ Dominik.
2 A: _____ _____ _____, please?
  B: _____ Patricia Pérez.
3 A: Hello. _____ _____ David Cooper.
  B: _____. _____ Lisa Smith. Nice to _____ you.

b Match the three dialogues to the three photos on the left.

c Practise the dialogues with your classmates.

2 a **1.2** Listen and repeat this phone number.

020 651 347

b **1.3** Now listen and write the phone numbers.

01452 946 713

c Practise with a partner.

A: Say a phone number from Exercise 2b.
B: Point at the correct number.

Grammar	subject pronouns + positive forms of *to be*
Can do	talk about where you are from

Vocabulary | countries and nationalities

1 Find the countries on the map.

United States of America [A]   Australia [ ]
Britain [ ]   Brazil [ ]   China [ ]   Finland [ ]
France [ ]   Germany [ ]   Greece [ ]   Italy [ ]
Japan [ ]   Poland [ ]   Russia [ ]   Spain [ ]
Turkey [ ]

2 **a** Look at the photos and the box. Ask and answer.

> Gong Li   Penélope Cruz   Nicole Kidman
> a Nokia phone   a Jaguar car   Will Smith
> a Gucci handbag   ~~Paulo Coelho~~
> Roman Polanski   Ralf and Michael Schumacher
> Catherine Deneuve and Gerard Depardieu

1 A: *Who is he?*   B: *He's Paulo Coelho.*

2 A: *Who is she?*   B: *She's ...*

3 A: *What is it?*   B: *It's ...*

4 A: *Who are they?*   B: *They're ...*

b Match the photos to the countries.
Paulo Coelho - Brazil

3 **a** Ask and answer about the people and objects in the photos.

A: *Where is Paulo Coelho from?*
B: *He's from Brazil. He's Brazilian.*
A: *Where are Nokia phones from?*
B: *They're from Finland. They're Finnish.*

b `1.4` Listen and check your answers.

4 Complete the table. Then listen again and check.

COUNTRY	NATIONALITY	ENDING
Australia	1 *Australian*	*(i)an*
2 _____	American	
Brazil	3 _____	
Italy	4 _____	
5 _____	German	
Russia	Russian	
6 _____	Spanish	*ish*
Poland	7 _____	
Britain	8 _____	
9 _____	Finnish	
Turkey	Turkish	
China	10 _____	*ese*
Japan	Japanese	
11 _____	French	
Greece	Greek	

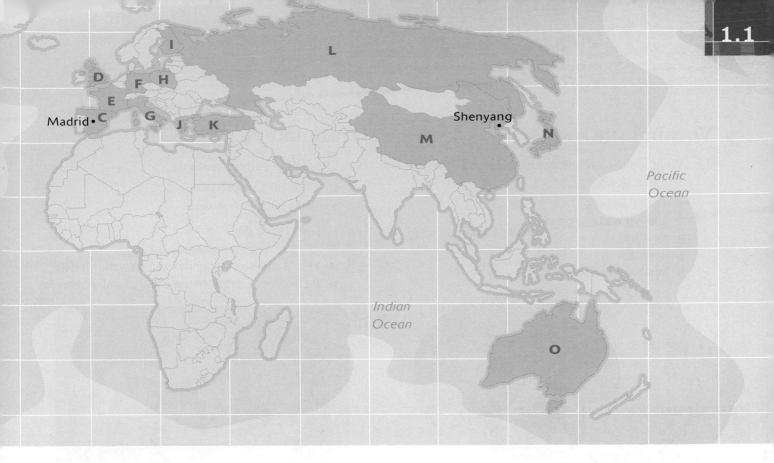

Madrid • C   G   J   K

Shenyang

Pacific Ocean

Indian Ocean

Pronunciation

5   **a**   **1.5**   Listen and repeat the nationality words.

> ### Lifelong learning
>
> **How to record stress**
> <u>Underline</u> the syllable with the strong sound.
> Aust<u>ra</u>lian

b Listen again. Write the words and <u>underline</u> the stress.

c Practise the words. **Student A:** say a name. **Student B:** say the nationality.

A: *Roman Polanski*

B: *He's Polish.*

6   **a**   Where are the people from? Write the names.

I'm from Rio de Janeiro. = *Paulo Coelho*

1   I'm from Philadelphia. = _____
2   We're from Germany. = _____
3   I'm from Madrid. = _____
4   I'm from Shenyang. = _____
5   We're from France. = _____

b Imagine you are one of the people in the pictures. Who are you? Ask and answer.

A: *Where are you from?*

B: *I'm from Rio de Janeiro.*

A: *You're Paulo Coelho.*

B: *Yes, that's right.*

Grammar | *to be* (positive)

7   **a**   Complete the Active grammar box with *am, is* or *are*.

> ### Active grammar
>
> I _____ (I'm)
> You __are__ (you're)
> He _____ (he's)
> She _____ (she's)   from
> It _____ (it's)   Russia.
> We _____ (we're)
> You _____ (you're)
> They _____ (they're)

see Reference page 13

b Complete the sentences.

I '<u>m</u> Brazilian. *I* 'm from São Paulo.

1   Jennifer López _____ American. _____'s from New York.
2   We'_____ Polish. _____'re from Warsaw.
3   A: Excuse me, where _____ you _____?
    B: I'_____ from Colombia.
4   A: What is _____? B: It'_____ a dictionary.
5   A: Who are _____? B: They'_____ students in my class.

8   Race your classmates. Work in pairs. Say the name of a country to another pair. Write names of famous people and things from the country in two minutes.

1.2 Family ties

Vocabulary | families

1 What are their relationships? Match 1–5 to the pictures (A–E).

1 father and son ☐
2 mother and daughter ☐
3 brothers ☐
4 sisters ☐
5 husband and wife ☐

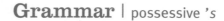

2 Match the sentence halves.

1 Julio Iglesias is   a   Bill's wife.
2 Hillary Clinton is   b   Serena's sister.
3 Venus Williams is   c   Enrique's father.
4 Prince Harry is   d   Madonna's daughter.
5 Lourdes is   e   Prince William's brother.

Grammar | possessive 's

3 Choose the correct sentence.

1 Bill is Hillary husband.
2 Bill is Hillary's husband.

see Reference page 13

4 **a** This is the Bundy family from TV's *Married ... with Children*. Complete the Bundy family tree.

b Make eight sentences about the family. Use 's.

> ~~wife~~   ~~son~~   husband   sister   brother
> mother   father   daughter

Peggy is Al's wife. Bud is Al and Peggy's son.

5 **a** Match the family words to the meanings.

1 mother and father   a   uncle
2 sons and daughters   b   grandmother
3 father's or mother's brother   c   nephew
4 father's or mother's sister   d   parents
5 mother's or father's mother   e   aunt
6 mother's or father's father   f   niece
7 brother's or sister's son   g   children
8 brother's or sister's daughter   h   grandfather

b Find the meanings in a dictionary.

> stepbrother   father-in-law   girlfriend
> best friend   cousins   grandparents

Pronunciation

6 a **1.6** Listen to the underlined sound /ʌ/.

m**o**ther   br**o**ther

b **1.7** Listen and repeat these family words. Underline the sound /ʌ/ in five words.

1 husband   2 father   3 grandmother
4 sister-in-law   5 daughter   6 cousin
7 uncle   8 nephew   9 grandson   10 niece

Grammar | possessive adjectives

7 Read about the Bundy family. Complete the Active grammar box with the underlined words.

Hi. Welcome to my crazy family – my husband Al and our children Bud and Kelly!

Meet the Bundy family: Al Bundy is married to Peggy, his beautiful wife, and Bud and Kelly are their children. Kelly is sixteen and her little brother, Bud, is thirteen. They're a crazy family!

Active grammar

Subject pronouns	Possessive adjectives
I	_____
you	your
he	_____
she	_____
we	_____
you	your
they	_____

see Reference page 13

8 Complete the gaps with possessive adjectives.

Clare is *our* sister. (we)

1 _____ teacher is English. (I)
2 Mr and Mrs Schegel are _____ parents. (they)
3 What is _____ homework? (we)
4 How old is _____ best friend? (you)
5 A: Are _____ grandparents from Madrid? (you)
  B: Yes, they are.
6 A: Are _____ sisters married? (she)
  B: No, they are single.
7 A: Is _____ boyfriend American? (you)
  B: No, he's Australian.
8 A: Is Tomas _____ brother? (he)
  B: Yes, he is.

Grammar | *to be* (questions)

9 Look at sentences 5–8 in Ex. 8 again. Complete the Active grammar box with *is* or *are*.

Active grammar

	he she it	American?	Yes,	he she it	___.
___	we you they	American?	Yes,	we you they	___.

see Reference page 13

Listening

10 a Complete the questions and answers with *she, he, my, your, is* or *are*.

1 She's nice. Is she _____ mother?
2 She's young! How old _____ she?
3 Really? And this man, is _____ your uncle?
4 Where _____ he from?
5 The girls are beautiful. Are they _____ sisters?
6 How old _____ they?

a No. Clare's _____ sister and Liz _____ her best friend.
b Well, she _____ forty-eight.
c No, he's _____ sister's boyfriend.
d No, _____'s my mother-in-law, Jack's mother.
e Clare _____ eighteen and Liz _____ twenty-two.
f He _____ from Warsaw.

b **1.8** Listen and match 1–6 to a–f.

Person to person

11 Write the names of five people in your family. Show them to your partner. Ask and answer.

A: *Who's Elena?*
B: *She's my aunt.*
A: *Is she your mother's sister?*
B: *No, she's my father's sister.*

1.3 Work on the web

A B C D E F G H I

Vocabulary | jobs

1 **a** Look at the photos and choose the correct words. Talk to a partner.

> an architect   an artist
> a bank clerk   a dentist
> a doctor   an electrician
> an engineer   a teacher
> a journalist   a judge
> a lawyer   a nurse
> a police officer
> a secretary
> a housewife/husband
> a shop assistant
> a student   a traffic warden
> a computer programmer
> retired   unemployed

A: *A is a secretary.*

B: *No, I think she's a journalist.*

A: *H is unemployed.*

B: *Yes, that's right.*

b Write the correct jobs.

Grammar | *a/an*

2 Look at the jobs in Ex. 1a again. Complete the Active grammar box with *a* or *an*.

> ### Active grammar
>
> Use _____ before vowel sounds (a, e, etc.). *She's* _____ *artist.*
>
> Use _____ before consonant sounds (b, h, w, etc.). *He's* _____ *lawyer.*

see Reference page 13

3 Write *a* or *an*.

_a_ mother

1 ___ answer   2 ___ uncle   3 ___ hamburger   4 ___ taxi

5 ___ aunt   6 ___ number   7 ___ family   8 ___ handbag

Person to person

4 **a** Guess other students' jobs. Use a dictionary.

A: *Are you a taxi driver?*   A: *Are you a ...*

B: *No, I'm not a taxi driver.*   B: *Yes, I am./No, I'm not a ...*

b Ask and answer about your partner's family or friends.

> ~~brother~~   mother   father
> sister   uncle   best friend

A: Is your brother a manager?

B: No, he isn't. He's an accountant.

Grammar | *to be* (negative)

5 Complete the Active grammar box with *'m not* and *isn't*.

> **Active grammar**
>
> | I | _____ | : | We aren't |
> | He | _____ | : | You aren't |
> | She | _____ | : | They aren't |

see Reference page 13

6 Complete the sentences with the correct negative form of *to be*.

We *aren't* from the United States.

1 My sister _____ married.
2 I _____ a shop assistant, I'm the manager!
3 My cousins are sixteen but they _____ at school.
4 Uncle John is old now but he _____ retired.
5 You _____ English. Where are you from?
6 I _____ unemployed; I'm retired.

Reading

7 Look at the form on the website. Match the questions to the parts of the form.

a How old are you? `3`
b What's your (mobile) phone number? ☐
c What's your surname? ☐
d What's your email address? ☐
e Where are you from? ☐
f What's your job? ☐
g What's your first name? ☐
h What's your address? ☐
i What's your nationality? ☐

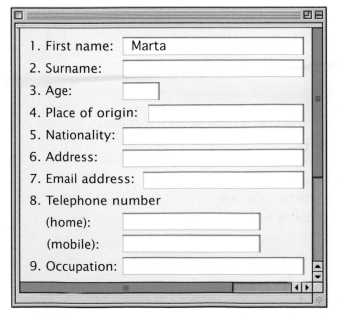

1. First name: Marta
2. Surname:
3. Age:
4. Place of origin:
5. Nationality:
6. Address:
7. Email address:
8. Telephone number
   (home):
   (mobile):
9. Occupation:

Listening

8 **a** 🔊**1.9** Listen. Who are Marta and Jake?

b Listen again and complete the form on the website.

c Check your answers with a partner.

A: *What's her surname?*
B: *Nowak. How old is she?*
A: *She's twenty-two.*

Speaking

9 Copy the form in Ex. 7. Ask your partner the questions to complete the form.

10 Work in pairs. Complete the forms.

Student A: ask and answer about the forms below.
Student B: look at page 125.

A: *OK. Let's start with Form A. Anne – what's her surname?*
B: *Simons – S-I-M-O-N-S.*
A: *What's her nationality?*

A

First name: A N N E
Surname:
Age: 3 4
Place of origin: V A N C O U V E R   C A N A D A
Nationality:
Address: 1 2   H Y T H E   S T R E E T
L O N D O N
Email address:

Telephone number (home): 0 2 0 8 1 4 2 9 0 5 5
Telephone number (mobile):
Occupation: L A W Y E R

B

First name:
Surname: M A R S H A L L
Age:
Place of origin:
Nationality: A U S T R A L I A N
Address:

Email address: d . m a r s h a l l @ t o t a l .
c o m
Telephone number (home):
Telephone number (mobile): 0 7 9 5 4 0 0 6 8 9 3
Occupation:

1 Communication

Making conversation

1 a 🔊 **1.10** Listen to two dialogues and tick (✓) the expressions you hear.

Excuse me … ☐   See you later. ☐
Bye. ☐   Hello. ☐   Hi. ☐
Good morning. ☐
See you tomorrow. ☐   Goodbye. ☐

b Listen again. Complete the How to box.

HOW TO …

start and finish a basic conversation

Start	*Hello.*
	_____
	_____
	_____
Finish	*See you tomorrow.*
	_____
	_____
	_____

2 a Complete the dialogues with the expressions in the box.

> What's your job?
> No, I'm not. I'm single.
> I'm from Barcelona.
> Hello Maria, I'm Clara.
> Excuse me, are you Silvio?
> What's your email address?

1 A: Hello, I'm Maria.
   B: _____
   A: Pleased to meet you.

2 A: _____
   B: Yes, I am. What's your name?
   A: My name's Jordi.

3 A: Where are you from?
   B: _____

4 A: _____
   B: It's silvio77@hotserve.com.

5 A: _____
   B: I'm a student at the university.

6 A: Are you married?
   B: _____

b 🔊 **1.11** Listen and check your answers.

3 Practise the dialogues in Ex. 2a with a partner. Use real information!

4 a Match a–d to numbers on the application form.

a your birthday ___

b married or single ___

c exams and certificates ___

d name of a relative (husband or wife, mother or father) ___

⟳ Saver Bank plc

JOB APPLICATION FORM
Please complete in pen and sign at the bottom.

1 Surname: _____

2 First name: _____

3 Date of birth: _____ 4 Age: _____

5 Marital status: _____

6 Place of origin: _____

7 Nationality: _____

8 Passport or identity card number: _____

9 Address: _____
   _____

10 Email address: _____

11 Telephone number: _____

12 Occupation: _____

13 Qualifications: _____

14 Languages: _____

15 Next of kin: _____

Please sign here:

b Complete the form with information about *you*.

5 a Exchange your forms with other students. Find:

• a married student.

• a student with two languages.

• a student with the letter 'Y' in his/her name.

• a student with a university degree.

• a student with a different place of origin.

b Tell the class your results.

A: *Maria. She's married.*

Subject pronouns, possessive adjectives and possessive *'s*

There are eight subject pronouns in English. Use subject pronouns before verbs. There are also eight possessive adjectives. Use possessive adjectives before nouns.

Subject pronouns	*I* *you* *he* *she* *it* *we* *you* *they*	+ verb	Possessive adjectives	*my* *your* *his* *her* *its* *our* *your* *their*	+ noun

Possessive adjectives and noun + *'s* have the meaning *belongs to* (for things). With people they show relationships.

*This is John's phone.   This is **his** phone.*

*Peggy is Al's wife.   Peggy is **his** wife.*

Verb *to be*

⊕	*I*	*'m*	
	You	*'re*	*German. / from Germany.*
	He / She / It	*'s*	
	We / You / They	*'re*	
⊖	*I*	*'m not*	
	You	*aren't*	*Italian. / from Italy.*
	He / She / It	*isn't*	
	We / You / They	*aren't*	

❓						
Am	*I*			*I*	*am. ('m not)*
Are	*you*	*American?*	*Yes, (No,)*	*you*	*are. (aren't)*
Is	*he / she / it*			*he / she / it*	*is. (isn't)*
Are	*we / you / they*			*we / you / they*	*are. (aren't)*

In informal English we usually use the contracted forms:
'm = am, 's = is, 're = are, isn't = is not, aren't = are not

*I am British. = **I'm** British. He is Brazilian. = **He's** Brazilian.*

*I'm not Italian. He/She/It **isn't** Italian. We/You/They **aren't** Italian.*

We don't use contracted forms in questions and short affirmative answers.
A: *Are you Russian?*   **B:** *Yes, I am.*

Wh- questions

We form *wh-* questions with a question word.

Who asks about a person.

What asks about a thing.

Where asks about a place.

How old asks about age.

Question word + *am/is/are* + subject pronoun.

Where *are you from?*

How old *is she?*

a/an

Use *a/an* to introduce singular nouns: *a teacher, an address.*

Use *a* before consonant sounds: *a burger, a handbag.*

Use *an* before vowel sounds: *an engineer, an uncle.*

Use *a/an* with nouns: *a doctor,* but we don't use *a/an* with adjectives: *she's unemployed*

Key vocabulary

Jobs

a bank clerk   an architect
a computer programmer
an artist   a dentist
an electrician   a doctor
an engineer   a housewife
an accountant   a househusband
a journalist   a judge   a lawyer
a nurse   a police officer
a secretary   a shop assistant
a student   a teacher
a traffic warden   a manager
a taxi driver   retired   unemployed

Family

Male:	Female:
father	mother
husband	wife
son	daughter
brother	sister
uncle	aunt
nephew	niece
grandfather	grandmother
stepfather	stepmother
father-in-law	mother-in-law

Male or female:

parents   children   cousins

1 Review and practice

1 Choose the correct word in italics.

Excuse me. Is this *my/your* bag?

1 John is twelve and *his/her* sister is fourteen.

2 This is Mariana. She's *my/her* wife's best friend.

3 Mr and Mrs Silva are teachers and *they/their* children are students.

4 We are German. *Our/Their* parents are from Frankfurt.

5 Jennifer López is American but *her/their* parents are from Puerto Rico.

6 My sister is married. *His/Her* husband is forty-three.

7 I am from Rio de Janeiro but *my/our* boyfriend is from El Salvador.

8 Tessa is married. *Her's/Tessa's* husband is Canadian.

9 Martin Sheen is a film star. Emilio Estevez and Charlie Sheen are *his/their* sons.

2 Make sentences.

Pilar and Esteban/Spain

Pilar and Esteban are from Spain.
They are Spanish.

1 Elizabeth/the United States

2 Ivan and Katia/Russia

3 I/France

4 You/Britain

5 Pavlos/Greece

6 His camera/Japan

7 I/Poland

3 Complete the questions and answers. Use information from Ex. 2.

A: (1) _*Is*_ Elizabeth British?

B: No, she (2) _*isn't*_. She's (3) _*American*_.

A: (4) _____ Katia and Ivan from Mexico?

B: No, they (5) _____. They (6) _____ from (7) _____.

A: (8) _____ Pavlos (9) _____ Greece?

B: Yes, he (10) _____.

A: (11) _____ his camera German?

B: (12) _____, it (13) _____. It's Japanese.

4 Write about you. Correct the false sentences.

I'm an English student.

That's right.

I'm from the United States.

No, I'm not from the United States. I'm from ...

1 I'm seventeen years old.

2 My parents are doctors.

3 My best friend is a student.

4 Our teacher is British.

5 My mobile phone is German.

6 My brother/sister is married.

5 Complete the dialogue with questions.

A: _*Hi, what's your name?*_

B: My name's Andreas Schmidt.

A: (1) _____

B: Yes, it is, and Schmidt is my surname.

A: (2) _____

B: I'm from Germany.

A: (3) _____

B: I'm twenty-three.

A: (4) _____

B: I'm an engineer ... This is David and Gina.

A: (5) _____

B: They're my cousins.

A: (6) _____

B: No, they aren't. They're British. My aunt is married to a British man.

6 Write *a/an*.

_*an*_ American president

1 ___ email address

2 ___ Australian actor

3 ___ first name

4 ___ Polish surname

5 ___ Japanese television

6 ___ British taxi

7 ___ Italian car

7 Find the jobs and family words in the word chains, and write them in the table.

journalisteacheretiredentistaxidriver

cousinstudenttrafficwardenursengineer

parentsonniecelectricianephew

JOBS	FAMILY
journalist	*cousins*
	parents

2 Activities

Lead-in

1 a Which activities can you see in the photos?

> go to work   leave work   have dinner   have lunch   get up
> go to bed   have breakfast   get home   leave home

b Match the activities from Ex. 1a to the parts of the day.

in the morning ___*get up,*___

in the afternoon _____

in the evening _____

at night _____

2 a **2.1** Listen and complete the times with these words.

> quarter past   half past   quarter to   o'clock

What time is it?

1 It's _____ six.

2 It's _____ five.

3 It's three _____.

4 It's _____ eight.

b What time is it? Complete the times then ask and answer.

1 It's _____ o'clock.

2 It's half past _____.

3 It's quarter to _____.

4 It's quarter past _____.

1

A fun job
for fun people!

Are you 18-25?

Be a rep for
Fun Club Holidays

- organise parties
- sell tickets for excursions
- help our clients

Call 0800 007007 now!

2

Fun Club Holidays

Fun package holidays
for young people age 18–30

Hotels, food and entertainment
included in the price!

Meet people, play games and have FUN

with **FUN CLUB**

Reading

1 Match the advertisements to the descriptions.

advertisement for a package holiday = ___
advertisement for a job = ___

Vocabulary | holidays

2 **a** Match the words to the pictures A–F.

1 restaurant ☐ 2 swimming pool/games ☐
3 entertainment ☐ 4 beach ☐
5 holiday rep and client ☐ 6 nightclub ☐

b Read the advertisements and match the verbs to the nouns.

VERB	NOUN	ADVERTISEMENT
1 have	a games	____
2 organise	b people	____
3 sell	c fun	2
4 meet	d clients	____
5 play	e parties	____
6 help	f tickets	____

c Now match each word pair to an advertisement.

Listening

3 **a** 2.2 Jenny is a holiday rep. Listen and tick (✓) the eight activities she mentions.

1 Get up ☐
2 Have breakfast ☐
3 Go to the hotels ☐
4 Tell clients about parties ☐
5 Have lunch ☐
6 Go to the office ☐
7 Organise games at the pool ☐
8 Take clients to a restaurant ☐
9 Go to a nightclub ☐
10 Get home ☐

b Listen again. Write Jenny's activities and the times in the correct place in her diary.

Morning

1 *get up* - 10.00.

2 _____

3 _____

Afternoon

4 _____

5 _____

Evening

6 _____

7 _____

8 _____

Grammar | Present Simple: *I/you/we*

4 Look at the tapescript on page 150 and complete the Active grammar box.

Active grammar

⊕	*I meet the clients.*
	Sometimes we _____ special parties.
Yes/no questions	*Do you cut with the clients?*
	_____ the games?
	Yes, I _____.
	No, I _____.
Wh- questions	*What do you do in the afternoon?*
	Where _____ for dinner?

---

see Reference page 23

5 Match the questions and answers.

1 Where do you work?   a I watch TV.

2 What do you do?   b No, I don't.

3 When do you have lunch?   c I work in a school.

     d At half past one.

4 Do you have lunch in a restaurant?   e I'm a teacher.

5 What do you do in the evening?

6 **a** Read the interview. Complete the dialogue and write the job at the end.

A: When (1) _____ you get up?

B: At ten in the evening.

A: (2) _____ you work at night?

B: Yes, I do.

A: What (3) _____ you (4) _____ in the afternoon?

B: I sleep.

A: (5) _____ do you have dinner?

B: I (6) _____ dinner at about eleven in the morning.

A: Do (7) _____ work in an office?

B: No, I (8) _____.

A: Where (9) _____ you work?

B: I (10) _____ in a hospital.

A: So, what do you do?

B: I'm a [_____].

b **2.3** Listen and check your answers. Then practise the dialogue with a partner.

7 Look at Jenny's diary in Ex. 3b. Make a diary about your daily routines.

8 Complete the How to box. Use the information from Ex. 6.

HOW TO ... **talk about your daily routine**

Ask about routines	*What _____ you _____ in the afternoon?*
Answer	*I sleep.*
Ask about times	*When _____ you get up?*
Answer	*_____ ten in the evening.*
Ask about places	*Where _____ you work?*
Answer	*I _____ in a hospital.*

Person to person

9 Interview a partner.

- What do you do in the morning?
- When do you go to work/school?
- Do you work in an office?

Jo Kinsey has an interesting job. She's a *hairdresser* – but a very special hairdresser. Jo works at Madame Tussaud's – the *wax model* museum. She starts work at 7.30. In the morning she checks the models for dirty hair and in the afternoon she washes and dries their hair.

Jeanette Ewart is a cleaner, but in a very dangerous place. She cleans the *shark tank* in the zoo in her city. She swims under the water every day to clean the tank, and she feeds the *sharks* three times a week. She's careful, but another diver waits by the tank and watches her. The visitors at the zoo watch her too.

John Wardley is an inventor. He invents exciting rides for his theme park. He walks through the theme park and he listens to people when they talk about a *ride*. He invents new rides, and the engineers make the rides. John likes his work – his theme park is the best place to work!

Reading

1 a Look at the photos. What are the jobs?

b Read the texts quickly and check your answers.

c Match A–E on the photos to the words in the texts in italics.

A _____   B _____
C _____   D _____
E _____

2 Write Jo, John or Jeanette.
This person ...
works under water. *Jeanette*

1 works in a museum.
2 thinks a lot at work.
3 starts work before eight o'clock.
4 listens to other people.
5 is very careful at work.

Vocabulary | verbs

3 Write a verb from the texts under each picture.

a

b

c

d

e

f

g

Grammar | Present Simple: *he/she/it*

4 **a** Complete the sentences with the correct form of the verbs in brackets.

1 Jo _____ (wash) and _____ (dry) the models' hair.

2 Jeanette _____ (clean) the shark tank.

3 Jo _____ (have) an interesting job.

b Complete the Active grammar box with *has, -s, -es* or *-ies*.

> ### Active grammar
>
> After *he, she* and *it,* add _____, but:
>
> 1 when the verb ends in *o, s, sh, ch* or *x,* add _____.
>
> 2 when the verb ends in consonant + *y,* omit *-y* and add _____.
>
> 3 the form of *have* after *he, she* and *it* is _____.

see Reference page 23

c Look at the texts. Which form of the verb do we use after *they* (e.g. the engineers)?

5 Complete the sentences with the correct form of the verbs in the box.

> clean have help play talk wash watch

1 My mother _____ our house.

2 The teacher _____ in English in class.

3 Jake _____ his hair every morning.

4 Matt _____ DVDs on his laptop computer.

5 Allie _____ her little sister with her homework.

6 My brothers _____ football every evening.

7 They _____ dangerous jobs.

Pronunciation

6 **a** **2.4** Listen to the endings of these three verbs. Are they all the same?

/s/ walks	/z/ listens	/ɪz/ organises

b **2.5** Listen and write the verbs in the table. Then repeat them.

Listening

7 **a** Complete the dialogue.

A: Does Jeanette like her work?

B: Yes, she does. She *loves* it.

A: _____ she clean the tank every day?

B: Yes, she _____.

A: _____ she feed the sharks every day?

B: No. She _____ them three times a week.

A: _____ she work every day?

B: No. She _____ five days a week.

b **2.6** Listen and check your answers.

8 Cross out the incorrect words in the questions.

1 ~~Does~~/Do the sharks eat/~~eats~~ every day?

2 Does/Do Jeanette clean/cleans the tank every day?

3 Does/Do Jeanette like/likes her work?

9 Complete the questions with the verbs in brackets.

Do you *work* every day? (work)

1 _____ Maria _____ her work? (like)

2 _____ your parents _____ DVDs? (watch)

3 _____ John _____ computer games? (invent)

4 _____ I _____ in my sleep? (talk)

5 _____ Anna _____ children? (have)

Speaking

10 Rob is a studio engineer. Ask and answer about his daily routine.

Student A: look at the diary on page 125.
Student B: look at the diary on page 129.

Writing

11 Write about part of Rob's day.

1 Choose morning, afternoon or evening.

2 Underline the verbs in the diary for that part of the day.

3 Write sentences with the verbs. Use *and* or *or* to join sentences.

Rob gets up at eight o' clock and he has breakfast.

Vocabulary | everyday objects and colours

1 **a** Look at the photo. Where are the people? What do they do here?

b **2.7** Listen and check your answers.

2 **a** Label the things in the picture.

> bags books watches DVD player
> laptop computer pictures shoes lamps
> suitcase video camera

fax machine

printer

8

1

5

chair

2

dishes

3 6

4 7 9

10

b **2.8** Listen and tick (✓) the things you hear.

3 Find examples of the colours in the pictures.

> ~~black~~ yellow grey brown white pink red
> orange blue purple green silver gold

The fax machine is black.

Grammar | *this, that, these, those*

4 **a** **2.9** Listen and complete the dialogues.

1

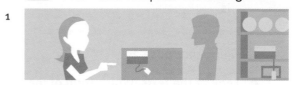

A: What's _____ ?   B: It's _____ .

2

A: What's _____ ?   B: It's _____ .

3

A: What are _____ ?   B: They're _____ .

4

A: What are _____ ?   B: They're _____ .

see Reference page 23

b Correct the <u>underlined</u> words in the sentences.

What <u>are</u> this? *What's this?*
<u>These are</u> a car. *This is a car.*

1 What colour is <u>those</u>?
2 These <u>is</u> very beautiful.
3 <u>Are</u> that your house?
4 <u>These</u> isn't very old.

Pronunciation

5 **a** `2.10` Listen to the vowel sounds. Repeat.

/ɪ/ this   /iː/ these

b `2.11` Listen and write these words in the table.

> green   listen   niece   pink   read
> sister   teacher   think

/ɪ/ this	/iː/ these

Vocabulary | adjectives

6 **a** Check these adjectives in a dictionary. Match the opposites.

> ~~bad~~ big ~~good~~ horrible modern nice old
> old-fashioned small useful useless young

bad – good

b Write sentences about you with six of the adjectives.

My house is big but my car is small.

Listening

7 **a** `2.12` Listen. Where are the people?

b Listen again. Match the dialogues to the pictures below.

c Look at the tapescript on page 151. Find six more words for everyday objects.

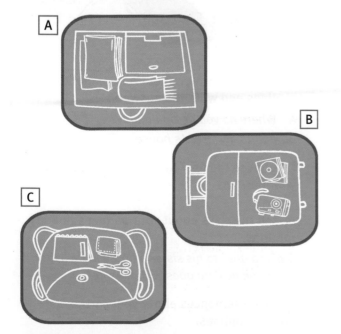

A

B

C

Grammar | noun plurals

8 **a** Complete the Active grammar box.

> ### Active grammar
>
> *one book, twenty* _____
>
> *one lamp, ten* _____
>
> *one phone, two* _____
>
> To make the regular plural of a noun, add _____.

see Reference page 23

b Some nouns change their spelling in the plural, and others are irregular. Write the plurals of these words.

regular	book → *books*, bag → _____, camera → _____, shoe → _____
word + *-es*	watch → _____, dish → _____
f → *-ves*	scarf → _____
consonant – *-y* → *-ies*	diary → *diaries*
irregular	person → *people*

> ### Lifelong learning
>
> **Irregular plurals**
>
> Use a dictionary to find irregular plurals:
>
> **diary** /ˈdaɪəri/ noun, plural **diaries**

c Find the plurals of these words and write them in the table in Ex. 8b.

> man   woman   child   wife   dictionary
> address   family   niece   class   bus

Speaking

9 Play a guessing game.

Student A: think of an object, e.g. my mobile phone.

Student B: ask *yes/no* questions. Guess the object. Use adjectives.

B: *Is it old-fashioned?*

2 Communication

Holiday routines

1 Match the photos to the captions.

1 In the city ☐
2 In the mountains ☐
3 At the beach ☐

2 a Complete the questions in the questionnaire with words from the box.

> do do get ~~go~~ go time what when ~~where~~ who

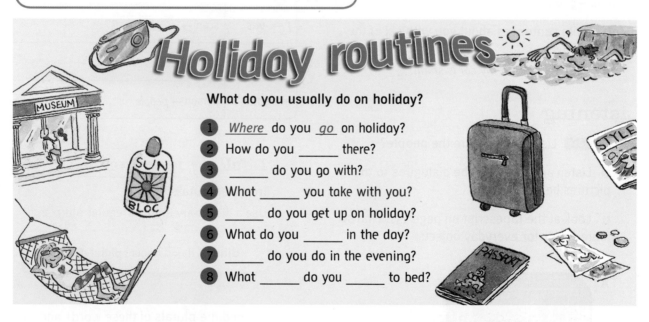

Holiday routines

What do you usually do on holiday?

1. _Where_ do you _go_ on holiday?
2. How do you _____ there?
3. _____ do you go with?
4. What _____ you take with you?
5. _____ do you get up on holiday?
6. What do you _____ in the day?
7. _____ do you do in the evening?
8. What _____ do you _____ to bed?

b Match the questions to these answers.

a my camera and a good book _4_
b to the beach ___
c at about ten in the morning ___
d go on excursions or swim ___
e at about half past eleven ___
f go to a nightclub or restaurant ___
g my friends ___
h by car ___

c What do you do? Answer the questions in the questionnaire in Ex. 2a.

3 a Ask your partner about his/her holiday routines and write the answers.

A: *Where do you go on holiday?*
B: *I go to my sister's house.*

b Choose the best holiday from the photos for your partner.

4 a Tell the class about your partner's holiday routines.

Stefano goes to his sister's house in the city. He takes the bus. He goes with his wife ...

b Make sentences about your partner's holiday routines.

Present Simple

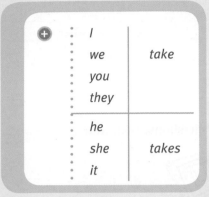

I we you they	take
he she it	takes

I **take** the train.

She **takes** the bus.

Use the Present Simple for daily routines and activities. With *I, we, you* and *they* the Present Simple form is the same as the infinitive. With *he, she* and *it* we add *-s* to the infinitive, but note these exceptions.

- verbs ending in *-ch, -s, -sh, -x* and *-o* add *-es*:

  watch → *watches, go* → *goes*

- verbs ending in *-y*, remove *-y* and add *-ies*:

  carry → *carries*

- *have* → *has*

Wh- questions

- *Wh-* word + *do* + *I/we/you/they* + infinitive

  When do you finish work?

- *Wh-* word + *does* + *he/she/it* + infinitive

  Where does he eat lunch?

- In questions, don't add *-s* to the verb.

Yes/no questions

- *Do* + *I/we/you/they* + infinitive

  Do you eat with the clients?

- *Does* + *he/she/it* + infinitive

  Does he finish at five o' clock?

- Note the short answers:

  Yes, I/we/you/they do.
  he/she/it does.

  No, I/we/you/they don't.
  he/she/it doesn't.

this, that, these, those

	Singular	Plural
Near	*this*	*these*
Far	*that*	*those*

What's **this**? Do you like **these** shoes? Look at **that** car! **Those** bags are horrible.

Noun plurals

We add *-s* to nouns to make the regular noun plural:

book → *book**s**, picture* → *picture**s***

There are some special rules.

- nouns ending *-ch, -s, -sh, -x* add *-es*:

  watch → *watch**es**, address* → *address**es***

- most nouns ending *-f*, remove *-f* and add *-ves*:

  scarf → *scar**ves**, knife* → *kni**ves***

- nouns ending consonant + *-y*, remove *-y* and add *-ies*:

  diary → *diar**ies**, city* → *cit**ies***

Note: nouns ending with a vowel + *-y* are regular: *day* → *days*

Some plural nouns are completely irregular:

man → *men, child* → *children*

Key vocabulary

Personal possessions

bag book camera car chair desk diary dish DVD player handbag fax machine lamp laptop computer magazine mobile phone picture printer scarf scissors shoes suitcase wallet watch

Basic verbs/verb phrases

Routines:

eat work watch sleep get up go to work/school/bed
have breakfast/lunch/dinner leave home/work start finish wash clean

Other verbs:

check dry feed help invent like make meet open organise play repair sell swim wait walk

1 Look at the pictures and write sentences about Clive's day. Use the verbs and phrases in the boxes.

watch   finish   eat   go   read   ~~get~~

a sandwich   the news   work   to bed
~~the bus to work~~   his emails

A   *He gets the bus to work at quarter past eight.*

2 Complete the sentences and questions with the correct form of the verbs in brackets.

She *finishes* work at five o'clock. (finish)

1   They _____ at ten o'clock on Sundays. (get up)
2   _____ he _____ a good job? (have)
3   I _____ to English lessons in the evening. (go)
4   She _____ the house in the morning. (clean)
5   What _____ you _____ on Saturday afternoons? (do)

3 Put the words in the correct order to make questions.

to you work When go do

When do you go to work?

1   she afternoon What does do in the ?
2   have Where does lunch he ?
3   to work Do take the train you ?
4   does finish he When work ?
5   What in you evening do do the ?

4 Six of these plural nouns are wrong. Find five more and correct them.

lunchs   ✗ *lunches*   4 pizzaes   _____
clients   ✔ _____   5 sandwichs   _____
1 holidaies   _____   6 sharks   _____
2 hotels   _____   7 studios   _____
3 partys   _____   8 knifes   _____

5 Complete the questions. Then write the answers.

What's *this* ?
It's a *laptop computer* .

What are _____?
They're _____.

What's _____?
It's a _____.

_____?
_____.

_____?
_____.

6 a Look at the 'personal possessions' vocabulary on page 23. Copy the table and write the objects.

PERSONAL	HOUSE/HOME	TRAVEL	EQUIPMENT
diary	chair	car	DVD player

b Look at the 'routines' vocabulary on page 23. Write the verbs in the order you do them during the day.

1 *get up* 2 *wash* 3 *have breakfast*

c Who does these things in their work? Write the jobs.

organises people on holiday *holiday rep*

1   washes people's hair _____
2   repairs cars _____
3   sells things in a shop _____
4   invents and makes machines _____
5   helps students at school _____
6   cleans the house _____
7   works in a bank _____

A

3 Free time

Lead-in

1 **a** Match the photos to verbs and verb phrases in the box.

cook   dance   go for a walk   go shopping   go to a concert
go to the gym   listen to music   meet friends   play football
play the guitar   read a book or magazine   sunbathe   swim
watch TV or a video

B

b Check the meanings of the verbs in the box with a partner.

A: *What does 'cook' mean?*
B: *It means make food, for example, lunch or dinner.*

c Where do you do the activities in Ex. 1a? Write them in the table.

C

AT HOME	IN THE PARK	AT THE SHOPS	AT A NIGHTCLUB	AT A CONCERT HALL	AT A SPORTS CENTRE/SWIMMING POOL

2 **a** Write two activities that you do, where you do them and when.

b Ask your partner questions.

What activity do you do? Where do you do it? When do you do it?

D

c Tell the class about your partner.

Mark plays the piano. He plays at home...

TRAFFIC JAMS. WE HATE THEM, BUT WHAT DO WE DO IN THEM?

Listening

1 Look at the photo and answer the questions.

1 When does this happen in your town/city?

2 What do you do in traffic jams?

2 a **3.1** Complete the quotes below. Compare your answers with a partner, then listen and check.

'Traffic jams are OK. I think about work and *plan* my day. I (1)_____ my diary. <u>My daughter doesn't like traffic jams</u> – she calls her friends, but I don't make phone calls in the car. It's dangerous.' (*Melanie, 39*)

· · · · · · · · ·

'Well, in the mornings I shave and listen to the radio. I (2)_____ the news. I like music, but unfortunately my car doesn't have a CD player.' (*Nathan, 28*)

· · · · · · · · ·

'I don't do a lot, really. I (3)_____ traffic jams – they're so boring! I think about things or (4)_____ the people in the other cars. Sometimes I sing.' (*Simon, 35*)

· · · · · · · · ·

'We (5)_____ computer games or (6)_____ friends on our mobiles. Or we just talk. We don't like the radio.' (*Lauren, 22 and Emily, 21*)

b Mark the sentences true (T) or false (F).

Melanie makes phone calls in a traffic jam. *F*

1 Melanie's daughter likes traffic jams.

2 Nathan listens to CDs.

3 Simon sings in his car.

4 Lauren and Emily work on their computers.

5 Lauren and Emily think mobile phones in cars are dangerous.

Grammar | Present Simple: negative

3 a Find the negative of the sentences below in the texts. <u>Underline</u> them.

1 My daughter likes traffic jams.

2 I make phone calls in the car.

3 My car has a CD player.

4 We like the radio.

b Complete the Active grammar box with *don't* or *doesn't*.

Active grammar

I	_____	
He/She/It	_____	work.
We/You/They	_____	

see Reference page 33

4 a Correct the false sentences in Ex. 2b. Use the negative verb form.

Melanie doesn't make phone calls in a traffic jam.

b What about you? Tick (✓) the true sentences. Correct the false sentences.

I like traffic jams.   *I don't like traffic jams.*

1 I listen to the news on the radio.

2 I write my diary every day.

3 I play football at the weekend.

4 I make phone calls in the car.

5 I sleep for ten hours every night.

Vocabulary | days of the week

5 a `3.2` Number the days of the week in the correct order. Then listen and check.

- ☐ Friday ☐ Monday ☐ Saturday ☐1 Sunday
- ☐ Thursday ☐ Tuesday ☐ Wednesday

b `3.3` Listen to Alistair talking about his lunchtime activities. Write the days.

Tuesday

Reading

6 a Read the text about Alistair. Find three mistakes with the days and correct them.

What I do
in my lunch **break**

Today we talk to Alistair Standing. Alistair works in the city. He doesn't go home at lunchtime, so how does he spend his time?

'Well, I have an hour and I want to use that time. I do a lot of different things,' says Alistair. He certainly does! On Mondays Alistair goes for a walk or he has a swim. On Tuesdays he sometimes meets friends and they have lunch in a restaurant. On Wednesdays he goes to the gym. On Thursdays he sometimes listens to a lunchtime concert. On Fridays he goes shopping. On Sundays he watches football on TV and sleeps!

b Write positive or negative sentences about Alistair. Use the corrected text to help you.

Mondays/play tennis

He doesn't play tennis on Mondays.

1 Thursdays/watch a film
2 Fridays/work
3 Saturdays/play football
4 Sundays/sleep

Speaking

7 a Read the questionnaire. Tick (✓) the things you do, and write the day you do them, if possible. Then add two more.

Activity	You (when)	Your partner (when)
talk to friends on the phone		
watch TV		
listen to music		
play computer games		
go for walks		
play a sport		
go to concerts	✓ (Friday evenings)	
go to the cinema		
read books		
go to the gym		
_____		

b Complete the questionnaire for your partner.

A: *Do you go to concerts?*

B: *Yes, I sometimes go to concerts on Friday evenings./No, I don't.*

Writing

8 a What do you do in your free time? Make a list.

Monday evenings – watch TV
Saturdays – read newspaper/go shopping

b Write a short article about your free time. Use your notes from Ex. 8a.

1 Start your article with a short introduction.

My name is ... I work in ..., but I do a lot of things in my free time. On Mondays I ...

2 Write your notes into sentences.

On Monday evenings I (sometimes) watch TV.

3 Join some of the sentences with *and, or* or *but*.

On Saturday mornings I read the newspaper or I go shopping.

4 Combine your introduction and sentences to write your article.

3.2 Skateboard style

Grammar	*can/can't*
Can do	talk about what you can and can't do

Vocabulary | sports and games

1 **a** Match the words from the box to the activities.

> aerobics computer games football running
> judo sailing skiing swimming tennis yoga

b Write the activities in the table. Then check in the Reference on page 33.

DO	GO	PLAY
do aerobics	*go running*	*play football*

c Ask and answer.

A: *Do you do yoga?*

B: *Yes, I do.*

A: *When?*

B: *On Thursday evenings.*

Tony Hawk
the man and the champion

Tony Hawk is American. He's 34. He's married. He has three children. He's a businessman. And he's the skateboarding champion of the world.

Reading

2 **a** Look at the photo. Answer the questions.

1 Do you go skateboarding?
2 What kind of people usually go skateboarding? (young/old)

b Read the introduction to the text above and answer the questions.

1 Where is Tony Hawk from?
2 What does he do?
3 Some people think he is unusual. Why?

3 **a** Look at the text (page 29) and find these things.

1 Tony's age   2 his son's name and age
3 the name of Tony's book

b Read the introduction and the text again and answer the questions. Write sentences.

How many children does Tony have?

He has three children.

1 How many prizes does he have?
2 What does he do on his skateboard?
3 What does his son ride?
4 Where does Tony take his show?
5 What do the people in the show do?

Tony has 73 prizes from skateboarding competitions. He's 34 but he can skateboard like a sixteen year old. He goes very fast and he does tricks on his skateboard. His four-year-old son, Spencer, can also ride a skateboard!

But Tony isn't only a fantastic skateboarder – he can do other things too. Tony writes computer games and books. Lots of people buy his books. *HAWK – Occupation: skateboarder* is a bestseller in the United States.

Tony also has a skateboarding and music show and he takes it all around the United States and Canada. Tony doesn't perform the music – he can't play the guitar or sing – but he and other skateboarders perform tricks, and their musicians play rock music. The show is very popular.

Grammar | can/can't

4 **a** Tick (✓) the things Tony can do. Cross (✗) the things he can't do.

play the guitar ☐   ride a skateboard ☐
use a computer ☐   sing ☐
play rock music ☐   perform tricks ☐

b Complete the sentences and questions with *can* or *can't*. Then complete the Active grammar box.

What _can_ Tony Hawk do?

1 He _____ ride a skateboard.
2 What _____ his friends do?
3 They _____ play the guitar and sing.
4 _____ you ride a skateboard?
5 No, I _____, but I _____ ride a bicycle.

Active grammar

⊕ : I/You/He/She/It/We/They _____ swim.

⊖ : I/You/He/She/It/We/They _____ swim.

❓ : _____ I/you/he/she/it/we/they swim?

Yes, I/you/he/she/it/we/they <u>can</u>.

No, I/you/he/she/it/we/they _____.

see Reference page 33

Pronunciation

5 **3.4** Listen. What can Jonny and Susie do? Tick (✓) the things they can do.

	Jonny	Susie
play the guitar	✓	✓
play the piano		
sing		
dance		
play football		
play tennis		
ski		
speak French		
speak Spanish		
ride a bike		
drive a car		

6 **a** **3.5** We say *can/can't* in different ways. Listen and repeat.

/ə/	/æ/	/ɑː/
<u>Can</u> you dance?	Yes, I <u>can</u>.	No, I <u>can't</u>.

b Ask and answer. Use the table.

A: *Can Susie speak French?*
B: *Yes, she can.*
A: *Can Jonny drive?*
B: *No, he can't.*

c Work with a partner. Ask and answer, using the activities in Ex. 5.

A: *Can you ski?*
B: *No, I can't. Can you ...?*

Speaking

7 **a** Work in groups. Find someone who ...

can ...
- speak three languages
- stand on their head
- write backwards
- move their ears
- play an unusual instrument
- write computer programs

can't ...
- cook
- swim
- write with their right hand
- get up in the mornings
- send a text message
- use a video or DVD player

b Tell the class about your group.

3.3 | Phone fun

Functions	making suggestions; using the phone
Can do	understand and leave a simple phone message

Listening

1 Do you use a mobile phone? Where? When? Who do you call?

2 **a** [3.6] Listen. Match the messages to the names.

Damian ☐ Jane ☒1 Mary Wilde ☐
Benson Cameras ☐ Steve Henshaw ☐

b Listen again and complete the messages with one word, a number or a time.

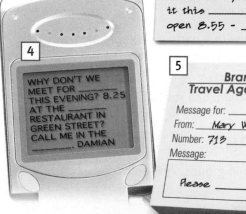

1
Message for: **Tony**
From: _____
Message:
Meet outside the _____ at 7.50.

2
Message for Mandy from Steve Henshaw.
Please _____ him – 068 919 _____.

3
Message for Michael _____.
Carol at Benson Cameras – your new _____ is there. Can you go and get it this _____? Shop is open 8.55 – _____.

4
WHY DON'T WE MEET FOR _____ THIS EVENING? 8.25 AT THE _____ RESTAURANT IN GREEN STREET? CALL ME IN THE _____. DAMIAN

5
Brandon Travel Agency 🌐
Message for: _____ Renton
From: _____ Mary Wilde
Number: 713 _____ 8834
Message:
Please _____ her.

c Listen to message five again. How do we say *88* in the phone number?

3 **a** [3.7] Number the sentences in the correct order. Then listen and check.

OK. What's your number? ☐
OK. Bye. ☐
She isn't here right now. Can I take a message? ☐
Hello. ☒1
Yes, please ask her to phone Jeffrey. ☐
It's 011 908 5561. ☐
Hello, can I speak to Laura, please? ☐

b Practise the dialogue with a partner.

4 Make two phone calls.

Student A: turn to page 125.

Student B: read the notes below.

Call 1 Your name is Carla. Phone Student A: You want to speak to Jason. Your number is 990 675 3551.

Call 2 Answer the phone and start the conversation. (Sylvia isn't here today. Take a message for Sylvia.)

Reading

5 **a** Read the text below quickly. Match the headings to paragraphs 1–3.

a The Mobile Phone Olympics
b The phone throwing competition
c Texting in Britain

b Read the text again. Match the numbers to the information.

1 1.54 billion   a words in Natalie's text message
2 50 million   b Natalie's age
3 2 million   c competitors
4 8   d messages a month
5 15,000   e messages an hour
6 18   f messages a day for each user
7 30   g messages a day

Texting at the Mobile Phone Olympics

In Britain people send 1.54 billion text messages every month. That's more than 50 **1** million messages a day or 2 million an hour! In fact, the average mobile phone user sends about 8 messages a day.

Now texting fans have the chance to show what they can do at the Mobile Phone Olympics. Every year about 15,000 competitors enter the competition in London. In the texting **2** event competitors send an 80-character message as fast as they can. This year's champion is 18-year-old Natalie Johnson from Leeds. She can send a 30-word text message in just 138 seconds!

Of course, some people hate mobile phones. One event at the Olympics is just for them. This is the 'Mobile Phone Throwing' **3** competition. In this event competitors throw their phones as far as they can. It's a lot of fun for mobile phone haters!

6 [3.8] How do we say these numbers? Choose from the words in the box. Then listen and check your answers.

6 *six* 16 60 600 6,000 60,000 600,000
6,000,000 6,000,000,000

> six million   six thousand   sixty
> sixty thousand   six billion   ~~six~~
> six hundred thousand   six hundred   sixteen

Pronunciation

7 **a** [3.9] Listen. <u>Underline</u> the strong sounds.

sixteen   sixty
fourteen   forty

b [3.10] Listen and tick (✓) the number you hear.

1	fourteen ☐	forty	☐
2	eighteen ☐	eighty	☐
3	seventeen ☐	seventy	☐
4	thirteen ☐	thirty	☐
5	nineteen ☐	ninety	☐
6	sixteen ☐	sixty	☐

c Test your partner.

8 Look at page 152 and complete the How to box with examples from the dialogues in Ex. 2a.

HOW TO …

make suggestions and requests

Make suggestions	*Let's* + infinitive
	Let's meet outside the cinema at ten to eight.
	Why don't we + infinitive + ?
	_____
	How about + noun + ?
	_____
Make requests	*Can you* + infinitive + ?
	_____

see Reference page 33

9 **a** Find these times in the tapescript on page 152 and write them in words.

7.50   *ten to eight*

1   3.20 _____   2   8.55 _____
3   6.30 _____   4   8.25 _____

b Complete these suggestions and requests. Write the times in words.

we meet – cinema – 7.00?
Why *don't we meet at the cinema at seven*?

1   have dinner – Chinese restaurant – 8.40
    Let's _____

2   you come – the office tomorrow – 9.55?
    Can _____?

3   3.10 – Greek café – Belmont Street?
    How _____?

4   we go – the bar – 10.45?
    Why _____?

10 **a** What can people do in your town in the evening? Tick (✓) the activities and make notes about where and when you can do them.

see a film ☐   have dinner at a restaurant ☐
go to a football match ☐   go to a bar ☐
go to a nightclub ☐   go to a concert ☐
get a takeaway meal ☐
go to the sports centre ☐

b Work in pairs. You want to do something together tonight. Make suggestions.

A: *What can we do tonight?*
B: *Let's …*
A: *OK. Let's meet at half past nine./No, I don't like … How about …?*

The perfect job

1 **a** Match the abilities to the jobs. Use a dictionary.

ABILITIES	JOBS
1 speak foreign languages	a sports teacher
2 design buildings	b taxi driver
3 play sports	c artist
4 drive	d carpenter
5 repair computers	e mechanic
6 play a musical instrument	f photographer
7 draw and paint	g tourist guide
8 repair cars	h musician
9 use a camera	i architect
10 make things in wood	j computer technician

b Work with a partner. Think of more abilities and jobs.

2 **a** Read the information below about Jane and Brian. Complete their agency notes on the right.

Jane Danby is thirty-two years old. She has a degree in Art from Edinburgh University. She can speak Spanish and German. She can paint and draw. She likes the Internet. She takes digital photos and she changes them on her computer. She can't drive.

Brian Winter doesn't have any qualifications but he can do a lot of things. He can repair cars and engines, and he can repair houses. He doesn't like cold weather. He makes furniture in wood and metal. He is twenty-five years old and he has a driving licence.

b **3.11** Listen and complete the notes for David and Lizzie.

3 **a** Work in groups. You work for the Perfect Employment Agency. Jane, Brian, David and Lizzie want new jobs. Choose the best job for each person. Talk about your reasons and complete the table.

A: *I think 'computer technician' is best for Jane.*
B: *Do you? Why?*
A: *Because she likes the Internet ...*

NAME	JANE	BRIAN	DAVID	LIZZIE
JOB	computer technician			
REASONS	She likes the Internet.			

b Compare your ideas with other groups.

PERFECT EMPLOYMENT AGENCY

Applicant notes

NAME: Jane Danby

AGE:

QUALIFICATIONS:

ABILITIES:

LIKES/DISLIKES:

PERFECT EMPLOYMENT AGENCY

Applicant notes

NAME: Brian Winter

AGE:

QUALIFICATIONS:

ABILITIES:

LIKES/DISLIKES:

PERFECT EMPLOYMENT AGENCY

Applicant notes

NAME: David Burford

AGE:

QUALIFICATIONS:

ABILITIES:

LIKES/DISLIKES:

PERFECT EMPLOYMENT AGENCY

Applicant notes

NAME: Lizzie Pereira

AGE:

QUALIFICATIONS:

ABILITIES:

LIKES/DISLIKES:

Present Simple: negative

Form the negative of the Present Simple with the verb *do* + *not* + infinitive.

I You We They	don't (do not)	
He She It	doesn't (does not)	work.

*I **don't live** in the city.*
*She **doesn't work** in the office.*

Note that we do not add *-s* to the infinitive in the Present Simple negative.

can/can't

Can is a modal verb. We use modal verbs before other verbs.

The negative of *can* is *cannot,* but we usually use the short form *can't*.

I You He She It We You They	can can't (cannot)	sing.

Modal verbs do not change their form after *he*, *she* or *it*.

He can play the piano.

Use *can* and *can't* to talk about ability. Use *can* to talk about things we are able to do, and *can't* to talk about things that we are not able to do.

*I **can sing** but **I can't dance**.*

Use *can* + *you* + infinitive to make requests – when we want someone else to do something.

***Can you take** a message?*

Making suggestions

When we want to do something with another person we make suggestions.

Let's + infinitive
***Let's meet** outside the cinema at ten to eight.*
Why don't we + infinitive + ?
***Why don't we have** dinner this evening?*
How about + noun + ?
***How about lunch** on Friday?*

play, do, go + activities

Use *play* + noun for games, and for sports we usually do in teams, e.g. *play football, computer games*.

Use *do* + noun for activities we can do alone (not in a team), e.g. *do aerobics, yoga*.

Use *go* with activity verbs that end in *-ing*, e.g. *go swimming, running*.

Key vocabulary

Days of the week
Sunday   Monday   Tuesday   Wednesday
Thursday   Friday   Saturday

Activities
cook
dance
do aerobics/judo/yoga
drive a car
get a takeaway meal
go for a walk
go running/sailing/shopping/skiing/swimming
go to the cinema/a concert/the gym/a nightclub/
   a football match/a bar
have lunch/dinner (at a restaurant)
listen to music/the news/the radio
meet friends
play computer games/football/tennis
play the guitar/piano
read a book/a magazine/a newspaper
ride a bike
see a film
sing
skateboard
sunbathe
swim
watch a DVD/a video/the TV

1 Make positive or negative sentences about Malcolm.

live in a nice house

Malcolm doesn't live in a nice house.

sleep in the park

Malcolm sleeps in the park.

1 have a job

2 have an address

3 go to work every morning

4 carry his things in a bag

5 eat in restaurants

6 like his life

2 Write four sentences about the activities that you and your friends <u>don't</u> do together. Choose from the box.

> watch TV go to a nightclub go to the gym
> listen to music   eat in restaurants
> go to concerts   play a sport go to the cinema
> play computer games   go shopping

We don't eat in restaurants.

1 _____   3 _____

2 _____   4 _____

3 Write a sentence with *can* and *can't* about the things below. Choose from the box.

> check spellings   drive   invent text messages
> play computer games   sleep all day
> play football   run   send photos   swim   think

Young children

can play computer games but they can't drive.

1 Computers

2 Sharks

3 Mobile phones

4 Cats

4 The text has eight mistakes. Find the mistakes and correct them.

> Andreas cans do a lot of things. He likes sports and he can plays basketball and football but he no can play tennis. He don't like tennis. He likes rock music and he play the guitar in shows. He sing too but he doesn't dances. He can't plays the piano.

5 Put the words in order to make suggestions and requests.

cinema to we tonight Why don't go the ?

Why don't we go to the cinema tonight?

1 six o'clock Let's at meet .

2 restaurant How the lunch at about Italian ?

3 a Can message you take ?

4 from takeaway Let's a McDonald's get .

5 give your Can number you me phone ?

6 we video don't watch this Why a evening ?

7 Saturday about on How dinner ?

6 Complete the diary with the correct verbs.

Monday

　play　football with the boys

1 _____ to the cinema (evening)

Tuesday

2 _____ Jack and Ellie for lunch

3 _____ the bikes to the park

Wednesday

4 _____ to the gym

5 _____ dinner for Emma

Thursday

6 _____ to a nightclub

7 _____ the piano for Sam

Friday

8 _____ yoga with Jane (morning)

9 _____ swimming with the girls

Saturday

10 _____ shopping

Sunday

11 _____ Harry's video

4 Food

Lead-in

1 Match eight words from the box to the things in the pictures.

> apples beef bread butter cheese cherries chicken
> eggs milk potatoes rice sugar tea trout watermelon

2 **a** In pairs, find the meanings of the other words. Then complete the table below with all the food words you know.

MEAT/FISH	DAIRY	FRUIT	DRINKS	OTHER
			water	

b Where do you buy food? How do you pay for it?

3 Match the pictures below with the words from the box. Ask and answer the questions.

> coin note cheque receipt credit card

1 Which pictures show cash? When do you use cash/credit cards/cheques?

2 How much money do you have in your wallet? How much does this book cost? How much does your journey to school cost?

I've got three euros fifty in my wallet.

35

Food around the world

Regan Ronayne and Craig Caven and their children, Andrea (5) and Ryan (3), live in California. They are a typical American family. Regan and Craig both work and they don't usually have time to cook, so they like convenience food. The children love hot dogs, cereal and cola. They eat at fast food restaurants once a week.

The Ukitas live in Tokyo, Japan. Kazuo Ukita lives with his wife, Sayo, and his daughters Mio (17) and Maya (14). He works in a bookshop. Sayo cooks breakfast before Kazuo leaves for work at 7.00 a.m. They have dinner together at home in the evenings. They eat a lot of fish and rice. Sayo cooks all the meals for her family.

Ramón Costa, his wife Sandra and their children, Lisandra (16) and Favio (6), live in Havana. Cuba is a tropical country so they eat a lot of fresh fruit – pineapples, watermelons, bananas, and papayas. Families in Cuba have ration books. These show how much food the family can buy every month.

Vocabulary | food and drink

1   Look at the photo and find these things.
orange juice ☐   cereal ☐   bananas ☐
carrots ☐   cola ☐   minced beef ☐ A   water ☐

Reading

2   **a**   Read the text quickly and tick (✓) the countries it talks about.
Japan ☐   Britain ☐   Spain ☐   Cuba ☐
Russia ☐   United States ☐

b   Read the text again and tick (✓) the correct answers.

Which family...	Ronayne	Ukita	Costa
1 eats a lot of fish?	☐	☐	☐
2 eats fresh fruit?	☐	☐	☐
3 has a ration book?	☐	☐	☐
4 eats at fast food restaurants?	☐	☐	☐
5 doesn't have time to cook?	☐	☐	☐
6 has dinner together?	☐	☐	☐

Grammar | countable and uncountable nouns

3   **a**   Look at the picture and answer the questions.

1   Can you count the eggs?
2   Can you count the cereal?
3   Which is uncountable, *eggs* or *cereal*?

b Here is the Ronayne family shopping list. Answer the questions.

1 Choose the correct alternatives.

a The red words are *countable/uncountable* nouns.
b The blue words are *countable/uncountable* nouns.
c Uncountable nouns do not have *singular/plural* forms.

> 12 hot dogs
> 450g cereal
> 12 eggs
> 4 litres milk
> 2 litres orange juice
> 18 bananas
> 1 pizza
> 675g minced beef

2 How do we measure uncountable nouns?

c Write the headings in the Active grammar box.

Uncountable nouns   Countable nouns

Active grammar

1 _____
- They have singular and plural forms.
- We can use numbers in front of them.

2 _____
- They do not have plural forms.
- We cannot use numbers in front of them.
- We often use quantity words (e.g. *litres, kilos*) + *of* in front of them.

see Reference page 43

4 a Here are the shopping lists for the Costa and Ukita families. Write the food words in the table.

> Costa
> 1 pineapple
> 4kg bread
> 1kg pasta
> 2 watermelons
> 3 papayas
> 500g coffee
> 12 bananas
> 750g cereal

> Ukita
> 5kg rice
> 4 litres milk
> 2 pizzas
> 2kg tuna
> 12 eggs
> 300g beef
> 1 kg tomatoes
> 2 litres cola

COUNTABLE	UNCOUNTABLE
pineapple	bread

b Answer the questions, then complete the Active grammar box.

1 How much coffee does the Costa family buy each week?
2 How many pineapples do they buy?

Active grammar

We use *How* _____ with countable nouns.
We use *How* _____ with uncountable nouns.

see Reference page 43

5 a Complete with words and phrases from the box.

> 2kg   coffee   much   tomatoes   many   six

A: How (1) _____ rice do you buy each week?
B: I usually buy (2) _____ of rice.
A: And how many (3) _____ do you eat?
B: About (4) _____.
A: How much (5) _____ do you buy?
B: I buy about 250g of coffee.
A: How (6) _____ pineapples do you get?
B: Oh, only one.

b 4.1 Listen and check your answers.

6 4.2 Listen and complete the quantities.
6 litres water

1 _____ milk   4 _____ coffee
2 _____ rice   5 _____ cheese
3 _____ bananas

HOW TO … say quantities and numbers

Number	Quantity
201 *two hundred and one*	litres (l)
450 *four hundred and fifty*	grammes (g)
675 *six hundred and seventy-five*	kilos (kg)
1.5 *one point five/one and a half*	

7 Ask questions about your partner's weekly shopping. Make notes and tell the class.

A: *How much rice do you buy?*
B: *500 grammes./I don't buy rice.*

Vocabulary | containers

1 **a** Look at the advert and discuss the questions.

  1 What is the TV programme about?

  2 Who introduces the programme?

  3 Which food in the bins is healthy (good for you)? Which food is unhealthy (bad for you)?

b Find examples of these containers in the bins. Use a dictionary to help you.

> bag bottle box can carton packet

Listening

2 **a** `4.3` Listen to the first part of the TV programme. Write A or B by the correct bin.

b Listen again. Write the names of food and drink in the correct column.

HEALTHY FOOD	UNHEALTHY FOOD
vegetables	*burgers*
pasta	*crisps*

Person to person

3 Discuss.

  1 Do you agree with Laurence about the diets of the two families?

  2 What other food is healthy/ unhealthy, do you think?

  3 Tell your partner about your diet.

In the rubbish bin

People's rubbish tells us about their lives. Tonight Laurence Redburn looks at the diet of two families.

Tuesday 9.00p.m. Channel 6

Grammar | *a/an, some* and *any*

4 Look at these sentences. Complete the Active grammar box with *a/an, some* or *any*.

We have some cans... We have a bottle ...

Do they eat any vegetables or any fruit? They eat some pasta ...

Active grammar

Noun	Singular countable	Plural countable	Uncountable
⊕	_____	_____	_____
⊖	*a/an*	*any*	*any*
?	*a/an*	_____	*any*

see Reference page 43

5 **a** Complete the gaps with *a/an, some* or *any*.

We don't have <u>any</u> potatoes.

  1 I want _____ potatoes and _____ carrots, please.
  2 Can I have _____ apple now?
  3 Can I have _____ bottle of water, please?
  4 I have _____ fruit here – do you want _____ banana?
  5 We don't eat _____ meat.

b Correct the <u>underlined</u> mistakes in this paragraph.

I like Italian food. Every Thursday evening we cook <u>a pasta</u> with <u>any minced beef</u> and <u>a tomatoes</u>. We have <u>some bottle</u> of water with the meal. We eat a lot of meat, but we don't eat <u>some chicken</u> – we don't like chicken. We also eat <u>any vegetables</u> every day.

Pronunciation

6 a Listen to the vowel sounds in these words. Can you hear the difference?

/æ/	/ʌ/
pasta	some

b Listen. <u>Underline</u> the /æ/ and /ʌ/ sounds. Then repeat the sentences.

1 He has lunch on Sundays in his club.
2 My family travels by taxi, but my young cousin takes the bus.
3 Anne and Sally have butter on their pasta.

Vocabulary | adjectives

7 a Match the pictures to the adjectives.

happy ☐	healthy ☐
hungry ☐	thirsty ☐
tired ☐	unhappy ☐
unhealthy ☐	fit ☐

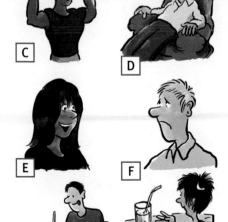

b Which adjectives have a positive meaning? Which have a negative meaning?

Reading

A

Dear Laurence
I'm always hungry. I eat three good meals a day but then I want crisps and biscuits too. Of course, now I'm quite fat! Can you help me?

Lois

B

Dear Laurence
I know I have an unhealthy diet. I work about ten hours a day and I get home late, so I don't have time to cook and I eat convenience food. What can I do?

James

C

Dear Laurence
I try to eat a good diet – I eat pasta and vegetables, and I don't eat any meat, fish or cheese – but I'm always tired. What's wrong with my diet?

Karin

8 a Laurence also writes about diet in a magazine. Read the letters above and match them to the problems.

1 He/She doesn't have time to cook.
2 He/She eats a lot.
3 He/She feels tired all the time.

b Read Laurence's answer to one letter.

1 Which letter does it answer?
2 How does he start his answer?
3 How does he make the two suggestions?

Dear ____
It's horrible when you feel tired all the time. You need some meat, fish or cheese in your diet – they give you energy. Also, why don't you take some exercise? That gives you energy too. How about a walk every evening after work? I hope that helps.

Laurence

Writing

9 a Read the other two letters again and look at Laurence's notes. Which notes are for which letter?

1 salads are quick and healthy *letter B*
2 eat fruit, not crisps and biscuits
3 go to the doctor
4 don't work ten hours a day
5 some food is quick to cook, e.g. fresh pasta
6 eat only small meals

b Make more suggestions for the writers of the two letters.

c In pairs, write an answer to one of the other letters.

1 Think of two or three suggestions.
2 Start the letter, write your suggestions and finish the letter.
3 Give your letter to another pair to correct and improve it.

4.3 Ready to order?

Grammar	object pronouns; *I'd like*
Can do	order food in a fast food restaurant

Listening

1 Discuss.

1 Where is the place in the photo?

2 Do you eat at places like these? Which places?

2 **a** **4.6** Listen to a dialogue in a fast food restaurant. Who orders these things? Write J for Jenny and S for Sam.

cheese sandwich ☐

fries ☐   salad ☐

coffee ☐   water ☐

b Listen again and complete the bill below (1–4).

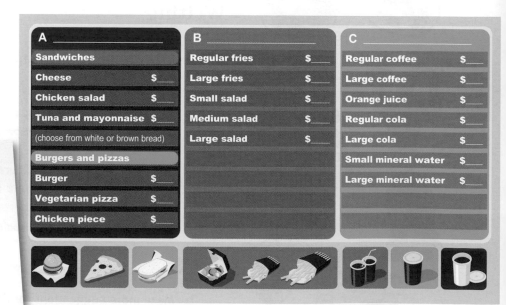

🍴 Restaurant

```
============================================
Cheese sandwich          x1 $4.50
Large (1) _____       x1 $3.00
(2)_____ salad        x1 $4.00
(3)_____ coffee       x1 $2.95
Small mineral (4)_____  x1 $2.25

TOTAL                    $ (5)_____

Service & tax included
```

3 **a** **4.7** Listen and complete number 5 in Ex. 2b.

b Listen again and answer the questions.

1 What does Jenny really like?

2 How does Sam ask for the price of the meal?

3 How does Sam pay for the meal?

4 **a** This is the menu from the fast food restaurant. Match the headings to A–C.

Drinks   Main dishes   Side orders

A _____		B _____		C _____	
Sandwiches		**Regular fries**	$___	**Regular coffee**	$___
Cheese	$___	**Large fries**	$___	**Large coffee**	$___
Chicken salad	$___	**Small salad**	$___	**Orange juice**	$___
Tuna and mayonnaise	$___	**Medium salad**	$___	**Regular cola**	$___
(choose from white or brown bread)		**Large salad**	$___	**Large cola**	$___
Burgers and pizzas				**Small mineral water**	$___
Burger	$___			**Large mineral water**	$___
Vegetarian pizza	$___				
Chicken piece	$___				

b Work in pairs.

Student A: turn to page 125.

Student B: ask your partner questions to complete the menu.

How much is a burger?

Grammar | object pronouns

5 a ⟨4.8⟩ Listen and complete the sentences.

1 OK. A large cup of coffee for _____ and a small glass of mineral water for _____.

2 No, that's not for _____.

3 Two vegetarian pizzas? I really like _____!

4 A medium salad for _____, sir.

5 Oh no, the salad's for _____.

b Look at the tapescript on page 153 and check your answers. Use the information to complete the Active grammar box.

Active grammar

Subject pronouns	Object pronouns
I	me
he	_____
she	_____
it	it
we	_____
you	_____
they	_____

see Reference page 43

6 Tell the waitress. Complete the sentences with object pronouns.

Well, who is this for?

you: 'It isn't for *me*.'

1 your boyfriend: 'It isn't for _____.'

2 your mother: 'It isn't for _____.'

3 you and your friend: 'It isn't for _____.'

4 your brother and sister: 'It isn't for _____.'

7 a Match 1–7 to a–g.

1 What
2 I'd like
3 Jenny, what would
4 Do you
5 Sam, do
6 How
7 Can I

a much is that?
b pay by credit card?
c can I get you today?
d a cheese sandwich, please.
e have salads?
f you like?
g you want some juice?

b Look at the tapescripts on page 153 and check your answers. Then complete the sentences in the How to box.

HOW TO... order in a fast food restaurant

Ask questions	_____ you have salads?
Say what you want	I'd _____ a cheese sandwich, please.
Ask about prices	How _____ is that?

c Use some of the words from Ex. 7a to complete this dialogue.

A: Hello, what _____ I get you today?

B: _____ like a vegetarian burger, please.

A: Any side orders?

B: _____ you have salads?

A: No, we don't. Do you _____ fries?

B: OK. Small fries.

A: Anything to drink?

B: Yes, I'd _____ an orange juice, please.

A: OK.

B: How _____ is that?

A: That's €10.95.

B: _____ I pay by credit card?

Speaking

8 Work in groups of three. Use the menu in Ex. 4a.

Student A: you are a waiter/waitress. Take the customers' order.

Students B and C: you are customers at the restaurant. Look at the menu, choose the things you want and order a meal.

Shopping at a market

1 a [4.9] Listen. What does the woman ask for? Tick (✓) the blue boxes.

apples ☐ ☐   carrots ☐ ☐   tomatoes ☐ ☐
bananas ☐ ☐   chicken ☐ ☐   potatoes ☐ ☐
beef ☐ ☐   melon ☐ ☐   tuna ☐ ☐

b Listen again. What things can she buy? Tick (✓) the red boxes.

c How much does the woman pay for all her shopping? Listen and check if necessary.

2 a [4.10] Listen to the intonation. Write ↗ if it goes up and ↘ if it goes down.

I'd like three bananas ↗, a kilo of apples ☐ and a melon ☐.
I'd like 500g of minced beef ☐, 200g of tuna ☐ and a chicken ☐.

b Listen again and repeat.

c Play a game in groups. Choose food and drink from the box below. Follow the example, and be careful to use the correct intonation. How long can you continue?

> minced beef   chicken   fish   lamb   tuna
> butter   cheese   eggs   milk   pasta   apples
> ice cream   bananas   carrots   melons
> papayas   pineapples   potatoes   tomatoes
> coffee   cola   orange juice   tea   water

Student A: *I'd like some coffee.*
Student B: *I'd like some coffee and a bottle of water.*
Student C: *I'd like some coffee, a bottle of water and three apples.*
Student D: *I'd like some coffee, a bottle of water, three apples and ...*

3 a Half the class are shoppers at a market. The other half are shop assistants. Read your roles.

b When you finish, tell the class about the things you have.

Shoppers

Work in pairs. Choose six things from the box in Ex. 2c and write your shopping list. You have 25 euros for all your shopping. Look at the tapescript on page 153 and prepare to go shopping. Ask the shop assistants and try to buy all your items. How much do you pay?

Shop assistants

1   Your teacher gives you a letter, A, B, C or D.
    A: you sell fruit and vegetables.
    B: you sell drinks.
    C: you sell meat and fish.
    D: you sell dairy food (butter, milk, etc.).
2   Look at the box in Ex. 2c and the list on page 43 and find the correct type of food for your shop. Choose four items and write them down. Write a price next to each item, e.g. *coffee – 3 euros for 250 g, water – 1 euro a bottle.*
3   Look at the tapescript on page 153 and prepare to answer your customers' questions.

Countable and uncountable nouns; *How much?/How many?*

Countable nouns are things that we can count. They have singular and plural forms and we can use numbers in front of them.

one banana   three bananas   twenty-five bananas

Use *How many ...?* to ask questions about the number of countable nouns.

***How many** bananas do you buy every week?*

Uncountable nouns are things we can't count. They do not have plural forms and we cannot use numbers in front of them.

Use *How much ...?* to ask questions about the quantity of uncountable nouns.

***How much** water do you drink every day?*

Show the quantity *(how much/many)* of countable and uncountable nouns by using another noun (e.g. *a bag*) or a measurement (e.g. *kilos*) + *of* in front of the noun.

***A bag** of bananas. **Half a kilo** of bananas.*
***A glass** of water. **A litre** of water.*

a/an, some and *any*

Singular countable nouns

Use *a/an* before singular countable nouns when there is only one of the noun. Use *a/an* in positive and negative statements and in questions.

⊕	:	We have a car.
⊖	:	We don't have a car.
?	:	Do you have a car?

Plural countable nouns

Use *some* and *any* to talk about a number of something, when we don't know how many, or the number isn't important. We usually use *some* in positive statements, and *any* in negative statements and questions. Use *some* and *any* with plural countable nouns.

⊕	:	We have some magazines.
⊖	:	We don't have any magazines.
?	:	Do you have any magazines?

Uncountable nouns

We also use *some* and *any* with uncountable nouns.

⊕	:	We have some cheese.
⊖	:	We don't have any cheese.
?	:	Do you have any cheese?

Object pronouns

Use subject pronouns (see page 13) before verbs and object pronouns after verbs.

Subject pronouns		Object pronouns	
	I		*me*
	he		*him*
	she		*her*
	it		*it*
	we		*us*
	you		*you*
	they		*them*

He loves **her**.

He loves **them**.

She loves **him**.

They love **me**!

Key vocabulary

Food

Dishes: burger fries pizza salad sandwich

Meat and fish: (minced) beef chicken lamb trout tuna

Dairy: butter cheese cream ice cream milk

Fruit and vegetables: apple banana carrot papaya pineapple potato tomato (water)melon

Drinks: coffee cola fruit/orange juice tea milk water

Other: biscuits (white/brown) bread cereal crisps eggs mayonnaise pasta rice sugar

Money

cheque coin credit card note receipt

Adjectives for physical and emotional states

fit happy/unhappy healthy/unhealthy hungry thirsty tired

1 Match the sentence halves.

1. I usually buy a
2. We often get ten
3. She puts 100g
4. I drink a carton
5. We need a can of
6. He takes a box

a. tuna for this recipe.
b. of chocolates to his girlfriend every Saturday.
c. of milk every day.
d. pizza on Friday evening.
e. bags of crisps at the supermarket.
f. of cheese in the omelette.

2 Choose the correct alternatives.

How *much/many* oranges do you eat?

1. How *much/many* students come to your lesson?
2. She drinks three litres of *waters/water* every day.
3. Let's have *2/2kg* of those nice brown eggs for breakfast.
4. How *much/many* money do you have in your pocket?
5. How *many/much* sugar do you eat every week?

3 Amanda phones her husband, but he doesn't answer. Complete her message with *a, some* or *any*.

Hello John. Oh, no, it's a message. He isn't there. Mmm. John, please listen to this message. Can you go to the shops and get _some_ things for dinner? We need (1) _____ fish, and (2) _____ box of eggs. Mmm, I think we have (3) _____ potatoes, but we don't have (4) _____ onions. Do we have (5) _____ carrots? Can you check? Please buy (6) _____ cheese, and I'd like (7) _____ carton of orange juice. That's it. Oh ... we don't have (8) _____ butter – can you get some? Thanks. See you later.

4 Replace the words in brackets ( ) with the correct pronouns and rewrite the sentences.

(Mr Bosgrove) takes (my friend and me) to work in his car.

He takes us to work in his car.

1. (My mother and I) go shopping with (Julia and Carla) every Saturday.
2. (My sister) gets up before (my brother and me).
3. (David and Serena) don't take (the children) on holiday.
4. (My uncle) uses (the computer) every day.
5. (My friend and I) have lunch with (Maria) every Tuesday.

5 Complete the dialogue with the correct pronouns.

A: Hello, Mrs Lovett. How are _you_ ?
B: Oh, hello Sonia. (1) _____'m fine thanks.
A: How's your husband?
B: (2) _____'s fine. He works in the supermarket now.
A: Yes, I know. I see (3) _____ when I do my shopping. And how are the twins, Jake and Jerry?
B: Oh, (4) _____ are very well.
A: Do they go to school on the bus?
B: No. I take (5) _____ with (6) _____ in the car every morning.
A: Who is their teacher?
B: It's Mrs Moore. Do you know (7)_____?
A: Yes, I do. (8) _____ lives in our street. She always says 'Hello' to (9) _____.

6 a Put the letters in the correct order to write the food words.

nseyaimaon   m_ayonnaise_

1. ntau   t_____
2. errbug   b_____
3. eabrd   b_____
4. onermwalte   w_____
5. otmotsea   t_____
6. ckechin   c_____
7. ilmk   m_____
8. apzzi   p_____
9. crie   r_____

b Circle the odd-one-out.

coffee   tea   (rice)   water

1. beef   chicken   trout   lamb
2. apple   fries   tomato   carrot
3. butter   ice cream   milk   sugar
4. sandwich   coffee   tea   water

5 Home

Lead-in

1   **a** Which rooms from the box can you see in the photos?

> bathroom   bedroom   dining room   garden   garage
> kitchen   living room

b **5.1** Where can you do these activities? Match the places in the box to the activities. Then listen and check.

sunbathe *You can sunbathe in the garden.*

1 cook   2 sleep   3 have a shower   4 put your car

5 eat   6 watch TV

2   **a** **5.2** Tick (✓) the landscapes in the photos. Listen and check.

a beach ☐   mountains ☐   a river ☐   a forest ☐   a city ☐
a lake ☐   a desert ☐   the sea ☐

b Which other words for landscapes do you know? Make a list.

c Answer the questions.

1 What is in the north of your country?
(the centre/the south/the west/the east)

2 What can you see from your living room window?
(bedroom window/kitchen window)

3 Play a game in groups. Think of a country and describe its landscape. Can other students guess the country?

This country has beaches in the north. It has a big city in the east, mountains in the south and a famous forest in the south-west.

Reading

1 What kind of home do you live in? Do you like your home? Why/Why not?

2 **a** Look at the text quickly and answer the questions.

1 Where is this text from?

2 What is unusual about the homes in the text?

b Read the text. Mark true (T) or false (F).

1 The ship has:

a 110 apartments. ☐

b six restaurants. ☐

c two swimming pools. ☐

d two gyms. ☐

2 The apartments have:

a a large living room. ☐

b a dining room. ☐

c a garden. ☐

d a private terrace. ☐

The World of ResidenSea

Own a private luxury home ... at sea!

There are 110 luxury apartments on our ship The World, but that's not all! There are four restaurants, two swimming pools and a gym. There are shops, but there aren't any factories or cars, so there's no city stress. All our apartments have a large living room (with dining area) and two or three bedrooms. Each bedroom has a private bathroom and there's a cooker, a fridge, a dishwasher and a microwave in each well-equipped kitchen. Of course, there isn't a garden but each apartment has a private terrace. All the living rooms have modern TV, DVD and CD players. Choose from four different styles for your sofas, chairs, beds and other furniture, and make your apartment on the ship a very comfortable home.

———————— The World of ResidenSea ————————

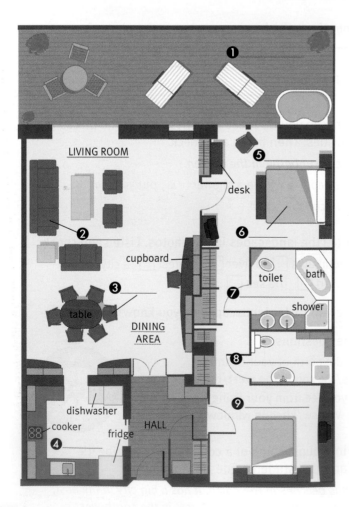

Vocabulary | equipment and furniture

3 **a** Look at the floor plan. Label the rooms and the furniture.

b Write the headings in the table. Then write two or three more things by each heading.

> furniture   kitchen equipment   ~~rooms~~
> living room equipment   ship's facilities

1	*rooms*	*kitchen*
2	_____	*cupboard*
3	_____	*fridge*
4	_____	*TV*
5	_____	*swimming pools*

Lifelong learning

Personalise it!

When you want to learn new words, it is useful to write them in a personal sentence.

fridge – *My fridge is very old – it's useless!*

cupboard – *I have a big cupboard in my bedroom.*

Grammar | *there is/there are*

4 Complete the Active grammar box with *'s, is, isn't, are* or *aren't*.

> ### Active grammar
>
> | | Singular | Plural |
> |---|---|---|
> | ➕ | There_s a gym. (There _is_) | There _____ 110 apartments. |
> | ➖ | There _____ a garden. | There _____ any cars. |
> | ❓ | _____ there a bookshop? | _____ there any music shops? |
> | | Yes, there is. No, there _____. | Yes, there _____. No, there aren't. |

see Reference page 53

5 Look at the text and the floor plan again. Complete the sentences with *'s, is, are, isn't* or *aren't*.

1 There _____ some shops on the ship, but there _____ any cars.
2 _____ there any factories? No, there _____.
3 There _____ a terrace in each apartment.
4 _____ there a dining room? No, there _____.

6 a Look at Ex. 2b. Make sentences.

There are 110 luxury apartments on the ship.
There aren't six restaurants.

b Ask and answer about the floor plan.

A: *Is there a bath in the apartment?*
B: *There's a bath in bedroom one, but there isn't a bath in bedroom two.*

7 Tell your partner about your home.

There are three bedrooms in my apartment but there's only one bathroom.

Listening

8 a `5.3` Jon Nott wants to buy an apartment on the ship. Listen and answer the questions.

1 What is Jon interested in?
2 Are there two-bedroom or three-bedroom apartments for sale?
3 What is the price of an apartment with two bedrooms?
4 Does Jon think the apartment is expensive?
5 Do you think he has the money for the apartment?

b Listen again. Number Jon's questions in the correct order. Then answer them.

1 How many bathrooms are there? ☐
2 Can I ask you some questions? ☐
3 How much space is there? ☐
4 Are there any apartments for sale now? ☐
5 How much does the apartment cost? ☐
6 How many bedrooms are there? ☐

Speaking

9 Work in pairs.

Student A: read the information below.
Student B: look at the information on page 126.

> **Student A**
> You are interested in a town house. Student B has the details. Ask questions to find out these things about the house:
>
> | | |
> |---|---|
> | 1 how big? | 4 garden/terrace? |
> | 2 how many rooms? | 5 where? |
> | 3 what rooms? | 6 price? |
>
> Do you want to buy the house?
>
> Now answer Student B's questions about the house below.

beautiful country cottage
- 120 square metres
- three bedrooms, two bathrooms
- living room, dining room
- kitchen/breakfast room
- two large gardens, front and back
- two kilometres from village with shops

€240,000

Vocabulary | possessions

1 **a** In pairs, look at the four rooms. Which room(s) do you like? Why?

b What's in the pictures? You have three minutes. Make a list of all the things you can see.

tables, cooker, mobile phone

c Close your books. In pairs, try to remember the things in the pictures.

There's a sofa in every room.
There's a plant in one room ...

Listening

2 **a** **5.4** Amanda Myers asks Pete Morgan some questions. Listen. Which picture shows Pete's flat?

b Listen again. Tick (✓) the things Pete has got and cross (✗) the things he hasn't got.

studio apartment ☐   house ☐   garden ☐   terrace ☐   fridge ☐
cooker ☐   sink ☐   microwave ☐   coffee table ☐   chairs ☐
sofa ☐   dining table ☐   TV ☐   music system ☐   laptop computer ☐
mobile phone ☐

Grammar | *have got*

3 **a** **5.5** Listen to the first part of the dialogue again and complete the gaps.

Amanda: Have you _____ your own house?

Pete: No, I _____. I _____ got a modern studio apartment in the centre of town.

Amanda: _____ it got a garden?

Pete: No, it _____ got a garden, but it _____ got a small terrace.

b Complete the Active grammar box.

Active grammar

⊕	I/We/You/They	_____	got
	He/She/It	's _____	
⊖	_____	haven't	got
	He/She/It	_____	
?	_____	I/we/you/they	got ...?
	_____	he/she/it	
	Yes, No,	I/we/you/they	have . _____.
	Yes, No,	he/she/it	has. hasn't.

see Reference page 53

4　**a** Find the false sentences and correct them.

He's got a house.　✗　*He hasn't got a house.*

1 He's got an apartment in the centre of town.
2 It hasn't got a kitchen.
3 He's got a laptop computer.
4 He hasn't got a dining table.
5 He hasn't got any chairs.
6 He's got a garden.

b Make questions from the prompts and write **true** short answers.

London/five airports?

Has London got five airports? Yes, it has.

1 your town/a theatre?
2 your parents/a car?
3 you/a computer?
4 your teacher/any pens?

Pronunciation

5　**a** ▣ 5.6 Listen to the underlined sounds. Which sound is different?

He's got a lapt<u>o</u>p, a c<u>a</u>t and a w<u>a</u>tch.

b ▣ 5.7 Listen and tick (✓) the word you hear.

1	hot ☐		hat ☐
2	on ☐		an ☐
3	top ☐		tap ☐
4	pocket ☐		packet ☐

Speaking

6 Work in pairs to describe rooms.

Student A: choose one of the rooms from Ex. 1 but don't tell your partner. Talk about your room. Use *there is/are* and *have got*.

Student B: listen to your partner. Ask questions. Which room is it?

7　**a** Make a list of your family members and important personal possessions. Use the ideas in the box.

Family: *husband, two children*
Accommodation: *two-bedroom apartment*
Furniture: *desk*
Electrical equipment: *CD player*
Pets: *cat*
Transport: *bicycle*
Other: *Swiss watch*

b In pairs, find four things that ...

• your partner has got but you haven't got.

1 _____ 2 _____ 3 _____ 4 _____

• you've got but your partner hasn't got.

1 _____ 2 _____ 3 _____ 4 _____

A: *Have you got a car?*
B: *No, I haven't but I've got a motorbike.*

Writing

8 Write a paragraph about where your partner lives and the things he/she has and hasn't got. Use the How to box to help you.

Mariela lives in a house with a garden. She's got two sisters. She's got a computer and a printer but she hasn't got a mobile phone.

HOW TO ...

add information

Use *and* to join similar sentences or parts of sentences.
He's got a mobile phone. He's got a TV. =
He's got a mobile phone and a TV.

Use *but* to give different/contrasting information.
I've got a house. I haven't got a car. =
I've got a house but I haven't got a car.

5.3 World class

Grammar	modifiers (*very, quite, really*)
Can do	write an informal email about your country

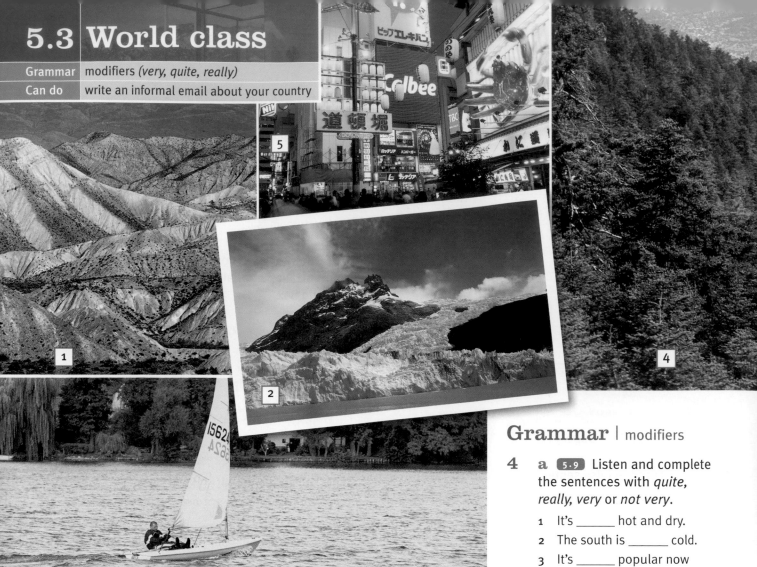

Listening

1 **a** Match these places to the photos. You don't need one word.

mountain ☐ desert ☐ forest ☐ city ☐ river ☐ lake ☐

b Work with a partner. In which countries are the places in the photos?

2 **5.8** Listen to five people talking about their homes and check your answers to Ex. 1a and Ex. 1b.

3 **a** Listen again. Make notes about the places in the table.

PLACE	LANDSCAPE	WHICH PART?
1 *Spain*	_____	_____
2 _____	_____	*south*
3 _____	*beautiful lakes*	_____
4 *Kefallonia*	_____	_____
5 _____	_____	*west*

b Make sentences about the places with *There's* or *There are*.
There's a famous desert in the south of Spain.

Grammar | modifiers

4 **a** **5.9** Listen and complete the sentences with *quite, really, very* or *not very*.

1 It's _____ hot and dry.

2 The south is _____ cold.

3 It's _____ popular now with people from other countries.

4 It's _____ busy and noisy, and it's _____ friendly.

b Write the correct modifiers next to the thermometer.

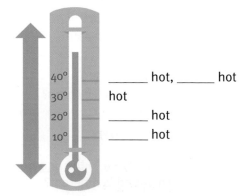

40° _____ hot, _____ hot
30° hot
20° _____ hot
10° _____ hot

see Reference page 53

5 Make sentences.

Russia/big *Russia is very big.*

1 New Zealand/big

2 Mount Everest/high

3 The Pyrenees/high

4 Mexico City/busy

5 Canada/cold

6 Britain/cold

Vocabulary | adjectives to describe places

6 **a** Which adjectives can we use with *desert*?
Look at the word map and add two adjectives
from the box.

hot —— desert

> beautiful busy cold dry
> famous green high hot
> huge noisy popular

b Make word maps for *mountain, island,
forest, beach* and *city*.

Pronunciation

7 **a** [5.10] Listen and answer the questions.

river   desert

1 How many syllables do the words have?
2 Is the second syllable strong or weak?

> ### Lifelong learning
>
> Use your dictionary ...
> to find how many syllables there are in a word.
> two: moun•tain three: mic•ro•wave

b [5.11] Look at the words in the box. Mark the
syllables and <u>underline</u> the strong syllable.

riv/er   des/ert

> centre island Japan Poland China

c Listen and check your answers.

Speaking

8 **a** Write answers to these questions. Use the
How to box to help you.

1 Where do you live?
2 What kind of landscape is there in your
country? Where is it?
3 Which parts of your country do you like/not like?

HOW TO...	**describe where you live**	
	Say where you live	*I'm from ... I live in ...*
	Describe the landscape	*There are ... in the south/north of ...*
	Give your opinion	*I like/don't like ... because ...*

b In pairs use your answers to describe where
you live and your country. Then describe where
a friend lives, or another country.

Writing

9 **a** Read the email and answer the questions.

Are there mountains in Australia?
Yes, there are. They're in the south.

1 What is there in the north of Australia?
2 Where are the deserts in Australia?
3 Is there a big city in the west?
4 Where are the famous beaches?

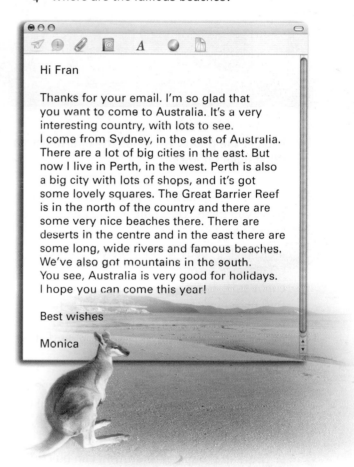

Hi Fran

Thanks for your email. I'm so glad that
you want to come to Australia. It's a very
interesting country, with lots to see.
I come from Sydney, in the east of Australia.
There are a lot of big cities in the east. But
now I live in Perth, in the west. Perth is also
a big city with lots of shops, and it's got
some lovely squares. The Great Barrier Reef
is in the north of the country and there are
some very nice beaches there. There are
deserts in the centre and in the east there are
some long, wide rivers and famous beaches.
We've also got mountains in the south.
You see, Australia is very good for holidays.
I hope you can come this year!

Best wishes

Monica

b Match these expressions from the email to
their purpose.

1 Hi Fran
2 Thanks for your email.
3 I hope you can come this year!
4 Best wishes

a opening sentence
b closing sentence
c starting the email (greeting)
d ending the email

10 Write an email to a friend about your country.

1 Look at your answers to Ex. 8a. Which
information do you want to put in the email?
2 Use *and* and *but* to join sentences.
3 In groups, read each other's emails. Add to the
information if possible.

Furnishing an apartment

1 Look at the photo. What has the apartment got? What hasn't it got?

2 **a** This is your new apartment. What do you think you need? Use a dictionary and choose ten things.

armchair ☐   bed ☐   bookshelves ☐
CD player ☐   coffee machine ☐   computer ☐
cupboard ☐   desk ☐   dining table and chairs ☐
DVD player ☐   lamp ☐   microwave ☐
phone with answering machine ☐   sofa ☐
television ☐   vacuum cleaner ☐   video ☐
washing machine ☐

b Compare your list with a partner. Agree on ten important things and put the things in order 1–10 (1 = very useful, 10 = not very useful).

3 **a** Work in groups of three. You can buy things for your apartment but you've only got €1,000!

You each have information from a different place. You can talk about your information but you can't show it to your partners. Talk about the things you want for your apartment, compare the prices and complete the shopping list of the things you want to buy and their cost. Remember you only have €1,000!

Are there any sofas in your list?

How much do they cost?

What have we got now?

NEW APARTMENT SHOPPING LIST

ITEM	SUPPLIER	COST
lamp	Furnishyourapartment.com	€45

Student A: you have information from the Internet. Turn to page 126.

Student B: you have a catalogue. Turn to page 129.

Student C: you have information from a local shop. Look at the bottom of this page.

b When you finish, compare your list with other groups.

Student C: you have this information from a local shop.

Davis Electrical
Today's bargains!

Home cinema
(DVD and flatscreen TV)
Only ų600!

Combination DVD player and TV
ų225

Japanese large TV and video combination
ų400

Washing machine
ų330

Vacuum cleaner
ų125

CD player
ų195

Digital phone and answering machine
ų130

Italian coffee machine
ų150

there is/there are

	Singular	Plural
➕	There's ... (There is)	There are ...
➖	There isn't ... (There is not)	There aren't ... (There are not)
❓	Is there ...?	Are there ...?
	Yes, there is./ No, there isn't.	Yes, there are./ No, there aren't.

Use *there is* (+ a singular noun) and *there are* (+ a plural noun) to talk about people or things for the first time. We often use them to describe places.

Use *there's*, *there isn't* and *there aren't* when you speak.

There's a huge forest in the west.

Use *There's*, not *There are*, to introduce a list of singular objects.

There's a swimming pool, a lake and a restaurant at the holiday village.

have got

	I/We/You/They	He/She/It
➕	've got (have got)	's got (has got)
➖	haven't got (have not got)	hasn't got (has not got)
❓	Have ... got?	Has ... got?
	Yes, we have. No, I haven't.	Yes, it has. No, she hasn't.

We usually use the contracted forms: *'s got ...,* *'ve got ...,* *hasn't got ...,* *haven't got ...*

There are no contracted forms for questions.

Have you got a DVD player?

We often use short answers when we answer *have got* questions.

A: *Have you got a television?*
B: *Yes, I have./No, I haven't.*

Use *have got* to talk about our possessions and family/friends. Don't use *have got* in very formal English.

I've got a sports car.
They've got two sisters.

Modifiers

The words *(not) very*, *quite* and *really* are modifiers. We put them in front of an adjective to make it stronger or weaker. Use *very* and *really* to make the adjective stronger.

This car is very/really expensive!

Use *quite* or *not very* to make the adjective weaker.

This car is quite expensive.
This car isn't very expensive.

Adjectives and places

Use adjectives to describe nouns. These adjectives describe places:

a hot, dry desert
a busy, noisy city
a long, wide river
a beautiful lake
a high mountain
a lovely beach
a green forest
a popular island

We usually put adjectives in front of the noun. We often put a comma between two adjectives in front of a noun.

Key vocabulary

Types of home
house   apartment   studio   cottage   town house

Rooms and parts of a house
bathroom   bedroom   dining room   garden   garage   hall   living room   roof terrace   terrace

Furniture
armchair   bed   bookshelves   chair   coffee table   cupboard   desk   dining chairs/table   sofa   table

Equipment and possessions
answering machine   bath   CD player   coffee machine   cooker   dishwasher   DVD player   fridge   microwave   MP3 player   music system   shower   sink   toilet   vacuum cleaner   video   washing machine

1 Look at the floor plan and complete the dialogue with *there is* or *there are*.

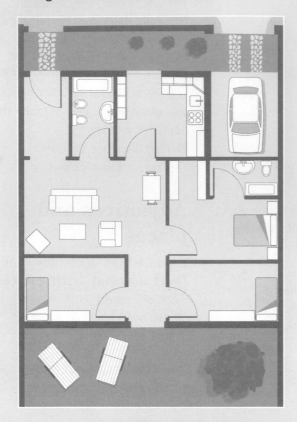

A: Good morning. Can you give me some information about the apartment on Chandos Road?

B: Yes, of course. It's a very nice, big apartment. (1) *There are* three bedrooms, ...

A: (2) _____ a bathroom with each bedroom?

B: No, (3) _____ . The main bedroom has got a bathroom, and then (4) _____ one other bathroom in the apartment.

A: OK. Is the kitchen big?

B: Yes, it is, and it's got a lot of equipment.

A: What about the dining room?

B: Ah, well, (5) _____ a dining room. But (6) _____ a large living room with a dining area.

A: I know there's a garden but (7) _____ any terraces?

B: No, (8) _____, I'm afraid.

A: And finally, (9) _____ a garage?

B: Yes, (10) _____ a garage at the front of the house.

2 Write negative sentences.

We've got an apartment in London.

We haven't got an apartment in London.

1 I've got a video camera.
2 She's got a mobile phone.
3 They've got a lot of money.
4 Their car's got a CD player.
5 England's got a lot of mountains.

3 Write questions and short answers.

Simon/sports car? No, _____.

Has Simon got a sports car? No, *he hasn't.*

1 Rachel/laptop computer? Yes, _____.
2 they/big house? No, _____.
3 your flat/garden? No, _____.
4 Kelly/washing machine? Yes, _____.
5 Spain/king? Yes, _____.

4 Complete the sentences with modifiers. You choose the modifier.

English is _quite_ easy to learn.

1 My town/city is _____ beautiful.
2 People in my country are _____ friendly.
3 My country is _____ popular with tourists.
4 My diet is _____ healthy.
5 My home is _____ noisy.

5 Match the words in the box to the places on the map (A–I).

> a beach   a city   a̶ ̶d̶e̶s̶e̶r̶t̶   a forest   an island
> a lake   mountains   a river   the sea

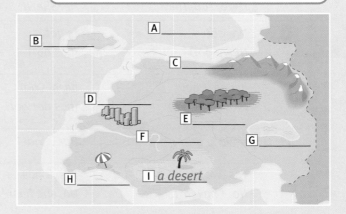

6 Write the things from the box in the rooms where you usually find them. Some things can go in two or three rooms.

> armchair   bed   bookshelves   CD player
> coffee table   cooker   cupboard   dishwasher
> fridge   sofa   table   washing machine

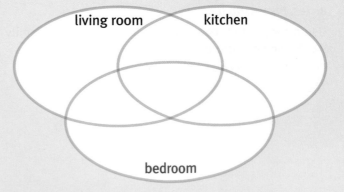

6 City life

Lead-in

1   **a** Look at the photos. Which places in the box can you see?

> art gallery   bank   bar   bookshop   café   church   cinema
> factory   hospital   library   museum   newsagent's
> phone shop   police station   post office   restaurant   school
> square   supermarket   train station

b **6.1** Listen to the words from Ex. 1a. How many syllables does each word or phrase have? Practise saying the words.

art/gal/le/ry – 4   bank – 1

c What can you do in these places?

A: *What can you do in a bookshop?*
B: *You can buy books in a bookshop.*

2   **a** **6.2** Listen and complete the directions.

Turn *left* at the bookshop.

1 _____ straight on to the post office.
2 The bank is _____ the right.
3 _____ right at the church.
4 _____ along the road next to the park.
5 The school is on the _____.

b Match the directions to the diagrams.

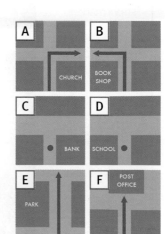

6.1 | Changes

Grammar	past of *to be*: all forms; Past Simple of regular verbs: positive
Can do	talk about your past

Reading

1 **a** What are the buildings in the photos? Read the text and check your answers.

     b Match the buildings with *now* and *in the past*.

		Now	In the past
1	The Hoover Building	an office	a hospital
2	The Musée d'Orsay	a supermarket	a train station
3	The Reina Sofía	an art gallery	a school
4	The Smolny Institute	a museum and art gallery	a factory

Grammar | past of *to be*

2 Choose the correct words in the rules in the Active grammar box, then complete the table in the Active grammar box.

Active grammar

We use *is* and *are* with *now/the past*.
We use *was* and *were* with *now/the past*.

	I/He/She/It	We/You/They
➕	was	_____
➖	_____	weren't
❓	_____ I/he/she/it?	Were we/you/they?
	Yes, I/he/she/it was.	Yes, we/you/they _____ .
	No, I/he/she/it _____ .	No, we/you/they weren't.

see Reference page 63

Changing **buildings**

You live in an apartment now, but was it an apartment fifty years ago? Maybe it wasn't an apartment, but a school or a factory …

The Hoover Building in London is a famous building from the 1930s. It was the main office and factory of the Hoover Company. It is now a supermarket.

The Musée d'Orsay in Paris was a train station in the early twentieth century. It is now an art gallery.

The Reina Sofía building was a hospital. It is now one of Madrid's main museums and art galleries.

The Smolny Institute in St Petersburg is now the office of the Governor of the city. It was a school for rich girls in the nineteenth century. The offices were classrooms.

3 Make two true sentences about each building.

The Hoover Building was a factory. It is now a supermarket.

Person to person

4 Where were you at these times? Ask and answer.

> ten minutes ago   an hour ago
> ~~six hours ago~~   yesterday at midday
> at eight o'clock last night
> last Sunday afternoon
> last Saturday evening

A: *Where were you six hours ago?*
B: *I was at home.*
A: *Were you in the living room?*
B: *No, I wasn't. I was in bed.*

Listening

5 **a** 〔6.3〕 Listen to four speakers. Which of the buildings in the photos does each speaker talk about?

Speaker 1 _____
Speaker 2 _____
Speaker 3 _____
Speaker 4 _____

b Look at this summary and find one new piece of information about each building.

The Hoover Building was a factory and offices: some people (1) _____ in the factory. They produced electrical equipment. Other people worked in the offices.

Doctors and nurses lived and worked in the San Carlos Hospital. They (2) _____ after sick people. The museum now has Picasso's *Guernica*.

Young women studied in the school. It (3) _____ into Lenin's main offices when he (4) _____ to come here in 1917, and he planned the Revolution here.

The Musée d'Orsay was a train station. It (5) _____ in 1900 but it (6) _____ in 1937. The museum opened in 1986, and France's Impressionist collection (7) _____ there.

Grammar | Past Simple of regular verbs (positive)

6 **a** Find the Past Simple of these verbs in the summary in Ex. 5b.

live _____   work _____   study _____
plan _____   open _____

b Match the verbs in Ex. 6a with these Past Simple endings. Then check in the Reference on page 63.

1   + -ed   3   + n + -ed
2   −y + -ied   4   + -d

c Complete gaps 1–7 in Ex. 5b with suitable verbs. Listen again to check.

7 Make sentences in the Past Simple from the prompts.

Doctors/work/in the San Carlos hospital
Doctors worked in the San Carlos hospital.

1   The Hoover Factory/produce/vacuum cleaners
2   Alicia/study/at the Sorbonne
3   My brother/start/a new job yesterday
4   My mother/marry/my father in 1977
5   That church/change/to apartments in 2002

Pronunciation

8 **a** 〔6.4〕 Listen to the Past Simple endings of these verbs. Are they all the same?

/t/	/d/	/ɪd/
work**ed**	open**ed**	decid**ed**

b 〔6.5〕 Listen and write the verbs in the correct column. Then repeat them.

visited finished lived changed started looked produced planned studied

/t/ worked	/d/ opened	/ɪd/ decided

c Read a sentence from Ex. 7. Your partner listens and checks your pronunciation.

Speaking

9 Use the verbs from this lesson to make notes about your past. Tell your partner about your past.

When I was a child, we lived in Biarritz, but we moved in 1990 to Marseille.

Reading

1 Read the text and answer the questions.

  1 How many hours was Robin Andrews away from home?

  2 What does *missing* mean?

  3 Why is Robin confused?

2 **a** [6.6] Listen to an interview with Robin and answer the questions.

  1 Where was Robin the next morning?

  2 Who helped him?

  3 Who collected him?

b There are some mistakes in the interviewer's notes for her article. Listen and correct the underlined phrases.

  1 Robin disappeared <u>at 2.30</u>.

  2 He walked <u>three</u> kilometres to the village.

  3 He called <u>at the post office</u>.

  4 He wanted to go <u>to the bar</u>.

  5 <u>A young man</u> helped him.

  6 <u>His mother</u> collected him.

Vocabulary |
prepositions of place

3 **a** Listen to the dialogue again. Tick (✓) the phrases you hear.

in the bank ☐
next to the supermarket ☐
at the phone shop ☐
to the Internet café ☐
in front of a library ☐
on the ground ☐
behind the police station ☐
at the bus station ☐
under the bridge ☐
between the trees ☐

b [6.7] Listen to the phrases in Ex. 3a and repeat them.

Man goes missing for 16 hours

Robin Andrews, 24, of Loxton Close, Shelton, was missing for sixteen hours last Tuesday. Mr Andrews disappeared at 2.30 in the afternoon when he walked out of the house to get some things in the village. In the village centre, three kilometres from his home, Mr Andrews collected some money from the cashpoint and called at the post office, but he doesn't remember anything after that. Mr Andrews is very confused, 'I wanted to go to the bar but something strange happened.' It seems that Mr Andrews arrived in Marbury, eight kilometres from Shelton, where ...

Lifelong learning

Words and pictures

Pictures can sometimes help you to learn words, like the diagrams of prepositions below.

4 Write the correct preposition under the diagrams.

Grammar | Past simple: questions

5 Read the questions in the Active grammar box and complete the rule. Choose the correct words

Active grammar

1 *Did you get lost?*

2 *Where did you go then?*

3 *Did you go to sleep?*

To make questions in the Past Simple, use *do/did* and the *past form/infinitive* of the verb.

see Reference page 63

6   **a** Complete the questions from the interview with *did* or a question word. Then match the question to the answers. Check your answers in the tapescript on page 154.

1 _____ you get the money?

2 _____ did you go then?

3 _____ you have any money with you?

4 So _____ did you do?

a No, I didn't, not then.

b Yes, I did.

c I wanted to go to the Internet café ...

d I asked the old man for directions to the police station.

b Write questions for the sentences in Ex. 2b. Use these question words.

What time? How many?
Where? Who?

What time did Robin disappear?

7   **a** What happened to Robin? Tell your partner your story and decide which ending you like best.

Student A: look at page 126.
Student B: look at page 129.

b ⬛6.8 Listen. Which story is correct?

Person to person

8   Ask and answer. Find out what your partner did ...

> yesterday last night
> last weekend
> on their last holiday

You can ask only ten *yes/no* questions.

A: *Did you watch TV last night?*

B: *No, I didn't.*

Listening

9   **a** ⬛6.9 Listen. Follow the directions on the map. Write the letters of these places.

post office ___   bookshop ___   police station ___

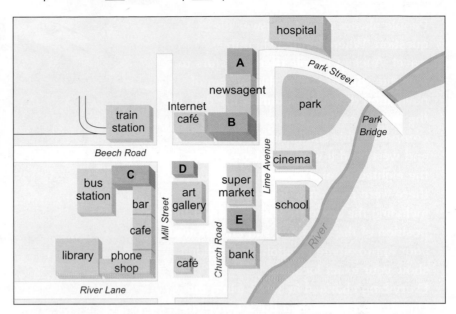

b Listen again and complete the expressions in the How to box. (You can check in the tapescript on page 155.)

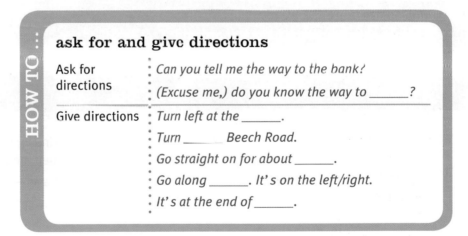

HOW TO ...

ask for and give directions

Ask for directions	Can you tell me the way to the bank?
	(Excuse me,) do you know the way to _____?
Give directions	Turn left at the _____.
	Turn _____ Beech Road.
	Go straight on for about _____.
	Go along _____. It's on the left/right.
	It's at the end of _____.

10 Work in pairs. Use the map. Ask for and give directions.

from	to
the bank	the bridge
the police station	the bus station
the library	the cinema
the hospital	the art gallery

11 Write two or three sentences to answer your friend's question.

Can you email me directions from the station or bus stop to your house? Thanks, and see you on Saturday.

People always need to answer the question 'Where am I?' when they travel. Ancient people used the *stars* to navigate. But of course this system of navigation didn't work during the day. In the twelfth century sailors invented the *compass* – this shows north, south, east and west, and it works at day or night. In the eighteenth and nineteenth centuries there were many new inventions, including the *sextant*. This measured the position of the stars and sun and showed your approximate location, but it didn't show your exact location.

Everything changed in 1973 when the United States launched the 24 *satellites* of the Global Positioning System (GPS). These go around the Earth at a height of 17,440 kilometres. Computers combine the signals from the GPS satellites with *maps* to show exactly where you are and how to get to another place.

Reading

1   Discuss.

   1   What do maps show?

   2   Are you good at using them?

   3   When was the last time you used a map?

2   **a** Read the text quickly. Choose the best title.

   a   What is GPS?

   b   How ancient people travelled

   c   Navigation past and present

b Read the text again. Use the words in italics to label the pictures below.

  A

  B

C

  D

  E

3   **a** Find words 1–6 in the text and match them to their meanings.

   1   travel   a   people who work on a ship

   2   navigate   b   not exact

   3   sailors   c   the place or position of something

   4   approximate

   5   location   d   find your position or direction when you travel

   6   signal

               e   electronic communication between machines

               f   go from one place to another

b Use information from the text to complete the sentences.

Ancient people *used* the stars to navigate.

1   The system of navigating by the stars _____ during the day.

2   There _____ many new inventions in the eighteenth century.

3   The sextant _____ an exact location.

4   In 1973 everything _____ .

Grammar | Past Simple: negative

4 Read the sentence in the Active grammar box. Complete the rule. Choose the correct words.

> ### Active grammar
>
> *This system of navigation didn't work during the day.*
>
> To make negatives in the Past Simple we use *don't/didn't* and the *past form/infinitive* of the verb.

see Reference page 63

5 Correct these false statements.

Ancient people used compasses.

Ancient people didn't use compasses.

1 The sextant showed exact location.
2 People used cars in the sixteenth century.
3 Leonardo da Vinci invented the compass.
4 Ancient people played computer games.
5 Beethoven painted the *Mona Lisa*.
6 Marco Polo owned a mobile phone.

Vocabulary | transport

6 **a** Look at the photo and answer the questions.

1 How did people travel around Bangkok 100 years ago?
2 How do they get around today, do you think?

b Match the forms of transport to the famous places.

transport

1 red buses 2 yellow taxis 3 water buses
4 high speed trains 5 electric trams 6 bicycles

places

a Japan b London c San Francisco
d Amsterdam e Venice f New York

Person to person

7 Discuss.

1 How do you get around your town/city? (by car/bus, on foot, etc.)
2 Which form of transport do you like?

Pronunciation

8 **a** **6.10** Listen and <u>underline</u> the stressed words in the answers.

A: Do you like buses?
B: No, I like <u>trains</u>.

1 A: Did you visit Venice? B: No, we visited Rome.
2 A: Was it nice? B: No, it was horrible.

b Make dialogues using the table.

LIKE	VISIT	WAS IT
coffee? (✗ tea)	the cinema? (✗ the theatre)	small? (✗ big)
rice? (✗ pasta)	Russia? (✗ Poland)	new? (✗ old)
bikes? (✗ cars)	your uncle? (✗ my brother)	good? (✗ bad)

A: *Do you like coffee?* B: *No, I like tea.*

Writing

9 **a** Read the paragraph. <u>Underline</u> all the verbs in the Past Simple.

> I visited Bangkok last year with my friend, Amanda. We liked the food but we didn't like the weather – it was very hot! We stayed in a hotel near the river. There were lots of tourists there and we talked to some girls from Australia. The city is enormous so we didn't walk very much. We travelled on the new overhead railway. It was very fast and comfortable. We looked at lots of temples and we watched the boats on the river. We wanted some presents so we visited the fantastic street markets ...

b Write a paragraph about your last holiday. Use the underlined verbs from Ex. 9a.

6 Communication

In shops

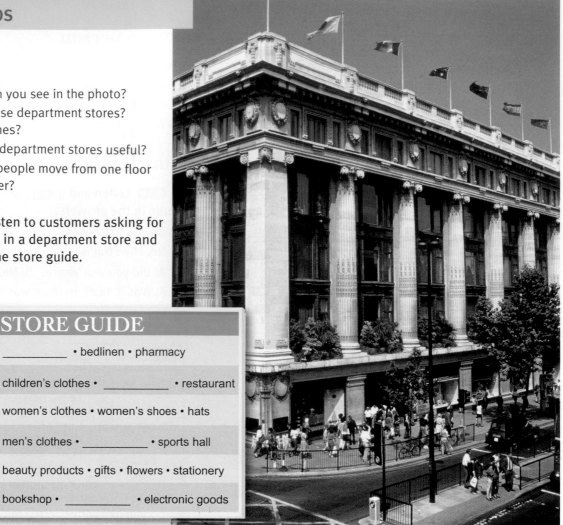

1 Discuss.

 1 What can you see in the photo?
 2 Do you use department stores? Which ones?
 3 Why are department stores useful?
 4 How do people move from one floor to another?

2 **a** **6.11** Listen to customers asking for information in a department store and complete the store guide.

STORE GUIDE

Fourth floor	_____ • bedlinen • pharmacy
Third floor	children's clothes • _____ • restaurant
Second floor	women's clothes • women's shoes • hats
First floor	men's clothes • _____ • sports hall
Ground floor	beauty products • gifts • flowers • stationery
Basement	bookshop • _____ • electronic goods

b Listen again (or look at the tapescript on page 155) and complete the How to box.

HOW TO ...

ask for what you want in a shop

Ask where something is	*Where _____ men's shoes?*
Ask for something	*_____ a store guide?*
	Can _____ a copy, please?
Ask about prices	*How _____ is that?*

c In pairs, ask and answer about where to find things. Use the information in the store guide.

> ~~sofa~~ football CD player aspirin printer
> women's jeans pencil dictionary

A: *Where can I find a sofa?*
B: *In furniture on the fourth floor.*

3 Work in pairs. You can be an A pair or a B pair.

A pairs: you work in a gift shop. Turn to page 126.
B pairs: you are customers. Read the information below.

It is your best friend's birthday next week and you want to buy her two presents. Decide how much you want to spend, then look at the categories below and decide on two suitable presents.

* travel guide books
* DVDs
* chocolates
* gifts (wallets, diaries, address books)
* stationery (pens, pencils, notebooks)

Let's buy her a guide book to New York and a box of Swiss chocolates.

Write down the things you want to buy then talk to different A pairs and find the things you want.

Excuse me, have you got any Swiss chocolates?
How much are they?
Can I have a box?

Past Simple

Use the Past Simple to talk about actions and situations in the past. The actions and situations are finished.

*My hair **was** red when I was a girl, but it's grey now.*

to be		
➕	I/He/She/It was	We/You/They were
➖	I/He/She/It wasn't (was not)	We/You/They weren't (were not)
❓	Was I/he/she/it?	Were we/you/they?
	Yes, I/he/she/it was.	Yes, we/you/they were.
	No, I/he/she/it wasn't.	No, we/you/they weren't.

*She **was** tired last night.*
*They **weren't** at the cinema yesterday.*
***Was** Karin at the office on Monday? No, she **wasn't**.*
***Were** the musicians good? Yes, they **were**.*

Regular verbs: positive

Make the Past Simple of most regular verbs by adding *-ed* to the verb.

work → *work**ed**, watch* → *watch**ed**, listen* → *listen**ed***

Note the spelling rules:

- add *-d* to verbs that end in *-e*,
  live → *liv**ed**, change* → *chang**ed***
- with verbs that end in consonant + *-y*, remove *-y* and add *-ied*, *study* → *stud**ied**, carry* → *carr**ied**.* (If the verb ends in vowel + *-y*, add *-ed*, *stay* → *stay**ed**.*)
- with verbs of one syllable that end in vowel + consonant, repeat the consonant and add *-ed*, *plan* → *plan**ned**, jog* → *jog**ged***

Negative

Did + not + infinitive

*Ancient people **did not use** compasses.*

In informal English, we use the contracted form *didn't*.

*People **didn't** know their exact location.*

Questions

Wh- questions

Wh-word + *did* + subject pronoun + infinitive
*When **did** you **finish** work yesterday?*

Yes/no questions

Did + subject pronoun + infinitive

Short answers

Yes, I/he/she/it/we/you/they did.
No, I/he/she/it/we/you/they didn't.
***Did** you **study** at university? Yes, I **did**.*

Prepositions of place

We use prepositions to show relationships of place. The prepositions *in, on, under, in front of, behind, between* and *next to* show clear location.

The books are **in** the cupboard. The picture is **on** the cupboard. The bin is **under** the desk. The chair is **in front of** the desk. The map is **behind** the desk. The desk is **next to** the cupboard. The plant is **between** the cupboard and the desk.

The preposition *at* can mean *in* or *near*.
I'm at the phone shop. (= in/in front of)
I'm at the door. (= next to/in front of)
We also use *at* with a very general meaning.
I'm at home. Are you at work?

Key vocabulary

Places in a town

art gallery   department store   pharmacy
bank   factory   phone shop   bar   police station
bookshop   hospital   post office   bridge
Internet café   restaurant   bus station   library
school   café   museum   square   cashpoint
newsagent's   supermarket   church   office
train station   tram   cinema   park

Forms of transport

bicycle   boat   bus   car   motorbike   ship   taxi
train   tram   water bus

1 Write the Past Simple form of the verbs in the correct column.

> ~~carry~~ ~~change~~ close decide ~~finish~~ ~~jog~~
> look live marry move own plan start
> stop want worry

+ -ed	+ -d	– -y + -ied	+ consonant + -ed
finished	changed	carried	jogged

2 There are ten mistakes in the text. Find and correct the other nine.

This is a photo of my great-grandparents – my mother's grandparents. They ~~live~~ *lived* in the middle of the last century. They was lovely people. My great-grandfather works in a car factory and he ownd a car when most people didn't know about them. My great-grandmother was very beautiful when she were a girl. She marryed my great-grandfather when she was only 17. She didn't work – she stays at home and looked after the children. My great-grandfather stoped work when he was 65, then every day they walked to the park and my great-grandmother always carries a little bag with sandwiches for their lunch. She died in 1983, when she was only 73, and after three months my great-grandfather dieed too – he didn't want to live without her.

3 Make Past Simple questions and answers from the prompts.

Albert Einstein/understand/Mathematics? (✓)
Q: Did Albert Einstein understand Mathematics?
A: Yes, he did.

Charles Darwin/French? (✗ British)
Q: Was Charles Darwin French?
A: No, he wasn't. He was British.

1 Pablo Picasso/Spanish? (✓)
  Q: _____
  A: _____

2 Mozart /play/the guitar? (✗ the piano)
  Q: _____
  A: _____

3 President Kennedy/Russian? (✗ American)
  Q: _____
  A: _____

4 the USA/launch/GPS satellites in 1983? (✗ 1973)
  Q: _____
  A: _____

5 the Hoover Building/a factory/70 years ago? (✓)
  Q: _____
  A: _____

6 Alexander Graham Bell/invent/the computer? (✗ the telephone)
  Q: _____
  A: _____

7 the ancient Romans/speak Latin? (✓)
  Q: _____
  A: _____

8 Neil Armstrong/walk/on a star? (✗ the Moon)
  Q: _____
  A: _____

4 Complete the text with prepositions of place.

Alan's room is really untidy! He's got an armchair in the room but there are some shoes _on_ it and there's a plant (1)_____ it. There's a phone and some credit cards (2)_____ the bed and there are CDs and books (3)_____ it. There's a cup of cold coffee (4)_____ the bed! There's a newspaper (5)_____ the sink. His suitcase is on the floor, open, (6)_____ the desk and the sink, and his laptop is (7)_____ the suitcase.

5 Write the names of two places where you can do these things.

1 have something to eat or drink _____
2 buy things to take home _____
3 look at paintings or old things _____
4 start a journey _____
5 sit for a few minutes _____
6 ask people for help _____

7 People

Lead-in

1 **a** Complete the descriptions of the people in the photos with A-H.

1 _C_ has got a pretty face
2 _____ has got blue eyes.
3 _____ has got fair hair.
4 _____ has got dark skin.
5 _____ has got grey hair.

6 _____ has got a beard.
7 _____ is slim.
8 _____ is young.
9 _____ is bald.
10 _____ wears glasses.

b **7.1** Listen and compare your answers.

2 Work in pairs.

Student A: describe a person from the photos.

This person's got fair hair and wears glasses.

Student B: point at the person.

3 **a** Who does it belong to? Match the things 1–4 with the people/places a–d.

1 Buckingham Palace
2 *The Mona Lisa*
3 20th Century Fox
4 Microsoft

a Rupert Murdoch
b Bill Gates
c Queen Elizabeth II
d The Louvre

b Check your answers in pairs.

A: *Who does Buckingham Palace belong to?*

B: *It belongs to Queen Elizabeth II.*

Reading and vocabulary

1 Marianne is twenty-two. She comes from New Zealand, but is at university in Brazil. Discuss.

  1 Where is the beach in the photo?

  2 What is the connection between Marianne and the beach, do you think?

Dear Carol

A Thanks for your letter about my old friends in New Zealand!

B Everything is fine here. I arrived in Rio de Janeiro a month ago to start my course and then I moved in with my host family. They live in a big apartment near the beach in Ipanema.

C The family is very nice. Mr and Mrs Silva are middle-aged and very friendly. They've got three children. Tina is my age, she's got dark hair and she's pretty. She's tall, like me. João is the middle one; he's fifteen. He's quite short and he's very tanned from playing football! Carlos is the young one, he's a bit fat. He's lovely, he laughs all the time.

D Every morning I go to college. The classes are tiring, especially the literature ones. I usually go to the beach in the afternoon. The beach here is beautiful and the sea is warm. There is a really handsome man on the beach. He watches me every day. I think he's nice but I'm quite shy so I don't look at him!

E Write to me soon and tell me all your news.

Love

Marianne

2 **a** Read the letter and answer the questions.

  1 What did Marianne do a month ago?

  2 Who does she live with now?

  3 What does she do in the afternoon?

b Read the letter again. Match the people and the adjectives.

  1 Mr and Mrs Silva   a tanned, short

  2 Tina   b handsome, nice

  3 João   c friendly, middle-aged

  4 Carlos   d dark, pretty

  5 the man on the beach e tall, shy

  6 Marianne   f young, fat

Lifelong learning

Opposite adjectives

A good way to remember adjectives is in pairs with opposite meanings.

old – young

3 **a** Find adjectives in Ex. 2b with the opposite meaning.

pale *tanned*

  1 fair _____   2 slim _____   3 horrible _____
  4 ugly _____/_____   5 old _____   6 tall _____

b Put the adjectives from Ex. 3a in the correct column. Which adjectives can go in more than one column?

BODY	FACE	SKIN	HAIR	HEIGHT	AGE	PERSONALITY
		tanned				

4 Think of someone in your class, or a famous person. Describe him/her to your partner but don't say his/her name! Can your partner guess the person?

She's quite short. She's got dark hair ...

Listening

6 **a** `7.2` Listen to the song and answer these questions.

1 Is the singer happy or sad? Why?

2 Who is 'The Girl from Ipanema', do you think?

b Listen again and complete the gaps.

Tall and (1) _____ and (2) _____ and lovely
The girl from Ipanema (3) _____ walking
And when she passes, each (4) _____ she passes goes – ah
When she (5) _____, she's like a samba
That swings so cool (6) _____ sways so gentle
That when she passes, each (7) _____ she passes goes – ooh

(Ooh) But I (8) _____ her so sadly
How can I tell (9) _____ I love her
Yes, I would (10) _____ my heart gladly
But each day, when she walks to the (11) _____
She looks straight ahead, (12) _____ at me

Tall and (13) _____ and (14) _____ and lovely
The girl from (15) _____ goes walking
And when she pauses, I smile – but she doesn't see (doesn't see)
She (16) _____ see, she never sees me ...

Grammar | pronoun *one/ones*

5 **a** Read the sentences in the Active grammar box and choose the correct meaning for the underlined words.

> ### Active grammar
>
> 1 *They've got three children. João is the middle* <u>one</u>.
> 2 *The classes are tiring, especially the literature* <u>ones</u>.
>
> **Meanings**
>
> a) classes b) class c) student d) child

see Reference page 73

b Read the paragraph. Find four more words you can change to *one* (or *ones*).

When I was a child I lived in three different houses. The first <s>house</s> *one* was lovely. The second house was quite small, but it was in a nice location. The third house wasn't very nice but there were six bedrooms. I used the bedroom on the second floor. The other bedrooms were on the first floor.

Writing

7 **a** Match the statements to paragraphs A–E in Marianne's letter in Ex. 2.

Marianne describes her host family. | C |
She asks Carol to do something. | ☐ |
She thanks Carol. | ☐ |
What she does. | ☐ |
Where she lives. | ☐ |

b Complete the How to box with words and phrases from Marianne's letter.

> **HOW TO ...**
>
> ### start and finish informal letters
>
> Start : (all letters) _____ + first name
> Finish : (close friends/family) _____ + your name
> : (friends) *Best wishes* + your name

8 Your family is a 'host family' for foreign students. Sue, an English friend, wants to stay with you. Write a letter to Sue and tell her about where you live and your family.

Listening

1   **a**   Jane Birch has a lot of friends. Match their names to the photos.

Mrs Clark wears glasses. ☐

Davy has got brown hair. ☐

Tara is quite tall. ☐

Mr Clark's got a grey beard. ☐

Gordon is bald. ☐

b   Add information to the descriptions in Ex. 1a. Then make guesses about each person's job.

Mrs Clark's got grey hair. I think she's retired.

2   **a**   Jane has got some presents for her friends. Match the words to the things in the picture.

clock ☐   electric drill ☐   wrapping paper ☐
diary ☐   trainers Ⓐ   handbag ☐   umbrella ☐

b   Who are the presents for? Discuss. Give reasons for your answers.

I think the handbag is for Tara because …

c   **7.3**   Jane went to work this morning. Her husband, Mike, phoned and asked her about the presents. Listen and check your answers to Ex. 2b.

Grammar | possessive pronouns

3 **a** Look at these examples. Choose the correct meaning (a–d) for the <u>underlined</u> words.

a our umbrella   b belong to Davy
c Davy's trainers   d belongs to us

1 A: The trainers. Are they Davy's?
B: Yes, the trainers are <u>his</u>.

2 A: There's an umbrella on the table.
B: It's <u>ours</u>!

b Read the tapescript on page 155 and complete the Active grammar box.

Active grammar

Possessive adjectives	Possessive pronouns
my	_____
his	_____
her	_____
its	_its_
our	_____
your	_____
their	_____

see Reference page 73

4 Rewrite the sentences. Use a possessive pronoun (and a verb if necessary) to replace the phrases in italics.

These aren't my CDs, they *belong to Jane*.

These aren't my CDs, they're hers.

1 Excuse me. Is this *your bag*?
2 Use the blue pen; the red one *belongs to me*.
3 Is this *Maria's watch*?
4 The house next to the church *belonged to them*.
5 Are these sandwiches *for us*?
6 That wasn't her phone number, it was *John's*.
7 They weren't our dogs, they were *Bob and Jo's*.
8 *Does* this *belong to your brother*?

Pronunciation

5 **a** **7·4** Listen to the *th* sound /θ/ in the word *birthday*. Is it the same as the sound in *brother* or *bathroom*?

b **7·5** Listen and circle the words you hear.

1 a) sick b) thick   4 a) first b) thirst
2 a) sink b) think   5 a) tree b) three
3 a) free b) three

c **7·6** Listen. Do you hear the sound /θ/? Tick (✓) for yes, cross (✗) for no. Listen and repeat.

1 ☐ 2 ☐ 3 ☐ 4 ☐ 5 ☐ 6 ☐ 7 ☐ 8 ☐

Vocabulary | ordinal numbers/months

6 **a** When are Jane's friends' birthdays? Look at the tapescript on page 155.

Gordon _the third of next month_ Davy _____
Tara _____

b Write the numbers from Ex. 6a on the red lines then complete the table.

1 _____	6 _____	11 _____	20 _____
2 _second_	7 _____	12 _____	22 _twenty-second_
3 _____	8 _eighth_	13 _____	30 _____
4 _fourth_	9 _____	14 _fourteenth_	31 _____
5 _____	10 _____	15 _____	

c **7·7** Listen and check your answers. Then repeat.

7 Choose the correct words.

1 My birthday is on the *first/one* of May.
2 Our new house has got *three/third* bedrooms.
3 America's Independence Day is on the *four/ fourth* of July.
4 This is my *three/third* holiday this year!
5 It's Lucy's *nine/ninth* birthday on Saturday.

8 **a** Find the names of two months in Ex. 7.

b Number the months 1–12 in the correct order.

c In pairs, answer the questions.

When is your birthday?
What dates are holidays in your country?

9 **a** Talk to your classmates. Find a student/ students with:

1 a birthday in the same month as yours.
2 the first and last birthdays of the year.
3 a birthday this month.
4 a birthday next month.
5 a birthday last month.

b Write the names of all the students in your class, in order of their birthdays.

Girls solve jigsaw puzzle and become rich!

One morning in December last year, schoolgirls Rachel Aumann and Maisie Balley were on their way to school when they saw lots
5 of pieces of paper on the ground. They picked up some pieces and looked at them: they were tiny pieces of banknotes, but where did they come from? Rachel and
10 Maisie noticed a bag in a rubbish bin – it had thousands of pieces of banknotes in it. The two 12-year-olds went to school and told their teachers, then, after school, they
15 took the bag to the police station and handed in the money. The police kept the money for six

months. During that time no owner asked for it, so the police gave back
20 the money to the girls. For the next few months the girls, with Rachel's stepfather Peter, spent time every evening matching the numbers on the pieces, and they put together a
25 lot of the banknotes. They now have £1,200 in £10 notes, but they think there's another £800 in the pieces of £5 and £20 notes. Whose money was it? The girls have no idea, but
30 they're happy that it belongs to them now! Rachel wants to keep her money for when she goes to university, but Maisie wants to go shopping right now!

Reading

1 Look at the headline. Discuss.

   1 What is a jigsaw puzzle?

   2 What games and puzzles do you like?

2 Read the text. What was the jigsaw puzzle?

3 Find words in the text with these meanings.

   1 small parts of something (*line 5*)

   2 paper money (*line 8*)

   3 saw (*line 10*)

   4 mother's husband (*line 22*)

4 Read the text again. Put the events in the correct order.

   a The police returned the banknotes to the girls. ☐

   b They handed the banknotes in to the police. ☐

   c They noticed a bag in a bin, with thousands of banknotes in it. ☐

   d The girls now have £1,200. ☐

   e Rachel and Maisie were on their way to school. ☐ 1

   f The girls matched the pieces of £10 notes. ☐

5 Answer the questions with a few words only.

What did Rachel and Maisie see on the way to school?

pieces of banknotes

   1 What was in the rubbish bin?

   2 Who did the girls tell about the money?

   3 Where did they take the banknotes?

   4 How long did the police keep the money?

   5 Why did the police give it back to the girls?

   6 How did the girls put together the notes?

   7 Whose money was it?

6 Look at Exs. 3–5 and put the strategies in the How to box in the correct order.

HOW TO…	**understand a narrative**	
	Identify the main events	⋮ ____
	Work out new words	⋮ ____
	Understand details	⋮ ____

Grammar | Past Simple: irregular verbs

7 Look at the Active grammar box. Match the verbs to their past simple forms. Check your answers with the text.

Active grammar

1	*go*	a	*took*
2	*give*	b	*put*
3	*have*	c	*spent*
4	*keep*	d	*went*
5	*put*	e	*saw*
6	*see*	f	*told*
7	*spend*	g	*gave*
8	*take*	h	*kept*
9	*tell*	i	*had*

see Reference page 73

8 Make Past Simple sentences about the text.

girls/see

The girls saw pieces of paper.

1 bag/have
2 girls/tell
3 girls/take
4 police/keep
5 girls/put together

Person to person

9 Write five sentences about you. Then ask and answer.

I saw an interesting film at the cinema yesterday.

~~yesterday~~ last weekend
last month   six months ago
last year

A: *What did you do yesterday?*
B: *I saw an interesting film at the cinema.*

Vocabulary | phrasal verbs

10 a Some English verbs have two parts. Complete these verbs from the text.

*pick **up*** 1 look _____ 2 hand _____ 3 give _____ 4 put _____

b Write the verbs from Ex. 10a under the correct picture.

1 _____ 2 _____ 3 _____ 4 _____ 5 _____

c Complete these sentences about the pictures.

1 _____ _____ that burger. It's huge!
2 Can I _____ _____ this wallet?
3 I always _____ _____ a lot of rubbish from the ground.
4 Jonathan! _____ _____ that toy to Harriet now!
5 Here's some glue. We can _____ _____ the pieces and glue them.

Pronunciation

11 **7.8** The first consonant in *wh-* question words can be /w/ (was) or /h/ (his). Listen to the questions from Ex. 5 and write the question words in the correct column.

/w/	/h/
what	

Speaking

12 a Find the Past Simple forms of these verbs on page 149. Make five *wh-* questions.

What did you buy last week?
Who did you go shopping with?

b In pairs, ask and answer the questions.

Identifying people

1 Look at the picture and discuss the questions.

1 Where is the young man?

2 What is his problem, do you think?

2 **a** [7.9] Listen and check your answers. Why did he go to the police station?

b Listen again and complete the form.

MISSING PERSON

Name: _____

Man ☐ /Woman ☐ Age: _____

Height: _____

Hair: _____

Body type: _____

Eyes: _____

Skin: _____

Other features: _____

_____

Last seen: _____

Name of person reporting: _David Kennedy_

Relationship to missing person: _____

---

c Which picture shows the missing woman?

A   B   C

3 Listen to the dialogue again or look at the tapescript on page 155. <u>Underline</u> the questions. Make questions to ask about the form.

4 **a** Your friend is missing. You are at the police station. Follow the stages to report the missing person to the police.

Person reporting: Turn to page 127 and choose one of the people. Decide the relationship of the person to you and when/how they went missing. Start the conversation:

Excuse me, I want to report a missing person.

Police officer: Ask your partner questions and find out about the missing person. (You can use the <u>underlined</u> questions in the tapescript on page 155 to help you.) Complete the form below. Then turn to page 127 and identify the person.

MISSING PERSON

Name: _____

Man ☐ /Woman ☐ Age: _____

Height: _____

Hair: _____

Body type: _____

Eyes: _____

Skin: _____

Other features: _____

Last seen: _____

Name of person reporting: _____

Relationship to missing person: _____

---

b Change roles and repeat. This time use the pictures on page 130.

Pronoun *one/ones*

Use *one* or *ones* to avoid repeating a noun. Use *one* after *this, that* or an adjective.

A: *Do you want the black **pen** or the blue **one**?*

B: *The blue **one**.*

Use *ones* to replace plural nouns. Use *ones* after *these, those* or an adjective.

A: *Did you buy the brown **shoes** or the black **ones**?*

B: *I bought the black **ones**.*

Possessive pronouns

Possessive pronouns show the person something is for, or who it belongs to. Use them in the place of a possessive adjective and a noun.

*This is **my coat**. = This is **mine**.*

Subject pronoun	Possessive adjectives	Possessive pronouns
I	*my*	*mine*
he	*his*	*his*
she	*her*	*hers*
it	*its*	*its*
we	*our*	*ours*
you	*your*	*yours*
they	*their*	*theirs*

(See also page 13)

*That book **is John's** (book).*
*That book is **for John**.* | = *That book is **his**.*
*That book **belongs to John**.*

Past Simple: irregular verbs

(See also page 63)

Many common verbs in English have an irregular past form, i.e. they do not end in *-ed* in the past.

have → had   do → did   go → went   make → made

*I **gave** my mother some flowers last week.*

There are no general rules for the formation of the Past Simple of irregular verbs. See page 149 for a list of irregular Past Simple forms.

These verbs are irregular only in the affirmative. They form the negative and questions with *did* and the infinitive, like regular verbs.

*He **went** to Australia on holiday last year.*

*He **didn't go** to Australia on holiday last year.*

***Did** he **go** to Australia on holiday last year?*

Phrasal verbs

Some verbs in English have two or three parts, usually a verb and a preposition. These verbs are very common. The phrasal verbs in Unit 7 are: *look at, give back, hand in, put together* and *pick up*.

Other phrasal verbs in Units 1–6 of Total English Elementary are: *get up* (Unit 2, Lead-in) and *look after* (Unit 6, Lesson 1).

Ordinal numbers

Use these numbers with nouns and when we talk about dates.

*My **first** child was a boy.*

*The **third** of September/September the **third**.*

We can write dates in different ways.

3 September 3rd September September 3rd

1	first	18	eighteenth
2	second	19	nineteenth
3	third	20	twentieth
4	fourth	21	twenty-first
5	fifth	22	twenty-second
6	sixth	23	twenty-third
7	seventh	24	twenty-fourth
8	eighth	30	thirtieth
9	ninth	31	thirty-first
10	tenth	40	fortieth
11	eleventh	50	fiftieth
12	twelfth	60	sixtieth
13	thirteenth	70	seventieth
14	fourteenth	80	eightieth
15	fifteenth	90	ninetieth
16	sixteenth	100	one hundredth
17	seventeenth		

We often write ordinal numbers like this.

first = 1st   second = 2nd   third = 3rd   fourth = 4th   fifth = 5th, etc.

Key vocabulary

Describing words

Adjectives:

Body	Face	Skin	Hair
slim	pretty	dark	dark fair
fat	handsome	fair	bald *
	ugly	tanned	short

Height	Age	Personality	
tall	middle-aged	nice	friendly
short	young	horrible	shy
	old		

Nouns: glasses   beard

---

* We say *He's bald*, not ~~He's got bald hair~~.

1 Read the dialogue. Find seven words you can change to *one* or *ones*.

A: There are so many sofas here, Philip. Which ~~sofas~~ do you like?   *ones*

B: Well, I like the brown ~~sofa.~~   *one*

A: No, it's ugly. What about the red sofa?

B: It's OK.

A: Fine. Now, chairs. Do you like modern chairs?

B: Yes. I like those chairs in the corner.

A: The metal chairs?

B: Yes.

A: Yes, they're quite nice. But how about this chair?

B: No, I don't like that chair. It isn't very attractive.

A: Well, I don't like this shop. Let's go to a different shop.

2 Match questions 1–7 with the questions with the same meaning.

1 Does this bag belong to you?
2 Is this his?
3 Is this Mary's CD player?
4 Are these our letters?
5 Are these theirs?
6 Is this present for me?
7 Are these mine or yours?
8 Does this umbrella belong to us?

a Are these ours?
b Is this hers?
c Is this mine?
d Do these books belong to them?
e Is this yours?
f Is this ours?
g Are these my keys or your keys?
h Does this belong to Mr McBride?

3 Complete these texts with the correct Past Simple form of the verbs in brackets.

4 Complete the sentences with ordinal numbers. The numbers in the box are clues.

| 1 | 8 | 9 | 16 | 18 | 25 |

Abraham Lincoln was the *sixteenth* president of the United States.

1 August is the _____ month of the year.
2 Christmas Day is on the _____ of December.
3 Neil Armstrong was the _____ man on the Moon.
4 British people can vote after their _____ birthday.
5 The _____ series of *Friends* was the last one.

5 Match the verbs and prepositions, then complete the sentences. (You need the Past Simple in one sentence.)

1 hand
2 give
3 look
4 put
5 pick

a together
b up
c in
d back
e at

Please *hand in* your completed forms to the tour guide.

1 Oh no! This dish is in pieces! Can you _____ it _____ again?
2 _____ your rubbish _____, please. Don't leave it on the floor.
3 Can you _____ _____ the dictionary when you finish your work?
4 A: How do you know the answer?
    B: I _____ _____ my grammar book.

Madame Chiang Kai-Shek died on Thursday in New York. She was 106. Madame Chiang Kai-Shek *met* (meet) her famous husband – Taiwan's leader Chiang Kai Shek – in 1920 and she married him in 1927. After her husband died in 1975 she (1) _____ (leave) Taiwan, and because she (2) _____ (speak) English, she (3) _____ (come) to the United States and (4) _____ (spend) most of her time in Manhattan.

Robert Atkins, famous for the Atkins Diet, died yesterday aged 72 after a fall in the street. Atkins, a doctor, studied at the University of Michigan. He (5) _____ (become) quite fat after he left university and he tried different diets to lose weight. He (6) _____ (think) that people (7) _____ (have) problems with weight because they (8) _____ (eat) the wrong things, and he (9) _____ (write) his first diet book in 1970. Not many people (10) _____ (buy) the book at first, but Atkins's diet is now very popular and his books are bestsellers.

8 Day to day

Lead-in

1 Answer the questions about photos A and B.

1 Where are the people?

2 What are the seasons? (spring, summer, autumn, winter)

2 **a** Check the words in a dictionary. Then find them in the photos. Which photo are they in? Write A–E.

coat $\boxed{B}$ hat ☐ jacket ☐ jeans ☐ pullover ☐ scarf ☐ shorts ☐
skirt ☐ suit ☐ T-shirt ☐ trainers ☐

b Can you name any other clothes in the photos?

3 **a** Match the clothes adjectives (1–6) with their meanings (a–f).

1	formal	a	comfortable, not small
2	casual	b	not thick or heavy
3	tight	c	tidy, in good condition
4	light	d	for important events, for business
5	loose	e	comfortable and informal
6	smart	f	feel small, fit closely

b **8.1** Describe the clothes in photos C–E. Then listen and check.

C – a smart suit

c Do you agree with these statements? Why/Why not?

1 I think jeans are uncomfortable.

2 It's OK to wear shorts to formal business meetings.

3 Winter coats are usually light.

4 Tight shirts and pullovers look good.

Reading

1 Discuss.

1 What type of clothes do you like?

2 Do you wear different clothes at different times/places?

3 Do you ever have problems with clothes?

2 **a** Read the text quickly and match the letters (1–3) to the answers (A–C).

b Read the letters again and find the names of the writers.

has a boyfriend *Sindy*

1 travels in the winter _____

2 sometimes goes to dinner parties _____

3 works for a bank _____

4 loves casual clothes _____

5 doesn't feel comfortable on a plane _____

Vocabulary | clothes

3 **a** Find words in the text with opposite meanings.

hot *cold*

1 uncomfortable _____   3 put on _____

2 informal _____   4 tight _____

b Find these words in the text and match them to the meanings.

1 cotton   a when things go together

2 wool   b one thing on top of another thing

3 matching   c fabric made from a plant

4 layers   d fabric made from animal hair

4 Look at the picture on page 77 and write all the clothes words A–P.

A = shirt

WHAT TO WEAR?
Alison Bering answers all your clothes questions.

1 Dear Alison

Can you give us some advice? We usually go to the Caribbean with our three young children in December. It's always really cold when we leave home, it's cool on the plane, but hot and sunny when we arrive – it's really difficult with children! So, what clothes can we all wear?
Mr and Mrs Jackson

2 Dear Alison

I work for an international bank and I wear a suit and tie all the time for work. I often travel for business and I am never comfortable on the plane in my formal clothes. Can you suggest anything?
Geoffrey W.

3 Dear Alison

I'm 22. I love casual clothes and I usually wear trainers, a T-shirt and jeans. I hardly ever wear skirts or shoes. And I hate dresses! We sometimes go to formal dinner parties and my boyfriend says I don't look smart. But I don't want to look middle-aged! So how can I wear casual clothes and be smart?
Sindy L.

A Buy a 'suit carrier' – that's a special bag for suits. You can take it on the plane. Put some comfortable loose clothes in the bag (for example, cotton trousers and a light wool pullover). At the airport, go to the toilet, take off your suit and change into the loose clothing. When you arrive you can change back into your suit.

B Casual clothes can be smart! Try black or white jeans, a nice white top and a smart jacket, but not trainers! Buy some smart shoes and a matching belt.

C My answer is simple – layers! You and your children can put on extra clothes when you are cold, and take them off when you are hot! For example, you can wear a T-shirt, a cotton shirt or top, a light pullover and a coat. Put sunglasses, scarves and gloves in your bags.

Grammar | Present Simple; adverbs of frequency

5 Find the adverbs of frequency below in the letters. Write them in the correct place in the Active grammar box. Then choose the correct words to complete the rules.

> ### Active grammar
>
> | Frequency | Adverbs | Letter 1 | Letter 2 | Letter 3 |
> |---|---|---|---|---|
> | 100% | *always* | *is always* | | |
> | ↑ | *usually* | *usually go* | | |
> | ↑ | *often* | | | |
> | ↑ | *sometimes* | | | |
> | ↑ | *hardly ever* | | | |
> | 0% | *never* | | | |
>
> We put adverbs of frequency *before/after* the verb *to be*.
> We put adverbs of frequency *before/after* other verbs.

see Reference page 83

6 Choose the correct adverb then rewrite the sentences.

We go to the cinema <u>twice a week</u>.   a) often ✓   b) sometimes

We often go to the cinema.

1 We go to the cinema <u>once a month</u>.   a) sometimes   b) always
2 He <u>doesn't</u> drink coffee.   a) hardly ever   b) never
3 He drinks coffee <u>with every meal</u>.   a) usually   b) always
4 I take the dog for a walk <u>six days a week</u>.   a) always   b) usually
5 I see my parents <u>once a year</u>.   a) hardly ever   b) sometimes

7 **a** Read the information about David and write one sentence with each adverb in the box.

David always wears a watch.

> I wear a watch every day.
> I don't smoke.
> I eat pasta once or twice a month.
> I see my brother twice a year.
> I wear a suit from Monday to Friday.
> I go to the gym three times a week.

> usually   often   sometimes   hardly ever   never   ~~always~~

b Write true sentences about your life with suitable adverbs.

I always have a sandwich for lunch.

Person to person

8 Ask and answer.

1 What do you usually wear ...
   • to work?   • at home?
   • at the weekend?
   • on holiday?
2 Where do you buy clothes? How often?
3 What's your favourite ...
   • clothes shop?
   • type of clothes?

Writing

9 **a** Look at letter 1 on page 76. <u>Underline</u> the phrases Mr and Mrs Jackson use to request advice from Alison.

b You and your partner work for the same company. Write a request to your partner. Then write an answer to his/her request.

Student A: look at page 127.
Student B: look at page 130.

Listening

1 Look at the picture and TV screens. Answer the questions.

1 Where are the people in the picture?

2 Where are the people on the TV screens?

3 Do you like this type of programme?

2 **a** 8.2 Listen. Write the number of the screen.

Adam and Rosa ☐   Cara ☐
Erica ☐   Gary ☐   Greg ☐
Jason ☐

b Write the correct names. Then listen again to check.

1 _____ is cycling in the gym.

2 _____ are talking.

3 _____ is digging in the garden.

4 _____ is preparing dinner.

5 _____ is looking for something.

6 _____ is crying.

Grammar | Present Continuous

3 **a** Look at these sentences and the ones from Ex. 2b. Complete the Active grammar box.

She isn't shouting.
Are they talking? Yes, they are.
Is she resting? No, she isn't.

Active grammar

⊕	⊖	?
I'm cycling.	*I'm not cycling.*	_Am_ *I cycling?*
He/She/It' _____ digging.	*He/She/It _____ digging.*	*_____ he/she/it digging?*
You/We/They' _____ shouting.	*You/We/They _aren't_ shouting.*	*_____ you/we/they shouting?*

Yes,	*I am.* *he/she/it _is_.* *we/you/they _____.*	No,	*I'm not.* *he/she/it _____.* *we/you/they _aren't_.*

b Complete the rules.

1 We use the Present Continuous when we talk about activities that:
a) happened yesterday/in the past.
b) are happening now.
c) happen every day.

2 To form the Present Continuous we use the verb _____ + the -ing form of the main verb.

c Look at Ex. 2b. Write the -ing forms.

1 look → *looking* talk → _____ cry → _____
2 ride → *riding* cycle → _____ prepare → _____
3 plan → *planning* dig → _____

see Reference page 83

4 a Write sentences about the people in the house.

Greg/shout *Greg is shouting.*

1 Greg/not prepare breakfast *Greg isn't …*
2 Cara/not sleep
3 Jason/dig up flowers
4 Erica/not jog
5 Erica/sing
6 Adam and Rosa/not write

b In pairs, describe a screen, but don't name the person. Your partner guesses the name.

Grammar | adverbs of manner

5 Look at the underlined words in the sentences in the Active grammar box. Complete the rule.

Active grammar

She's cycling <u>fast</u>. *They're talking* <u>quietly</u>.
He's looking very <u>carefully</u>.

1 Adverbs of manner give information about *the person doing the activity/the activity*.
2 They go *before/after* the verb.

---

see Reference page 83

6 Choose the correct explanation for each adverb.

1 She's cycling <u>fast</u>.
a) She's cycling at 25 kilometres per hour.
b) She's cycling at 5 kilometres per hour.
2 They're talking <u>quietly</u>.
a) We can hear them.
b) We can't hear them.
3 He's looking very <u>carefully</u>.
a) He's looking in every place.
b) He isn't looking in many places.

7 Complete the sentences with these adverbs.

> carefully happily healthily quietly well

1 You need to eat _____ to keep fit.
2 I couldn't hear him because he spoke very _____.
3 To get a job as a holiday rep. you need to speak English _____.
4 Maria's singing _____. Is she having a good day?
5 Write your essays _____ – I don't want to see any mistakes.

Pronunciation

8 a **8.3** Listen to the sentences. <u>Underline</u> the strong syllables. Then listen again and repeat.

She's <u>cycling</u> <u>fast</u>.

1 They're talking quietly.
2 He's looking very carefully.
3 You're speaking loudly.
4 We're living healthily.

b Play a mime game. One student mimes an activity from the box at the bottom of the page. The other students guess the activity.

A: *Are you digging?*
B: *Yes, I am.*
A: *You're digging fast.*
B: *That's right.*

Speaking

9 In pairs, write the missing names on the pictures.

Student A: look at the picture on page 127.
Student B: look at the picture on page 130.

Choose a verb to mime from A, and an adverb from B.

A: cook cycle dance dig drink eat laugh play a guitar run sleep swim teach use a computer walk write

B: badly well carefully carelessly fast slowly loudly quietly happily sadly comfortably uncomfortably

8.3 Under the weather

Grammar	Present Simple and Present Continuous
Can do	take part in a factual conversation on a simple topic

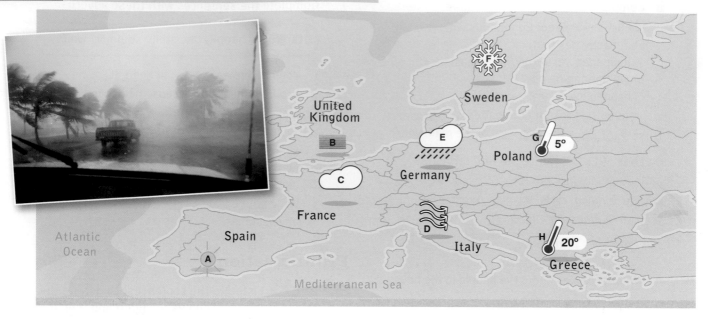

Vocabulary | the weather

1 a Match the symbols on the map to the weather descriptions.

1	It's foggy.	*B*	5	It's snowing. ☐
2	It's warm. ☐		6	It's cold. ☐
3	It's sunny. ☐		7	It's raining. ☐
4	It's windy. ☐		8	It's cloudy. ☐

b ▣8.4▣ Listen and check your answers.

c Listen again and complete.

It's _snowing_ in Sweden. It's (1) _____ in the east of the UK, and it's (2) _____ heavily in the north of Germany. It's quite (3) _____ today in Poland and it's very (4) _____ in France. It's very (5) _____ in the south of Spain and it's (6) _____ in Greece. Finally, it's very (7) _____ in northern Italy.

Pronunciation

2 a ▣8.5▣ Listen to these words. Is the vowel sound the same in all four?

c<u>o</u>ld   h<u>o</u>t   f<u>o</u>ggy   sn<u>o</u>wing

b ▣8.6▣ Listen and write the words in the correct column.

/ɒ/ hot	/əʊ/ cold

c ▣8.7▣ Listen and <u>underline</u> two /ɒ/ sounds and two /əʊ/ sounds in each sentence. Then repeat the sentences.

1 It often snows a lot in Poland.

2 The doctor told me not to get cold.

3 She wears tops and coats in orange and gold.

Reading

3 a Look at the website. Complete the title.

www.**yourhealth**.com

Your health and the _____

Last week we asked for examples of health problems in good or bad weather. We had hundreds of emails! Here are a few.

Your article was very interesting. I always get headaches when the weather changes from sunny weather to rain. My head isn't hurting now because it's summer and the sun is shining.
Pablo, Argentina

I live in Wales and it often rains here. My whole body aches sometimes when it rains – my legs, my arms. I'm aching badly at the moment because it's raining heavily today!
Miriam, Wales

The weather also affects our moods. In Norway a lot of people get depressed in the winter because it stays cold and dark all the time, especially in the north. We're all feeling depressed at the moment – it's November and there's another three months of darkness!
Lars, Norway

b Read the text. Complete the table.

PERSON/ COUNTRY	TYPE OF WEATHER	HEALTH PROBLEM
	change from sunny weather to rain	
Miriam/ Wales		
		feeling depressed

4 Match the words to their meanings.

1	ache	a	change, make different
2	heavily	b	sad and unhappy
3	affect	c	a lot
4	mood	d	when there is no light
5	depressed	e	hurt/feel bad
6	darkness	f	our feelings at one time

Lifelong learning

Nouns and adjectives

You can often work out the meaning of a word from its parts, e.g. *darkness* is the noun from *dark*. A lot of nouns from adjectives end in *-ness*.

5 Which adjectives do these nouns come from?

1 tiredness _____
2 happiness _____
3 fitness _____
4 sickness _____
5 baldness _____
6 craziness _____

Speaking

6 **a** **8.8** Listen to two people talking about the weather. Complete the expressions.

take part in a conversation

Giving your opinion	I _____ that it's the temperature.
Agreeing	Yes, I _____.
Disagreeing	I'm not _____.

b Look at the tapescript on page 156 and find more expressions for the How to box.

c Work with a partner. Have a conversation about the weather.

How do you feel about the weather in your country?
Does the weather affect your health?

Grammar | Present Simple/Continuous

7 **a** Look at the text again. Underline the verbs in the Present Continuous and circle the verbs in the Present Simple.

b Complete the rules in the Active grammar box.

Active grammar

1 Use this tense for actions happening now. _____

2 Use this tense for actions that happen often, every year, etc. _____

see Reference page 83

8 Choose the correct form of the verbs.

1 At the moment I *work/am working* in Paris.
2 We never *take/are taking* the bus to work.
3 I always *carry/am carrying* my umbrella in winter.
4 Kevin *doesn't wear/isn't wearing* jeans today.
5 We *study/are studying* a new tense in the English class.
6 My parents *don't drink/aren't drinking* coffee after 6.oop.m.

9 **a** Write what the people usually do and what they are doing today.

1 Peter – drive/sunbathe
Peter usually drives a bus. Today he's sunbathing.

2 Laura – walk to work/drive her new car
3 Sally – clean the house/play football
4 Anna – wear jeans/wear a dress

b Check your answers in pairs. Ask questions about the activities.

A: *Is Laura walking to work today?*
B: *No, she isn't. She's driving her new car.*

1 Match the phrases to the pictures. Write A–E in the picture column.

	picture	dialogue 1	dialogue 2
it doesn't work	☐	☐	☐
it doesn't fit	A	☐	☐
a receipt	☐	☐	☐
a refund	☐	☐	☐
an exchange	☐	☐	☐

2 **a** **8.9** Listen to dialogues 1 and 2 and match them to pictures A–E. Write 1 or 2 next to each picture.

b Listen again and tick (✓) the phrases you hear in the boxes in Ex. 1.

3 **a** Read the tapescript on page 156 and complete the How to box.

HOW TO…

make a complaint

Ask for help	*Excuse me. _____ you help me?*
Explain the situation	*I _____ this yesterday.*
Explain the problem	*It _____ fit/work.*
Ask for an exchange/ refund	*Can I _____ it?/ I'd _____ a refund.*

b In pairs, practise the dialogues from the tapescript on page 156.

4 Work in pairs.
Student A: look at the information below.
Student B: turn to page 127.

Roleplay 1
You bought an Ace Technology C100 computer at Computer Central in Danby Street, Dublin yesterday. You paid €1250. It doesn't work because the screen is broken. You want to exchange it for another one.

Roleplay 2
You are a shop assistant. Your shop doesn't give refunds, but you can exchange things.

5 **a** Read the letter and answer the questions.

> Dear Sir
>
> I bought a <u>Toshiba RX90 cooker</u> at your shop in the <u>Heaton Shopping Centre</u> on <u>20th June</u>.
> A <u>I'm afraid it doesn't work because the clock is broken.</u>
> I phoned the manager yesterday and she asked me to write to you.
> I would like a refund. I enclose a copy of my receipt.
>
> Yours faithfully
> Celia Smith

1 Why do we write letters like this?
2 Are letters like this formal or informal?
3 How do we start formal letters?
4 How do we finish formal letters?
5 What does *enclose* mean?

b Label the <u>underlined</u> phrases in the letter.

A a polite phrase to introduce a complaint
B details of the item
C the date when you bought it
D the place where you bought it
E details of the problem

6 You are the customer from Roleplay 1 in Ex. 4. Use the information and write a letter of complaint.

Adverbs of frequency

Use adverbs of frequency with the Present Simple to describe how regularly or how often something happens.

0%	→	→	→	→	100%
never	hardly ever	sometimes	often	usually	always

It **often** rains in England.
It **hardly ever** rains in the Sahara desert.

Put adverbs of frequency after the verb *to be* but before other main verbs.
The train **is usually** on time.
The train **usually arrives** on time.

Present Continuous

We make the Present Continuous with a present form of the verb *to be* and the *-ing* form of the main verb.

⊕	I	'm	staying at home today.
	He/She/It	's	
	We/You/They	're	

⊖	I	'm not	staying at home today.
	He/She/It	isn't	
	We/You/They	aren't	

❓	Am	I		staying at home today?
	Is	he/she/it		
	Are	we/you/they		
	Yes,	I am. he/she/it is. we/you/they are.	No,	I'm not. he/she/it isn't. we/you/they aren't.

The main verb in the Present Continuous is in the *-ing* form. Make this form by adding *-ing* to the base form of the verb, but note:

- with verbs that end in *-e*, remove *-e* and add *-ing*, *cycle* → *cycling*
- with verbs of one syllable that end in one short vowel + consonant, repeat the consonant and add *-ing*, *dig* → *digging*

Use the Present Continuous to describe actions that are happening **now**, at the moment of speaking:
I'm looking for your hat right now.

Present Simple and Present Continuous

Use the Present Simple to talk about routines: what we do every day/year, and to talk about facts.
*We always **have** a pizza on Friday evenings.*

Use the Present Continuous to talk about actions happening now, at the moment of speaking.
*We **'re having** our pizza now so we can't talk to you at the moment.*

Use phrases like *at the moment* and *(right) now* with the Present Continuous.

Use adverbs and expressions of frequency with the Present Simple.

Adverbs of manner

We usually use adverbs of manner with a verb. They describe the way that we do the action of the verb.
She's running. → *She's running **slowly**.*

We usually form adverbs of manner from adjectives. Add *-ly* to most adjectives.
quick → *quick**ly**, loud* → *loud**ly***

When the adjective ends in *-y*, we remove the *-y* and add *-ily*.
happy → *happ**ily**, healthy* → *health**ily***

Some common adverbs are irregular.
good → *well, fast* → *fast*

Adverbs of manner usually come after the verb, and often after any other words linked to the verb.
I drank it quickly.

Key vocabulary

Clothes

belt coat dress gloves hat jacket jeans pullover scarf shirt shoes shorts skirt suit tie top trainers trousers T-shirt

Clothes adjectives

casual comfortable formal heavy informal light loose smart thick tight warm

The weather

Good weather: It's sunny. It's hot. It's warm.
Bad weather: It's raining. It's snowing. It's cold. It's cloudy. It's windy. It's foggy.

1 Choose the best word or phrase.

I am quite fit because I *hardly ever/<u>often</u>* play sport.

1 Russians wear heavy coats in the winter because it is *never/usually* cold.

2 I don't like formal clothes. I *sometimes/hardly ever* wear a suit and tie!

3 Dario is quite fat because he *always/hardly ever* eats a lot.

4 Vegetarians *sometimes/never* eat meat.

5 Swiss watches *sometimes/hardly ever* cost a lot of money.

2 **a** Write the *-ing* form of these verbs.

come   *coming*

1	dig	_____	7	study _____
2	make	_____	8	swim _____
3	plan	_____	9	use _____
4	read	_____	10	wait _____
5	ride	_____	11	write _____
6	sit	_____	12	carry _____

b Sandra is writing a letter to her friend. Complete the gaps with some of the verbs from Ex. 2a in the Present Continuous.

Dear Geena

Thanks for your letter. I <u>'m sitting</u> in Luigi's café at the moment – do you remember it? We had a really good meal here in March. I (1) _____ this letter from here because I (2) _____ for Jacob. He's at college at the moment; he (3) _____ Art. He (4) _____ a computer in his Art classes and he really enjoys it – he (5) _____ some amazing pictures on the computer. There's a travel guide to Canada on the table – do you know why? I (6) _____ it because Jacob and I (7) _____ a visit to Canada! Really! We want to ...

3 Write questions and answers.

sun shine ✗ (rain)

Is the sun shining? No, the sun isn't shining. It's raining.

1 you/read/good book ✓

2 you/study German ✗ (English)

3 she/cook dinner ✗ (prepare tomorrow's lunch)

4 he/work at home today ✓

5 they/play tennis ✗ (badminton)

4 Read the paragraph. Then write sentences in the Present Simple or the Present Continuous.

> Amélie is a computer programmer. She works in a big, formal office. She has one hour for lunch. Today is her office summer excursion – every year they take their clients out for the day and buy them a big lunch. Today they are at a football match.

use/computer

Amélie usually uses a computer.

take/photos/match

She's taking photos of the football match today.

1 wear/formal business suit

2 wear/jeans and a T-shirt

3 talk/to people in the office

4 talk/to clients at the match

5 have/sandwich for lunch in the office

6 have/big meal in a restaurant

5 **a** Match the adverbs with their opposites.

1	badly		a	fast
2	happily		b	carefully
3	slowly		c	quietly
4	loudly		d	uncomfortably
5	carelessly		e	well
6	comfortably		f	unhappily

b Complete the sentences with an adverb from Ex. 5a.

1 Julie watched Philip <u>unhappily</u>.

2 He's shouting _____.

3 They're sitting _____.

4 'Shh! Please talk _____!'

5 She's writing her essay very _____.

6 Complete the sentences with suitable clothes.

I wear <u>shorts and a T-shirt</u> when it's sunny.

1 I wear _____ when it's snowing.

2 I wear _____ when it's raining.

3 I wear _____ for a country walk.

4 I wear _____ when I go to parties.

5 I wear _____ when I go to work.

6 I wear _____ for formal meetings.

9 Culture

Lead-in

1 **a** Put the letters in the correct order and match the art forms to the photos.

1 S C I U M _____ ☐
2 M I L F _____ ☐
3 R E I H E A T _____ ☐
4 A N I G N I P T _____ ☐

b Look at the words and phrases in the box. In pairs, name one example of each.

> ballet cartoon classical music comedy dance horror literature
> modern art novels opera plays painting poetry rock music sculpture

2 **a** Complete the word map with the art forms from Ex. 1a and words and phrases from the box. Then compare with a partner.

b 9.1 Listen to two people. Is your word map the same as theirs?

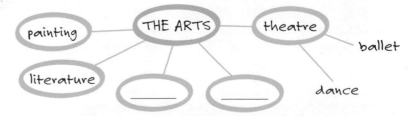

c Add more words to your word map if you can.

3 Work in groups. Discuss the questions. What or who is your favourite:
- film? • book? • play? • opera or ballet? • classical composer?
- poem? • painting? • group or singer?

Reading

1   a Discuss.

1   What's in the news today?

2   How did you get the news stories?

3   How do you usually get the news?

b Label the photos (1–6) with the names of the news sources from Ex. 2a.

Vocabulary | news media

2   a Look at the text and tick (✓) the correct adjectives in the table.

	fast	easy	detailed	cheap	new	exciting	versatile
Newspapers							
The radio							
The TV							
Teletext							
The Internet							
Text messages							

b Read the text carefully. Find advantages (good things) and disadvantages (bad things) about the different news sources. Can you think of any other advantages and disadvantages?

Advantages: *Newspapers are cheap and versatile.*
The radio is relaxing.

Disadvantages: *The radio is old-fashioned.*

c Do you agree with the opinions in the text?

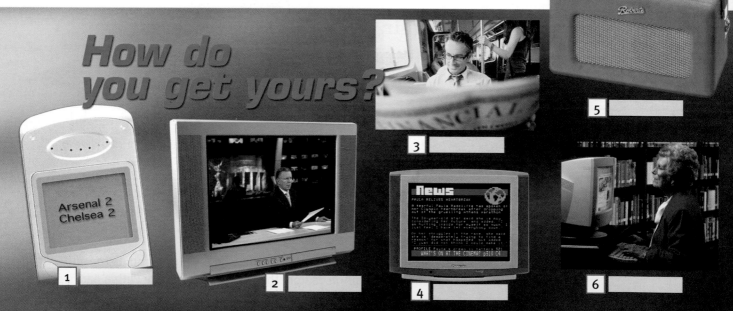

How do you get yours?

We all like to know what's in the news – world news, local news, sports news – and today there are many different ways of finding out about recent events. How do people choose, and what do they like about the different methods?

Newspapers – still the old favourite. Millions of people read newspapers because they're cheap, detailed and also versatile – you can read them at home, at work or on the train.

The radio – people listen to the radio because it's easy. You can listen in the car, when you're working or in bed, but some people think the radio is old-fashioned.

The TV – almost everyone watches TV and a lot of people get the news from it. It's interesting and exciting, because it's visual. There are lots of different news programmes to suit all types of people.

Teletext – this is a fast way of getting the news, but it doesn't give you a lot of detail.

The Internet – many people now use the Internet. It's detailed and it's very fast: news stories appear when they happen; but it can be expensive.

Text messaging – this way of getting news is popular because it's fast and very new. Messages arrive on your mobile phone, so you get the news immediately, but it is expensive.

Grammar | comparison of adjectives

3 a [9.2] Listen and complete the sentences with the correct news sources.

1. _____ are <u>cheaper than</u> the Internet.
2. _____ is <u>faster than</u> TV.
3. _____ is <u>more detailed than</u> teletext.
4. _____ is <u>more exciting than</u> newspapers.
5. _____ is <u>easier than</u> newspapers.
6. _____ is <u>better than</u> the radio.

b Complete the Active grammar box with the <u>underlined</u> words in Ex. 3a.

Active grammar

Adjective	Comparative
fast	*faster than*
cheap	_____
easy	_____
detailed	_____
exciting	_____
good	_____
bad	*worse than*

Write suitable comparative adjectives next to the rules.

1. Add *-er* to adjectives with one syllable only: *faster*
2. With adjectives that end in *-y*, remove the *-y* and add *-ier*: _____
3. With longer adjectives, we use *more* before the adjective: _____
4. Some adjectives have irregular comparatives: _____

see Reference page 93

4 Complete the sentences with the comparative form of the adjectives and another news source. Then compare with a partner.

TV news is ... (exciting)

more exciting than newspapers.

1. Teletext is ... (immediate)
2. Newspapers are ... (detailed)
3. Text messaging is ... (modern)
4. The radio is ... (good)

5 Write comparative sentences about the pictures.

1 Newspapers are usually more serious than magazines.

Pronunciation

6 a [9.3] Listen to these phrases and <u>underline</u> the syllables with /ə/. Listen again and repeat.

eas<u>ier</u> th<u>an</u>
1. f<u>aster</u> than
2. c<u>older</u> than
3. health<u>ier</u> than

b Write sentences comparing these things. Then read your sentences to a partner.

1. Iceland/Egypt/cold
2. Spanish/English/easy
3. fruit/chocolate/healthy
4. a Ferrari/a Fiat/fast

Writing and speaking

7 a Complete the table.

	I like ...	I don't like ...
TV programmes	*The Simpsons*	*Friends*
newspapers		
film stars		
books		
types of food		
holidays		

b Write sentences comparing the things in the table. Give reasons.

I like 'The Simpsons' because it's funnier than 'Friends'.

c Compare your sentences with a partner.

8 In groups, compare what you like.

A: *I like 'The Simpsons'.*
B: *I don't. I like 'The Sopranos' because it's more exciting than 'The Simpsons'.*

Vocabulary | films

1   **a**   Match the films in the photos to the types of film in the box.

> an action/adventure film   a cartoon   a comedy   a horror film
> a love story   a musical   a science fiction film   a thriller

A = _____   B = _____   C = _____   D = _____

b   Think of one film from each type.

'The Matrix' is a science fiction film.

c   Which of the types of film are/can be …

• sad?   • exciting?   • violent?   • clever?   • funny?   • scary?
• romantic?   • happy?   • interesting?

2   What types of films do you like/not like? Why? Use the adjectives in Ex. 1c and others.

I don't like horror films because they're usually scary and violent.

Listening

3   **9.4**   Listen to an interview and match the films with the opinions.

> American Beauty   Gladiator   The Sixth Sense
> All About My Mother   Pulp Fiction   Chicago

1   the best film in the last ten years
2   the scariest film
3   the most exciting film
4   the biggest surprise
5   the most interesting foreign language film
6   the most unusual film
7   the most violent film
8   the freshest musical for a long time
9   the best mixture of action and comedy
10   it had the best acting

Grammar | superlatives

4   **a**   Look at this sentence. Choose description 1, 2 or 3.

It was the best film in the last ten years.

It was …

1   better than some of the other films.
2   better than all the other films.
3   worse than all the other films.

b   Complete with superlative adjectives from Ex. 3. Then choose the correct words to make the rules.

Active grammar

Adjective	Superlative
bad	*the worst*
big	*the biggest*
exciting	_____
fresh	_____
scary	_____
good	_____
interesting	_____
unusual	_____
violent	_____

To make the superlative, we add *-est/-er* to one-syllable adjectives and we put *more/most* before longer adjectives.

see Reference page 93

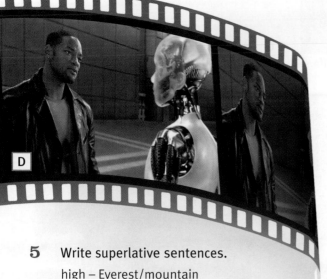

D

5 Write superlative sentences.

high – Everest/mountain

Everest is the highest mountain.

1 large – Asia/continent
2 deep – the Pacific/ocean
3 busy – Heathrow/international airport
4 comfortable – a Rolls-Royce/car

Reading and speaking

6 a Read the movie quiz. Complete the questions with the adjectives in the superlative form.

What do you know about movies?

Questions 1–6 are movie facts.
Questions 7–9 show the critics' choices.

1 What is *the most expensive* film ever made? (expensive)

2 What was _____ film with sound? (early)

3 Which film lasts _____ time? (long)

4 What is _____ cartoon? (successful)

5 Who is _____ film star? (rich)

6 Who is _____ Oscar winner? (young)

7 What is _____ love story? (romantic)

8 What is _____ horror film? (scary)

9 Who is _____ villain in a film? (bad)

b Do the quiz in groups of three. Each student has three answers. Discuss the questions and match the answers.

Student A: your answers are below.

Student B: turn to page 127.

Student C: turn to page 130.

See page 127 for answers.

Person to person

7 Discuss.

1 How many films in the quiz do you know?

2 What do you think is:
• the best film ever?
• the most exciting action film?
• the most romantic love story?
• the funniest comedy?
• the scariest horror film?
• the most boring film?

3 Who is the best film star at the moment?

Writing

8 a Read this film review and do the tasks.

> In my opinion, the best film of the last ten years was 'LA Confidential', from 1997. It's a thriller and it stars Russell Crowe, Guy Pearce, Kim Basinger and Kevin Spacey. The film is set in Los Angeles in the 1950s, and it's about problems in the police department. It's very exciting and the acting is excellent. Go and see it!

1 Find the sentences/phrases that give information about the following:
• the stars _____
• the writer's choice of film _____
• the story of the film _____
• the film's location _____
• a recommendation _____
• the type of film _____
• what the writer thinks is good about the film _____

2 Number the information in the order it appears in the review.

b In pairs, write a short film review.

1 Choose a film you like from the last ten years.

2 Make notes about the actors, the story and the location of the film.

3 Decide why you like the film.

4 Write a short review together.

Student A
Psycho Tatum O'Neal *Finding Nemo*

9.3 Is it art?

Reading

1 Look at the postcards and discuss.

1 What can you see?

2 Are these things 'art', do you think?

2 **a** Read the article quickly. Match it to one of the pictures.

> For many people modern art is a mystery and difficult to understand: abstract paintings; sharks in glass boxes and enormous steel angels. What do these works mean? Are they really art?
>
> One modern artist is different. Most people understand and enjoy his work. He is the American artist Christo. He wraps buildings and geographical features in fabric. One of his most famous works is the Reichstag in Berlin. He wrapped it in white fabric for fourteen days in 1995.
>
> We see everyday things in a new way in his work. And perhaps that is the greatest aim of modern art.

b Read the text again and answer the questions.

1 Why is modern art a mystery?

2 What is Christo's nationality?

3 What is the main aim of modern art?

c Find some words in the text that you don't understand. Use a dictionary to find the meanings and explain them to your partner.

Listening

3 **a** 〔9.5〕 Listen to Jenny and Serge. Match the artists to the postcards.

Christo ☐D☐ Damien Hirst ☐ Antony Gormley ☐
Kazimir Malevich ☐   Claude Monet ☐

b Listen again. What do they like? Write *J* or *S*. Then match the types of art to some of the postcards.

1 sculpture _____

2 Impressionist paintings _____

3 modern art _____

4 abstract paintings _____

Grammar | *prefer*

4 〔9.5〕 Listen to the dialogue again and complete the Active grammar box by choosing the correct statements. Then choose the correct word in italics to complete the examples.

> **Active grammar**
>
> 1 After *prefer* we can use:
>   a) a noun.
>   b) the infinitive of a verb (e.g. *buy*).
>   c) the -*ing* form (e.g. *buying*).
>
> 2 We use *prefer* for something we like:
>   a) more than another thing.
>   b) the same as another thing.
>
> I prefer Malevich *than/to* Monet.
> I prefer *buying/buy* postcards.

see Reference page 93

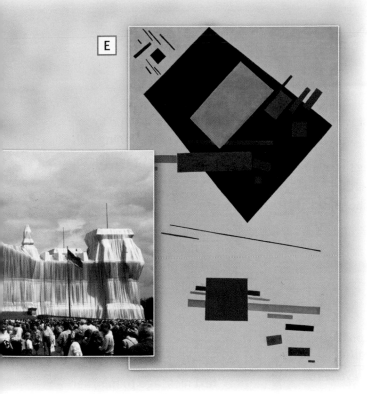

E

Grammar | *will* for spontaneous decisions and offers

7 **a** `9.6` Jenny and Serge are in London. Listen and tick (✓) two places they plan to visit.

Tate Britain ☐ Tate Modern ☐ Hayward Gallery ☐

b Listen again. Complete the phrases in the Active grammar box, then choose the correct words to complete the rule.

Active grammar

Jenny: *I'll get the _____.*
Jenny: *I'll look at the _____.*
Serge: *Right. We'll go there after _____.*

We use *will* for decisions and offers that we make *before/at the time of* speaking. In conversation and informal writing we use the short form *'ll*.

---

see Reference page 93

8 Look at the pictures and make offers. Use words and phrases from the box.

---

open carry find look after answer phone
ambulance door mother baby

A   B   C   D

Pronunciation

9 **a** `9.7` Listen. Does the voice go up (↗) or down (↘) at the end?

1 Any ideas?   2 Is it near?

b `9.8` Listen and write (↗) or (↘), then repeat.

1 Is it expensive?   4 It's boring.
2 It's expensive.   5 Are we late?
3 Is it interesting?   6 Does she know?

10 **a** Make questions. Practise them in pairs.

1 expensive *Is it expensive?*   4 new
2 he knows *Does he know?*   5 she smokes
3 cheap   6 they work

b Now write short dialogues with the questions.

---

5 **a** Which do you prefer? Ask and answer.

1 go to restaurants/eat at home?
2 watch videos /go to the cinema?
3 dogs/cats?
4 read books/listen to music?

A: *Do you prefer going to restaurants to eating at home?*

B: *No, I prefer eating at home.*

b Look at the tapescript on page 157 and complete the How to box.

---

talk about preferences

Say you like one thing more than another thing

⋮ *I _____ modern art _____ than traditional paintings.*
⋮ *I _____ Malevich to Monet.*

Person to person

6 **a** Discuss.

1 Do you agree with Jenny and Serge?
2 Which postcards do you prefer? Why?

I like … more than … because …

b Talk to your classmates and find out how many students prefer:

1 visiting museums to going to concerts.
2 cold weather to hot weather.
3 romantic films to action films.
4 modern art to traditional art.
5 city holidays to beach holidays.

Do you prefer visiting museums to going to concerts?

9 Communication

An evening out

1 **a** What do you usually do on Saturdays? Make a list with a partner.

b **9.9** Listen to these friends and tick (✓) the things they decide to do on Saturday.

go swimming ☐ watch a film ☐ have lunch ☐ go shopping ☐

c Listen again and complete the How to box.

HOW TO …

discuss and plan activities

Make suggestions	*How about a film?* *Why _____ we _____ to the sports centre?* *_____ go to the shopping centre.*
Express preferences	*I _____ watching films in the evening.* *I like shopping more _____ swimming.*
Make comparisons	*The shops are _____ expensive there.*
Decide what to do	*OK. _____ meet at eleven outside the bus station.*

2 **a** Look at this list of ways of spending an evening with a friend. Which ones can you see in the photos?

a a play at the theatre

b a meal in a smart restaurant

c an evening at a shopping centre

d a nightclub

e the cinema

f a classical concert

g an evening at the bowling alley

h a rock concert

i a football match

j an opera

b Which do you prefer? Rank them in order 1–10 (1 is the best).

c In pairs, compare your lists. Ask about your partner's list and explain your preferences.

My number 1 is 'classical concert' because I like classical music more than other types of music. So I prefer going to classical concerts.

3 **a** Work in groups to organise an evening out.

1 Ask about your classmates' preferences and find something you all like.

2 Talk about the things you can do in your area and make suggestions for tomorrow evening.

3 Agree a plan for your evening and arrange a time and place to meet.

b You want another friend to join you. Write a short text message to him/her with information about your group's arrangements.

> Plans for tomorrow: meet at …

9 Reference

Comparison of adjectives

Use comparative adjectives to compare two or more things.

This house is bigger than my old house.
The blue shoes are more expensive than the black ones.

This is how we form comparative adjectives:

Regular one-syllable adjectives:
old → older, cheap → cheaper, thick → thicker

Longer adjectives:
interesting → more interesting
comfortable → more comfortable

Two-syllable adjectives that end in -y:
funny → funnier

Irregular adjectives:
good → better, bad → worse

Use *than* to introduce the second noun in a comparative sentence.
This book is more interesting than his first book.

Superlative adjectives

Use superlative adjectives to compare one thing with all the others in a group.
This house is the biggest in the street.
The blue shoes are the most expensive.

This is how we form superlative adjectives:

Regular one-syllable adjectives:
old → oldest, cheap → cheapest, thick → thickest

Longer adjectives:
interesting → most interesting
comfortable → most comfortable

Two-syllable adjectives that end in -y:
funny → funniest

Irregular adjectives:
good → best, bad → worst

We usually use *the* before a superlative:
This is the most interesting book about mountain-climbing in the library.

Spelling rules

- add -r/-st to adjectives that end in -e,
  nice → nicer/nicest, large → larger/largest

- with adjectives that end in consonant + -y, remove -y and add -ier/-iest,
  busy → busier/busiest, heavy → heavier/heaviest

- with adjectives that end in a short vowel + consonant, repeat the consonant and add -er/-est,
  thin → thinner/thinnest, big → bigger/biggest

prefer

Use the verb *prefer* to talk about something we like more than another thing or things.

She likes coffee but she really loves tea. = She prefers tea (to coffee).

Use *prefer* with a noun (e.g. *tea*) or the *-ing* form of another verb.
I prefer tea to coffee.   I prefer drinking tea.

Use *to*, not *than*, to introduce a preference.
She prefers Mozart to Beethoven.

will for spontaneous decisions and offers

We use *will* + infinitive when we decide to do something or make an offer to do something at the same time as we are speaking. The action we are talking about usually happens in the immediate or near future.
A: *John. There's somebody knocking on our door.*
B: *OK. I'll answer it.*

In spoken English we use the contraction *'ll*, not *will*.
A: *Can somebody help me with these bags?*
B: *We'll do it.*

Key vocabulary

The arts
Fine arts:
painting (modern/impressionist/traditional/abstract art)
sculpture

Performance arts:
ballet
classical/rock music
dance
film/cinema
opera
theatre

Literature:
novels   plays   poetry

Film genres
an action/adventure film   a cartoon
a comedy   a horror film   a love story
a musical   a science fiction film   a thriller

1 Complete the paragraph with the comparative form of the adjectives in brackets.

Alan and Russell are brothers, but they look different. Alan is _younger_ (young) than Russell. He is also (1)_____ (tall) and (2)_____ (handsome) than his brother. Alan is (3)_____ (fit) than Russell. Russell is (4)_____ (fat) than Alan but he is also (5)_____ (happy) than his brother. Alan has (6)_____ (dark) skin than Russell and Russell has (7)_____ (short) hair than his brother.

2 Complete the table with the comparative and superlative form of the adjectives.

ADJECTIVE	COMPARATIVE	SUPERLATIVE
1 ancient	_more ancient_	_most ancient_
2 bad	_____	_____
3 beautiful	_____	_____
4 crazy	_____	_____
5 dry	_____	_____
6 fit	_____	_____
7 good	_____	_____
8 informal	_____	_____
9 noisy	_____	_____
10 private	_____	_____

3 **a** Match 1–8 to a–h.

1	deep/freshwater lake	a	Kilimanjaro
2	high/mountain in Africa	b	the Great Wall of China
3	large/museum in the world	c	Edvard Grieg
4	old/national flag	d	William Shakespeare
5	big/structure in the world	e	the Louvre
6	famous/Norwegian composer	f	Lake Baikal
7	scary/film	g	Denmark's
8	translated/British writer	h	_Psycho_

b Write sentences about Ex. 3a using superlative adjectives.

Lake Baikal is the deepest freshwater lake.

4 Find the mistakes in each sentence and write the correction.

Lucinda doesn't like tennis, she prefers play golf.
playing

1 I like the radio but my children prefer to watching television. _____
2 We reading books prefer. _____
3 Isabel prefers romantic films than science fiction ones. _____
4 Some people are preferring living in the country. _____
5 The bus is very slow so I prefer drive my car to work. _____
6 I prefer playing the guitar than listening to CDs. _____
7 Dario prefers to swimming to sunbathing. _____

5 Match 1–7 to a–g.

1	The phone's ringing!	a	I'll look at the map.
2	The coffee's ready.	b	We'll get the instructions.
3	Can you get me some milk?	c	I'll answer it.
4	Where is it?	d	We'll go to the shops later.
5	How does this video work?	e	I'll get a cup.
6	Can you write down her address?	f	I'll phone the doctor.
7	I think she's really ill.	g	I'll get a pen.

6 Do you know all of these examples of different types of art? Write one of the categories from the list on page 85 next to each one.

Toy Story   _a cartoon_

1 _Hamlet_
2 _The Mona Lisa_
3 _The Four Seasons_
4 _Carmen_
5 _The Exorcist_
6 _Anna Karennina_
7 Michelangelo's _David_
8 Queen's _Bohemian Rhapsody_

A

10 Journeys

B

C

D

Lead-in

1 Match the photos to the captions.

1 A businessman commuting to a meeting.
2 Rush hour traffic in Delhi.
3 Cycling to the office.
4 Commuting from the suburbs into Tokyo.

2 Find these forms of transport in the photos.

> car   plane   motorbike   underground train   bus   bicycle

3 Match the words to the meanings.

1	commuting	a	full of people
2	suburbs	b	travelling to work every day
3	park	c	the busiest time of day
4	rush hour	d	cars moving on a road
5	crowded	e	leave a car somewhere
6	traffic	f	places around a city where people live

4 Put the words from the box into the correct column. (Some words can go in more than one column.)

> ~~airport~~ car drive flight garage journey park passenger
> plane platform station ticket traffic train

AIR	RAIL	ROAD
airport		

10.1 Experiences

Grammar	Present Perfect (*been* with *ever/never*): *I/you/we/they*
Can do	talk about personal experiences

Reading and listening

1 a Read the text and find a word or phrase to describe the activity in each photo.

19.10 ***The Countryside Today***

Horse-riding and hiking are pleasant country activities that many people enjoy. But for farmers they can have negative results.

19.30 ***The Holiday Show***

Jason Morris joins a young British family for an action adventure holiday in Australia. After a long-haul flight of 22 hours they are ready for the experience of a lifetime.

20.25 ***Extreme Sports Challenge***

This week Liam and Terri go bungee jumping for the first time. There's only one problem – Terri is afraid of heights!

b Which do you think is the most exciting activity?

2 a 【10.1】 Listen to an extract from one of the programmes. Which programme is it?

b Read this extract from the TV programme. Is the plane journey Derek's first long-haul flight?

Derek: I've never been on a long-haul flight before so it's my first time.

c Listen again. Do they plan to do these things for the first time in Australia? Or is it their second time? Write *1st* or *2nd* in the table.

	Moira	Derek	Todd	Alicia
long-haul flight	*2nd*	*1st*		
visit Australia				
horse-riding				
hiking				
bungee jumping				

Grammar | Present Perfect (been with ever/never)

3 **a** Read the extracts from the TV programme and answer the questions below.

a *I've never been on a long-haul flight before.*
b *Have you ever been to Australia?*
c *We've all been hiking.*
d *We went horse-riding when we were in Scotland two years ago.*

1 Which extract refers to a particular time in the past? When?
2 Which extracts do not refer to a particular time in the past?
3 Which tense do we use when we do not refer to a particular time in the past?

b Listen again or read the tapescript on page 158 and complete the Active grammar box. Then choose the correct words to complete the rules.

Active grammar

⊕ subject + 've (or *have*) + past participle
  We've _____ to America.

⊖ subject + *haven't* (or *have not*) + past participle
  We _____ _____ bungee jumping.

  subject + 've (or *have*) + *never* + past participle
  I'_____ never _____ on a long-haul flight before.

❓ *Have* + subject (+ *ever*) + past participle
  Have _____ ever _____ to Australia?

  Yes, I/we/you/they have.
  No, I/we/you/they _____.

1 We use the Present Perfect with *ever* to ask about an activity at *any time up to now/a particular time in the past.*
2 *been* is a *past tense/past participle.*

see Reference page 103

4 **a** Complete the questions and answers.

1 A: Have you _____ been to New York?
  B: Yes, I _____.
2 A: _____ your mother ever been to the opera?
  B: No, she _____.
3 A: Have you ever _____ to Canada?
  B: Yes, we _____ last summer, it was great!

b Find the mistakes and correct them using the Present Perfect.

Have you ever go to England? *been*

1 I was never been bungee jumping.
2 They never been to Scotland.
3 Have you ever went to a classical concert?
4 Has you ever been on an adventure holiday?

Pronunciation

5 **a** [10.2] Listen to this extract from the TV programme. Are the vowel sounds in the underlined words /ɪ/ or /iː/?

1 But have you ever <u>been</u> to Australia?
2 No, we've never <u>been</u> there.

b [10.3] There are four /ɪ/ sounds in each of these sentences. Listen and <u>underline</u> the sounds. Practise the sentences.

1 Have you ever been to the cinema in Italy?
2 I've never been on a ship with him.
3 Has she ever been to dinner in Finland?
4 We've never been to Paris in spring.

6 Write questions with *ever* about the pictures in Ex. 1. Then ask and answer.

Speaking

7 Work in groups of three.
Student A: look at page 128.
Student B: look at page 130.
Student C: look at this page.

Student C
Ask your partners questions with *Have you ever been to ...?* If they answer *Yes*, find out when and where he/she did the activity, and if he/she liked it.

• an IMAX cinema?
• a bullfight?
• a rock concert?
• a wedding?
• a theme park?
• a circus?

A: *Have you ever been to an IMAX cinema?*
B: *Yes, I have. I went last week.*
A: *Did you like it?*

10.2 Holiday heaven

| Grammar | Present Perfect with regular and irregular verbs *(he/she/it)* |
| Can do | understand key points in a brochure; write a holiday postcard to a friend |

Vocabulary | holidays

1 **a** Match the symbols to the holidays in the box.

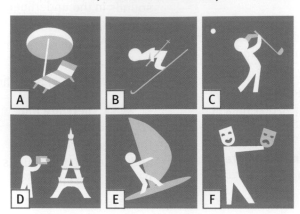

> activity ~~beach~~ cultural sightseeing
> water sports winter sports

A = a beach holiday

b Have you been on these types of holiday? Where? When? What did you do?

Reading

2 **a** Read the text. What can you do at Seagaia?

b Match the adjectives to their meanings.

1	luxurious	a	the best of its type
2	artificial	b	not real
3	first-class	c	very good
4	exclusive	d	very comfortable and beautiful
5	wonderful	e	expensive, for a few people

3 **a** Read the text again. Write questions for answers 1–5.

1 a luxurious resort *What is Seagaia?*
2 in Japan
3 an indoor beach and sea
4 in hotels, cottages or apartments
5 the zoo, theme park and gardens

b What do you think of Seagaia? Does this type of holiday interest you? Why/Why not?

Have you ever sunbathed on a rainy day? No?
Well, at Phoenix Seagaia, you can!

Seagaia is a luxurious holiday resort on Japan's Pacific coast. The Ocean Dome is the largest indoor artificial beach and sea. The water is warm, clean and safe, and the roof of the Dome opens when it's sunny, but closes in bad weather.

But Seagaia isn't only the Ocean Dome.

There's a lot more here:
- stay in a first-class hotel, a comfortable cottage or a traditional Japanese apartment
- play golf at our world-class courses
- surf and sail in the Pacific Ocean
- improve your tennis, horse-riding and golf at our exclusive clubs
- visit the wonderful zoo, theme park and gardens

For the holiday of a lifetime, choose Phoenix Seagaia!

Grammar | Present Perfect

4   **a**   Read the postcard. Who is it from? Where is she at the time of writing?

Dear Karen

1 Well, we've arrived at Seagaia, and it's amazing! We're staying in a nice little Japanese apartment.

2 The weather has been wonderful so I've spent hours at the Ocean Dome – the water's lovely. I've seen the golf courses but I haven't played any golf.

3 Patrick has had a great time in the sea. He has been surfing, sailing and swimming. Melanie loves animals, so she's visited the zoo and she's taken a horse-riding lesson.

4 Well, it's time for dinner. See you soon.

Love Lara

---

b   Underline Present Perfect verbs in the postcard and add them to the table.

REGULAR VERB	IRREGULAR VERB
have arrived	has been

5   Choose the correct words to complete the sentences in the Active grammar box.

Active grammar

1 Lara uses the Present Perfect to describe her holiday activities because *she is still on holiday/her holiday has finished*.

2 In the Present Perfect, we use *have/has* + past participle with *I, you, we* and *they*. We use *have/has* + past participle with *he, she* and *it*.

3 *Regular/Irregular* past participles have the same form as the regular Past Simple.

see Reference page 103

6   Complete the text with the Present Perfect of the verbs in brackets.

We *have arrived* (arrive) at our hotel. It's got a fantastic swimming pool and Leon and I (1) _____ (go) swimming. Zosia and Basia (2) _____ (not spend) any time in the sea because they noticed the tennis court – they (3) _____ (play) three games of tennis so far! I (4) _____ (also spend) an hour in the beauty salon – so relaxing. Leon (5) _____ (visit) the town and he (6) _____ (see) some lovely things but he (7) _____ (not take) any photos – he forgot his camera!

Lifelong learning

Record past participles

Make a table of irregular past participles.

VERB	PAST PARTICIPLE
be	been
go	been
do	done

7   Copy the table in the Lifelong learning box. Add the irregular past participles from Ex. 4b, and these:

buy   eat   get   write

Pronunciation

8   **a**   **10.4**   Listen to these long and short vowels, then repeat the words.

LONG	SHORT
/ɑː/ parked	/æ/ had
/iː/ seen	/ɪ/ written
/ɔː/ bought	/ɒ/ got

b   **10.5**   Listen. Underline the word you hear.

1	have	half	4	park	pack
2	feet	fit	5	bald	bad
3	short	shop	6	sleep	slip

Speaking and writing

9   Imagine you are on a weekend away. It is Sunday. In pairs, discuss the questions and make a note of the answers.

1 Where are you?
2 Where are you staying?
3 What has the weather been like?
4 What have you done?

10   **a**   Answer the questions about Lara's postcard.

1 Which tense does the writer use to describe what she has done?
2 Which paragraph:
   • describes the writer's activities?
   • describes her family's activities?
   • gives a reason for ending the postcard?
   • describes the apartment?

b   Write a postcard. Use your notes from Ex. 9.

City Profiles

This week we look at commuters around the world ...

Fatima da Costa lives in Patriarca, a suburb in the east of São Paulo, Brazil. She works in the centre of the city, near Praça Republica. Every day Fatima takes an underground train to work in the morning and back home in the evening. She thinks travelling on the São Paulo underground system – the Metro – is quick and convenient. But the trains are very crowded in the rush hour and she often can't find a seat.

Jan van Looy works in the main train station in Amsterdam. He works for the Dutch Railways but he doesn't catch a train to work. He cycles from his home in the suburb of Sloterdijk. Cycling is very popular in Amsterdam because the city is flat and the distances are not very great. Jan cycles to work because it is very cheap, but it's quite slow and it's horrible when it rains!

Reading and listening

1 Look at photo A. What can you see? Have you been in this situation? When? Where?

2 **a** Read the text quickly and match it to two of the photos A–E.

b Read the text again and complete the table for Fatima and Jan.

NAME	Fatima	Jan	Julia	Billy
PICTURE				
CITY				
FORM OF TRANSPORT			rollerblading	
ADVANTAGES	quick,			
DISADVANTAGES		slow,		

3 **10.6** Listen to Julia and Billy and complete the table.

Person to person

4 Discuss. Use your own opinions and the information in the table in Ex. 2b.

   1 Which form of transport is:
- the safest?
- the cheapest?
- the most comfortable?
- the most expensive?
- the most convenient?
- the fastest?

   2 Which form of commuting is best? Why?

Grammar | *-ing* form as noun

5 Look at the examples of the *-ing* form in the Active grammar box. Then find and <u>underline</u> two examples in the text. Choose the correct words to complete the sentences in the box.

> ### Active grammar
>
> <u>*Rollerblading*</u> *is a bit dangerous when you cross busy roads.*
> <u>*Commuting*</u> *is really difficult in London.*
>
> **1** *Swimming is/are my favourite sport.*
> **2** *Parking/Park isn't easy in the centre of big cities.*

see Reference page 103

C

D

E

Listening

7 **a** **10.7** Billy wants to take his family on holiday. Listen and answer the questions.

1 Which country does Billy want to go to?

2 When does he want to leave?

3 How much does it cost?

b Match words 1–7 to the meanings a–g.

1 destination   a go and come back
2 one-way   b more comfortable but expensive seats
3 return   c the place you want to go to
4 economy class   d when you leave
5 business class   e no stops on the journey
6 departure   f the journey to your destination only
7 direct   g the cheapest seats

c Read the tapescript on page 158 and complete the How to box.

HOW TO ...

book a travel ticket

Make enquiries	Do you sell airline _____ for New Zealand?
Give details	I'd like to _____ on Friday the 5th of next month. We _____ to come back one month later.
Ask for more information	What _____ does the flight leave London? Is it a _____ flight?
Ask about prices	How _____ is that?
Ask for tickets	I'd like _____ tickets, please.

6 Make sentences from the prompts.

park/impossible/in central London

Parking is impossible in central London.

1 eat/vegetables/good for your health

2 cycle/popular/in Amsterdam

3 wait/for a bus/boring

4 live/in a big city/exciting

5 take/taxis/expensive

8 Use words from Exs. 7b and 7c to complete the dialogue.

A: Do you sell airline (1) _____ for Mexico? I'd (2) _____ to go to Cancun on Wednesday the 12th.

B: One way or (3) _____?

A: One way. And I'd like to fly business (4) _____.

B: OK. We have flights with United Airlines.

A: (5) _____ much is that flight?

B: It's €800.

A: Is it a (6) _____ flight?

B: No, it stops in Miami.

9 Work in pairs.

Student A: you are a travel agent. Turn to page 128.

Student B: you want to book a flight. Look at this information then telephone the travel agent (your partner). Which airline do you choose?

You want to fly from Paris to Miami with a friend. You want to leave next Wednesday and return two weeks later. You can afford a maximum of €1,000.

Phone the travel agent, get information about flights, dates and prices, then book your tickets.

Booking a hotel room

Hotel Europa
R E C E P T I O N

PRICES
Single room €85
Double/twin room €120
Suite €160
Breakfast €10 (6.00–10.00)

FACILITIES   OPENING HOURS
Restaurant 12.00–23.30
Swimming pool 8.00–22.00 (free to guests)
Gym/sauna 8.00–22.00 (free to guests)
Shops 8.00–20.00
Beauty salon 10.00–18.00 (price list at reception)
Tennis/golf 10.00–18.00 (price list at reception)

1 Do you like staying in hotels? What's the best hotel you have ever stayed in?

2 Look at the hotel information and answer the questions.

  1 How much is a room for one person? For two people?

  2 What do we call a room for two people, but with only one bed?

  3 Is breakfast included in the room price?

  4 Can you have a beauty treatment before breakfast? (Why/Why not?)

  5 How much does it cost to go swimming?

  6 Where do you find out the prices of tennis and golf?

3 **a** **10.8** Listen to someone making a booking at this hotel. What kind of room do they book, and when? Do they want anything else, for example, a quiet room?

  b Look at the tapescript on page 158 and complete the How to box.

HOW TO …

book a hotel room

Ask to book a room	*I'd like to _____.*
Say which type of room	*I'd like a _____.*
Ask about the bathroom	*Does it have _____?*
Ask about the price	*How _____?*

4 Work in pairs. Book a hotel room.

Student A: close your book. Then decide on the type of room you want, the dates and anything else you want. Call Student B (the receptionist).

Student B: you are the receptionist. Use the hotel information and your imagination to answer Student A.

Now swap roles.

5 **a** **10.9** Listen to the complaints and complete the table.

	THE GUEST ASKED FOR …	WHAT HAPPENED?
1		
2		
3		

  b Work in pairs.

Student A: look at the information below.

Student B: turn to page 128.

B: *Hello/Reception. Can I help you?*

A: *Yes, I'm afraid there's a problem. I booked …*

Student A

Roleplay 1: you are the guest. You booked a double room in the hotel but they have given you a single room. Make a complaint.

Roleplay 2: you are the receptionist. The guest asked for breakfast at 7.00a.m. in his/her room, but it hasn't arrived. Offer to ask the kitchen to send it immediately (*I'll ask …*). You start the roleplay.

Present Perfect

Form the Present Perfect with *has/have* + the past participle, e.g. *been*.

	I/You/We/They	He/She/It
⊕	*'ve (have)* + past participle	*'s (has)* + past participle
⊖	*haven't (have not)* + past participle	*hasn't (has not)* + past participle
	Or *have* + *never* + past participle	Or *has* + *never* + past participle
?	*Have* + *I/we/you/they (+ ever)* + past participle	*Has* + *he/she/it (+ ever)* + past participle
	Yes, I/we/you/they have.	*Yes, he/she/it has.*
	No, I/we/you/they haven't.	*No, he/she/it hasn't.*

Have you ever been to New Zealand?

I've seen the golf courses but I haven't played any golf.

She's taken a horse-riding lesson.

We usually use the contracted forms, but in formal writing we use the full forms.

The past participle of most verbs is the same as the regular Past Simple form.

INFINITIVE	PAST SIMPLE	PAST PARTICIPLE
play	*played*	*played*
arrive	*arrived*	*arrived*

But there are a lot of irregular past participles. Some of them are the same as the Past Simple form.

INFINITIVE	PAST SIMPLE	PAST PARTICIPLE
buy	*bought*	*bought*
have	*had*	*had*

But many of them are different from the Past Simple form.

INFINITIVE	PAST SIMPLE	PAST PARTICIPLE
see	*saw*	*seen*
take	*took*	*taken*

Note that the past participle *been* is the past participle of both *be* and *go*.

It's a nice day. → *It's been a nice day.*

I go shopping on Saturdays. → *I haven't been shopping this week.*

Use the Present Perfect to talk about actions in the past when:

• we are talking about any time up to now: *Have you ever been to Cuba?*

• we don't say a definite time: *We've met the President.*

• it is still possible to do/repeat an action (because the time is still continuing): *Keith has written four books.* (He can write another book, because he is still alive.)

We often use the Present Perfect with *ever/never* to talk about experiences at any time up to and including the present.

Have you ever been to Rome?

No, I've never been to Italy.

Don't use the Present Perfect with a specific past time. Use the Past Simple.

I didn't have a holiday last year.

We saw her yesterday.

Use the Present Perfect to talk about a past experience for the first time.

We've been to Florida ...

But when we give more information, use the Past Simple.

We went to Miami two years ago.

-ing form as noun

We sometimes use the *-ing* form of a verb as the subject of a sentence.

Parking is really difficult in Madrid.

Use singular verbs with *-ing* verb subjects.

Flying is expensive.

Key vocabulary

Types of holiday
activity holiday
beach holiday
cultural holiday
sightseeing holiday
water sports holiday
winter sports holiday

Travel
commuting departure
journey one-way/return ticket
passenger
Railway:
train platform station
underground (metro)
Flying:
airport flight
long-haul flight direct flight
economy class/business class
Car:
drive garage park traffic
Other:
cycling rollerblading

Hotels
Rooms:
single double twin suite
Facilities:
reception restaurant shops
beauty salon gym sauna
swimming pool tennis golf

1 Put the words in the correct order to make sentences.

been to China Have ever you ?

Have you ever been to China?

1 never a long-haul I've flight been on

2 adventure holiday you been Have ever on an ?

3 to We've New York and Boston been

4 horse-riding in been She's Scotland

2 Some of the past participles in these sentences are wrong. Tick (✓) the correct sentences. Cross (✗) the incorrect ones and write the correct past participle.

Have you visited the wax museum? ☑ _____

Jonathan has ~~saw~~ a very good film. ☒ *seen*

1 I've spended a lot of money. ☐ _____

2 We've never bought a new car. ☐ _____

3 Has she took her last exam yet? ☐ _____

4 We've never play volleyball. ☐ _____

5 Mum and Dad haven't arrived yet. ☐ _____

6 He has wrote over 100 books. ☐ _____

3 Max and Lorena are on holiday in India. Look at the list of things they have/haven't done and complete Max's postcard.

	Max	Lorena
see the Taj Mahal	✓	✓
visit the Bollywood studios	✗	✗
have lots of Indian meals	✗	✓
go swimming in the Indian Ocean	✓	✗
take an elephant ride	✓	✓
buy some spices	✗	✓
play golf with some friends	✓	✗
go on a boat trip	✓	✓

Dear Paul

Well, we're in India – the holiday of a lifetime! *We've seen* the Taj Mahal – it's amazing – but *we haven't visited* the Bollywood studios. (1) _____ lots of Indian meals, of course – she loves Indian food – but I have only eaten in the hotel. (2) _____ in the Indian Ocean. Lorena hasn't because she's worried about sharks! (3) _____ an elephant ride. That was interesting but not very comfortable. (4) _____ some spices from the market and (5) _____ with some friends. (6) _____ on a boat trip. It was really relaxing.

See you soon.

Love Max

4 Find the mistakes in the Past Simple/Present Perfect in this dialogue, and correct them.

Liz: Have you ever been skiing?

Sue: No, I ~~didn't~~. *haven't*

Liz: It's fantastic.

Sue: When did you go?

Liz: We've been last winter.

Sue: And where did you go?

Liz: Switzerland.

Sue: I never went to Switzerland. Was it nice?

Liz: Yes, it was beautiful.

Sue: Was it cold?

Liz: Yes, we've been in January so it was very cold.

Sue: Did you ever go there in the summer?

Liz: No, I haven't.

5 Complete the sentences with a verb in the box.

swim take go commute fly pay drive

Flying in business class is quite expensive.

1 _____ by credit card is very convenient.

2 _____ is a good way to get fit.

3 _____ to the cinema is my favourite activity.

4 _____ a fast car is very exciting.

5 _____ photos is the best part of a holiday.

6 _____ takes a long time in big cities.

6 Complete each sentence with a travel word.

1 It doesn't stop. It's a _____ flight.

2 Excuse me. Can I have a _____ ticket? I want to come back tomorrow.

3 I prefer flying in business _____ because the seats are more comfortable.

4 Trains to Edinburgh leave from _____ 10.

5 I park my car on the street because I don't have a _____.

6 A Boeing 747 can take more than 300 _____.

7 Write the type of holiday where you can do these activities.

1 swimming and surfing _____

2 swimming and sunbathing _____

3 visiting museums and art galleries _____

4 skiing _____

5 walking and cycling _____

11 Learning

Lead-in

1 Look at the photos. What are the four learning situations? Which ones have you been in?

2 **a** Which learning situation does each rule come from?

1 Drive on the left.
2 Speak English.
3 Follow my movements.
4 Don't go over the speed limit.
5 Put your right hand here.
6 Don't shout out the answers.

b Discuss.

1 What were the main rules when you were at school?
2 Did you usually obey them?
3 What was the punishment when you broke the rules?

3 **a** Put the words and phrases in the box into two groups: school subjects or educational institutions.

> Biology Chemistry college Geography History kindergarten
> Languages Mathematics Physics polytechnic primary school
> Science secondary school university

b **11.1** Listen and write the number of syllables for each word in the box. Which word has the most syllables? Listen again and check your answers.

Bi/o/lo/gy – four

c How many other school subjects can you add to the list?

11.1 Rules of the road

Grammar	can/can't, have to/don't have to
Can do	understand signs and rules

Reading

1 Discuss.

1 Do you drive? Do you enjoy driving?

2 Do you always obey the rules of the road?

3 What happens when people break them in your country?
   • fines? • prison?
   • points on their licence?

2 **a** Read the text quickly. Which country is it about?

b Read the text again. Mark the statements true (T) or false (F).

1 You can't drive after you get a certain number of points on your licence.

2 Offenders have to do a course at Traffic School.

3 You have to pay to do Traffic School courses.

4 Offenders at Traffic School have to pass a driving test.

c Do you think Traffic School is a good idea? Does this happen in your country?

Traffic School

Have you ever driven faster than the speed limit or driven through a red traffic light? The answer is probably 'yes'. Every year thousands of motorists become 'offenders' – they break the rules of the road. But what are the punishments for this offence?

In most countries drivers have to pay a fine, usually €50–€200. But in the USA, Australia and some European countries offenders also get points on their driving licence. After they get a certain number of points, they can't drive.

Life is difficult when you can't drive so some states in the USA have introduced a new way to avoid this – Traffic School. Offenders have a choice, they can get points on their licence or they can do a course at Traffic School.

Traffic Schools run 'driver improvement courses'. They cost about $80 and take eight hours. Motorists learn the rules of the road and they learn how to be better drivers. They don't have to take a driving test, but at the end of the course they have to pass a written examination.

Grammar | can/can't, have to/don't have to

3 **a** Match the pictures A–F to the explanations 1–6 below.

1 You can pay by credit card.

2 He doesn't have to have a driving licence.

3 You can't smoke.

4 You have to wear a seat belt.

5 You don't have to pay.

6 She has to show her passport.

b Match 1–4 to a–d.

1 can ——————— a necessary

2 can't   b not possible

3 has/have to   c not necessary

4 doesn't/don't have to —— d possible

see Reference page 113

4   5   6   7   8   9   10

4 Look at the road signs above. Write the rules with *can, can't* or *have to*. Use the words and phrases in the box.

> ~~stop~~   go   ~~turn right~~   turn left   enter   get petrol
> park   overtake   give way   go faster than

1 You have to stop.   2 You can't turn right.

5   **a** 〔11.2〕 Listen to part of a tourist information line. What information is not mentioned?

     1 transport   2 immigration   3 driving   4 flights   5 hotels   6 museums

     b Listen to the second part of the tourist information line and complete the form with *can, can't, have to* or *don't have to*.

DRIVING IN BRITAIN

Visitors to Britain with a valid driving licence

● _can_ drive in Britain without a British licence for six months.
● _____ get a British driving licence after six months.

To rent a car, you

● _____ have a driving licence from your country.
● _____ have a credit card.
● _____ be 18 or over.

When driving in Britain, you

● _____ keep your documents with you.
● _____ turn right at a red traffic light.

---

6 Sami comes from Egypt. He wants to rent a car to drive when he is on holiday in Britain. Write four sentences using *have to, don't have to, can* and *can't*.

     1 Sami has to have an Egyptian driving licence.

Person to person

7 In pairs, ask and answer. In your country, what do you have to do to:

get a passport?   get a place at university?   open a bank account?
rent a car?   get a credit card?   get a mobile phone account?

Pronunciation

8   **a** 〔11.3〕 Listen. Do the underlined words sound the same?

     You don't have to be a British citizen to take a British driving test but you have to have a valid British visa.

     b 〔11.4〕 Listen and underline the word you hear. Then repeat.

     1   a) leave   b) leaf
     2   a) few   b) view
     3   a) fan   b) van
     4   a) V   b) we

     c 〔11.5〕 Listen to the sentences. Practise them.

     1   Philip finds French films very violent.
     2   Very few fines feel fair.
     3   Fiona Philips never gives fitness advice to fresh fruit fanatics.

Speaking

9   **a** 〔11.6〕 Listen to Steve talking about the USA and write sentences.

     military service
     Americans don't have to do military service.

     1   identity cards
     2   driving
     3   guns
     4   bars and nightclubs
     5   smoking
     6   doctors and hospitals

     b Work in small groups. Compare the rules in the USA with your country/countries.

     In my country you have to do military service when you are eighteen.

A

B

Reading and vocabulary

1 a Discuss.

1 How old are the people in the photos?

2 Which photos show: pre-school education, primary education (4/5–11/12), secondary education (11/12–17/18), higher education (18+)?

3 What do you call these types of education in your country?

b Complete the Education column of the table with the types of education from Ex. 1a.

EDUCATION	AGE	THE UK	JAPAN	NEW ZEALAND	YOUR COUNTRY
pre-school	3	nursery			
	4				
	5	primary school	elementary school		
	6				
	7				
	8				
	9				
	10				
	11				
	12	secondary school			
	13				
	14				
	15				
	16				
	17				
	18				
	19	college/ university		polytechnic	
	20				

2 a Read the text and answer the questions. (Ignore the gaps.)

1 How many years of compulsory education are there in Japan?

2 What is the name of the last compulsory school?

3 How many students stay at high school for six years?

b Read the text again and complete it with the red words in the box.

> academic college of education
> ~~compulsory~~ intermediate
> kindergarten optional
> primary private secondary
> specialised subjects
> university

c Use the information from the text to complete the table in Ex. 1b for Japan.

THE EDUCATIONAL SYSTEM IN JAPAN

Japan has nine years of <u>compulsory</u> education, from the age of six to fifteen. The schools are (1) _____ or public, and the (2) _____ year is from April to March.

Pre-school education

Pre-school education is not compulsory. Children can go to private or public kindergartens from the age of three.

Primary and secondary education

Children have to start school at six. They go to elementary school for six years (to the age of twelve). All the (3) _____ are compulsory.
They then spend six years at high school. They still have compulsory subjects but some subjects are now (4) _____. Students can leave high school after three years, but about 90 percent stay for another three years, to continue their general education but also to take some (5) _____ subjects, to prepare for work or university.

Higher education

Students can go to college or university at eighteen. They have to pay fees for their education and courses usually take four years.

C

D

Listening

3 **a** `11.7` Listen to an interview with Nicole Gardener. Where is she from and what kind of school does she teach in?

b Answer the questions. Listen again if necessary.

1 How many years of compulsory education are there?

2 Why did Nicole go to a college of education? How long was she there?

3 How much do students pay for their higher education studies?

c Listen again and complete the table in Ex. 1b for New Zealand. Use the blue words in the box in Ex. 2b.

Grammar | review of *wh-* questions

4 **a** Match 1–8 to a–h to complete the questions.

1 How

2 How long

3 When

4 How many

5 What

6 Where

7 Which type

8 How much

a years were you at primary school?

b of institution did you go to?

c did you go after primary school?

d did you start school?

e does the educational system work?

f does a student have to pay?

g subjects did you take?

h do students spend in the system?

see Reference page 113

b What do you know about question words?

1 You have studied three *wh-* question words that are not in Ex. 4a? Which ones?

2 Match the question words to the words and phrases in the box.

How? *the way something works*

How long? Where? What? When? How many?
Which? Whose? Why? How much? Who?

people   things and ideas   times   possession
places   prices or cost   numbers and quantity
a choice between two (or more) things
periods of time   ~~the way something works~~
reason

Pronunciation

5 **a** `11.8` Listen to the questions. Does the voice go up (↗) or down (↘) at the end?

1 What did you do there?

2 Was it interesting?

3 Who did you see?

4 Did you like it?

b `11.9` Listen and repeat the questions from Ex. 4a.

Speaking

6 Write ten *wh-* questions to ask about a person's education. Ask and answer in groups.

A: *Where did you go to primary school?*

B: *When did you leave secondary school?*

A: *What did you study at university?*

Writing

7 **a** In pairs, complete the Your country column in the table in Ex. 1b.

b Make some more notes about your country's educational system. Think about these things:

• private/public

• years of compulsory education

• length of college/university courses

• pay for university

c Using the table and your notes, write a short account of your country's educational system for an international students' magazine. Use the text in Ex. 2a as a model.

Reading

1 **a** Read the email quickly. What does Joanna plan to do? Where?

b Read again and mark the sentences true (T) or false (F).

1 Joanna wants to leave work.
2 She wants to study languages.
3 The Open University offers distance-learning courses.
4 Joanna can study from home.

January 25th

Hi Marisa

Thanks for your email before Christmas.
I've got some interesting news – I'm returning to studying!
My job is a bit boring now but I *can't afford* to leave work, so
I've joined the Open University. I'm starting the course next
month (February) and I'm taking *a degree* in Art History. As
you know, I haven't got any *academic* qualifications, so I think
it's a good idea. It's a *distance-learning* course, so I can study
at home in my free time. You have a personal *tutor* who helps
you. I'll tell you all about it when I start.
That's the only exciting news from here. We're having a few
days in the country next week, before my course starts, and
Geoff is working in the US again in March – he organised it
all last week. Are you doing anything exciting in the next few
weeks?
Write soon.

Love,
Joanna

Lifelong learning

Recognising word groups

When you don't understand a word in a text, first decide if it is a noun, verb or adjective.

2 **a** Are the words in italics in the text nouns, verbs or adjectives?

b Match 1–5 to the words in italics in the text.

1 university qualification
2 connected with education
3 teacher
4 haven't got the money to do something
5 learning from home, away from a school/college

Grammar | Present Continuous for future

3 **a** Look at the sentences in the Active grammar box and answer the questions.

Active grammar

I'm starting the course next month ...

Geoff is working in the US again in March ...

1 Which tense are the sentences?

2 Has Joanna decided to do the course?

3 Has Geoff organised his stay in the States?

4 Are the sentences describing an action in the present or in the future?

b <u>Underline</u> other examples of the Present Continuous for future in the text.

see Reference page 113

4 **a** Look at this list of activities for four flatmates. Write sentences in the Present Continuous.

Monday	Kimiko – cook dinner for friends, 7.30
Tuesday	Juan and Pilar – go to the cinema, 8.45
Wednesday	Radek – start his new English class, 6.30
Thursday	Juan – meet his brother at the Italian restaurant, 8.00
Friday	everyone – go to a nightclub, 10.30
Saturday	Kimiko – take the flight to Tokyo, 11.50

Kimiko is cooking dinner for her friends on Monday.

HOW TO ... ask about plans and arrangements

| Ask about plans | What are you doing next ...? |
| Express arrangements | I'm visiting my aunt. We're having dinner with some friends. |

b What arrangements do you have for these times? Discuss in pairs.

on Friday evening / on Saturday afternoon / on Sunday / the weekend after next

Listening

5 **a** Match the adverts below with these types of learning.

		Advert
1	distance learning	☐
2	evening classes	☐
3	professional training	☐
4	education for older people	☐

U3A
University of the Third Age

Lifelong learning for retired people

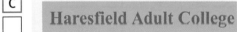

M **MicroMatters Ltd.**
COMPUTER TRAINING SPECIALISTS

Improve your computing skills on courses from one day to four weeks, all computing skills

Haresfield Adult College

Part-time day and evening classes for adults

Courses from life-saving to languages, hairdressing to history

TheOpen University

- study part-time in your own home
- improve your career prospects
- gain new skills and confidence
- study for pleasure

b (11.10) Listen to four people. Write 1–4 by the adverts in Ex. 5 in the order the speakers talk about them.

6 (11.10) Listen again and complete the table.

	Haresfield College	Open University	MicroMatters Ltd.	University of the Third Age
Where do you study?	*local schools, the centre*			
How much does it cost?		*about £500 a year*		
How much time does it take?			*two or three days, a week*	
Examples of subjects				*(He doesn't say.)*

Vocabulary | education

7 **a** Look at the words in the box. Then put some of the words into categories. In pairs, compare your categories.

higher education: college, degree, university...

people: pupil, student, trainee ...

> academic certificate classroom-learning college compulsory degree distance-learning full-time lecturer optional part-time pupil school student teacher trainee trainer tutor university vocational

b Use some of the words to write two or three sentences describing your education.

Speaking

8 Discuss.

1 Do you have all these types of learning in your country?
2 Have you ever tried/Would you like to try any of them?
3 Do you think that studying part-time is a good idea? Why/Why not?
4 Do you want to study any other subjects in the future? What? When?

1   a   Discuss.

1   Have you ever made an appointment to see …
    a doctor?   a dentist?
    a vet?   a hairdresser?
    a business client?
    a lawyer?

2   How did you do it?
    by telephone   by email
    by text message   by fax
    by going there

b   Do these expressions mean a) I can see you at 4.30, or b) I can't see you at 4.30?

1   I'm free at 4.30.
2   I'm busy at 4.30.
3   I'm available at 4.30.
4   I'm not available at 4.30.

2   a   `11.11`   Listen to Carlos's phone call and answer the questions.

1   What is Carlos trying to arrange?
2   Why?
3   When is his appointment?

b   Listen again and complete Jill's diary for next week.

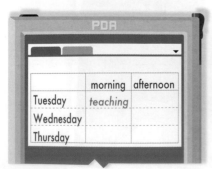

	morning	afternoon
Tuesday	teaching	
Wednesday		
Thursday		

c   Listen again or read the tapescript on page 160 and complete the How to box.

HOW TO …

make arrangements

Suggest a time	_____ you come on Thursday?
Refuse politely	I'm afraid I _____ come then …
Give reasons	… because _____ working.
Suggest alternatives	I _____ come on Tuesday. How _____ earlier in the morning?
Make arrangements	OK. _____ meet at nine o' clock.

3   a   Work in pairs to arrange an appointment.

Student A: you are a university lecturer. Turn to page 128.
Student B: you are a university student. Look at this information.
You want to see your personal tutor (Student A) next week. Phone him/her and arrange a one-hour appointment. This is your diary for next week. You can't change any of the things in your diary!

B: *How about nine o' clock on Monday?*
A: *No, I'm afraid I don' t start work until ten.*

	MONDAY	TUESDAY	WEDNESDAY	THURSDAY	FRIDAY
09.00			seminar from 9 to 11		
10.00	lecture from 10 to 12.45	lecture 10 to 12		take English test 10.30 to 12.30	lecture 11 to 12.30
11.00					
12.00		lunch with Emily 12 to 2			
13.00					
14.00			work in the computer centre all afternoon		doctor at 14.30
15.00		play badminton 3 to 5			
16.00					

b   Check with another pair. Are your appointments for the same time?

can/can't

Use *can* to say that something is possible or to give permission.
Hotel guests **can** *use the health club.*

Use *can't* to express prohibition – to say that something isn't possible or isn't allowed. We often use *can't* to explain rules.
You **can't** *drive through a red traffic light.*

Use *can* to ask about rules or ask for permission.
Can *we take photographs in the museum?*
Excuse me. **Can** *I use your telephone?*

have to/don't have to

	I/You/We/They	He/She/It
➕	have to	has to
➖	don't have to	doesn't have to
❓	Do ... have to?	Does ... have to?

Use *have to* to express an obligation, to say that something is necessary. Use it to explain rules.
In Britain you **have to** *drive on the left.*
My brother **has to** *do military service.*

Use *don't have to* when there is no obligation – to say that something isn't necessary.
It's informal – you **don't have to** *wear smart clothes.*
She's a member of the club so she **doesn't have to** *pay.*

Note the difference between *can't* and *don't have to*.
You **don't have to** *wear a suit.* (It isn't necessary, but you can wear one if you want to.)
You **can't** *wear jeans here.* (It isn't allowed.)

We can use *have to* to ask about rules.
Do I **have to** *get a visa?*

Wh- questions

The common *wh-* question words in English are *what, who, when, where, how, which, whose* and *why.*

We form a lot of questions with *How* + adjective/adverb: *how much, how many, how long, how tall.*

We usually answer these questions with a number, price, quantity, etc.
How much was your car? It was 3,000 euros.

Note the answers to *How long/tall/heavy/wide*, etc.
How tall are you? I'm 1.8 metres **tall**.
How high is Mount Everest? It's about 8,850 metres **high**.

In *wh-* questions, the verb *to be* and modal verbs (e.g. *can*) come after the question word but before the subject.
Where is your new apartment? Who can you see?

In all tenses the auxiliary verb usually comes before the subject and the main verb comes after it. We do not usually change this word order or omit the auxiliary.
When is Tim coming home?
Who did you see at the party?

Present Continuous for future

Use the Present Continuous to express plans and arrangements in the future. (For the form of the Present Continuous, see page 83.)
We're meeting Sonia at the station at six tomorrow.
John isn't starting his university course in October because he didn't pass his exams.

We often ask about plans with this tense.
What are you doing tomorrow evening?
Are you staying in Florida for two weeks?

We use it when the plans and arrangements are certain, e.g. when we have bought tickets/made arrangements/made a strong decision.
What are you doing tomorrow evening?
I'm having dinner with Yusuf. We're meeting in town.

Key vocabulary

Education

School subjects: Biology Chemistry Geography History Languages Mathematics Science

Institutions: kindergarten primary school secondary school college polytechnic university

Types of learning: classroom learning distance learning part-time full-time training

People: teacher tutor lecturer trainer student trainee

Qualifications: certificate degree

Adjectives: academic compulsory optional private public specialised vocational

Other: course skill fees

Driving and road signs

Driving: driving licence test overtake traffic lights (get) petrol rules of the road offenders fine points

Road signs: stop go turn right/left enter park give way go faster/slower (than)

1 Complete the rules using *have to/don't have to, can* or *can't* and the phrases in the box.

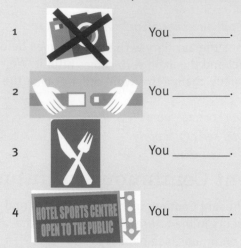

1   You _____.

2   You _____.

3   You _____.

4   You _____.

> take photographs   wear a seat belt
> be a hotel guest   find a restaurant here

2 Mike has made these notes about the rules in his new office. Complete the sentences with *has to, doesn't have to, can* or *can't.*

> <u>Office rules</u>
> Hours are from 9a.m. to 5.30p.m.
> But OK to go home at 4p.m. on Wednesdays.
> One hour for lunch (but anytime between 12 and 3).
> No smoking, eating or drinking in the office.
> Don't make personal phone calls.
> But personal emails from my computer are OK.
> Don't use my mobile phone in the office.
> Wear a suit and tie, but informal clothes OK on Fridays.

Mike <u>has to</u> start work at nine o'clock.

1   He _____ smoke in the office.
2   He _____ have more than one hour for lunch.
3   He _____ work after 4p.m. on Wednesdays.
4   If he wants to, he _____ have lunch at two o'clock.
5   Mike _____ wear a suit to work from Monday to Thursday.
6   He _____ make personal phone calls.
7   He _____ use his mobile phone in the office.
8   He _____ wear a suit on Fridays.
9   He _____ send personal emails from his computer.

3 Complete the questions with *wh-* question words. Then match the questions and answers.

1   <u>Where</u> did you go on your last holiday?
2   _____ did you go? Was it in the summer?
3   _____ did you get there? By plane?
4   _____ did you do there?
5   _____ did you stay, one or two weeks?
6   _____ did you go with? Friends from work?
7   _____ did you go there?
8   _____ did it cost?

a   We went skiing.
b   It was my mother's 60th birthday.
c   No, we went in February.
d   Three weeks, actually.
e   I went to Colorado, in the US.
f   It was very expensive!
g   Yes, by plane and bus.
h   No, I went with a big family group.

4 David is a film director. Read the dialogue and complete the gaps with the Present Continuous of the verbs in brackets.

David: Jules, hi. Can I check my diary for next week with you?

Asst: Of course. I've got your tickets, so *you're flying* (you/fly) to Cannes on Monday. (1) _____ (you/arrive) at 14.30.

David: OK. What (2) _____ (I/do) in the evening?

Asst: (3) _____ (you/not do) anything in the evening.

David: Good. Now, on Tuesday (4) _____ (I/watch) the films for the grand prize.

Asst: No, that's Wednesday. On Tuesday (5) _____ (you/meet) two American film directors for lunch.

David: That's Tuesday? OK. What time (6) _____ (they/show) my new film on Thursday?

Asst: At 2.00p.m.

David: OK. And when's the flight back?

Asst: (7) _____ (you/come) back at 10.50 on Friday morning.

5 <u>Underline</u> the odd-one-out in each group of words. Give your reason.

<u>compulsory</u> distance learning training
'Compulsory' isn't a type of learning.

1   Languages Mathematics college
2   tutor trainee trainer
3   certificate degree training
4   kindergarten polytechnic university
5   left petrol right
6   driving licence stop give way

A

12 Ambitions

B

C

D

Lead-in

1 Write labels for the photos, using one word or phrase from A and one from B.

A	trekking sailing cycling ~~white-water rafting~~
B	tunnel ~~river~~ bridge canyon

Picture A: white-water rafting on a river

2 **a** Work with a partner. Discuss.

1 Which photos show something that connects two places?
2 Do you think any of these activities are dangerous? Why?

b Make a list of other activities people can do in these places.

Horse-riding in a canyon

3 **a** **12.1** Listen to Dario and Mia. Which photos do they talk about?

b Listen again and answer the questions.
1 Which activity didn't Mia enjoy?
2 Which activity (not in the photos) do they talk about?
3 Where did they go cycling?
4 Which was their favourite activity?

4 In pairs, ask and answer.
1 Have you done any of the activities?
2 Did you like it or not? Why? Why not?
3 Do you want to try any of the activities in the future?

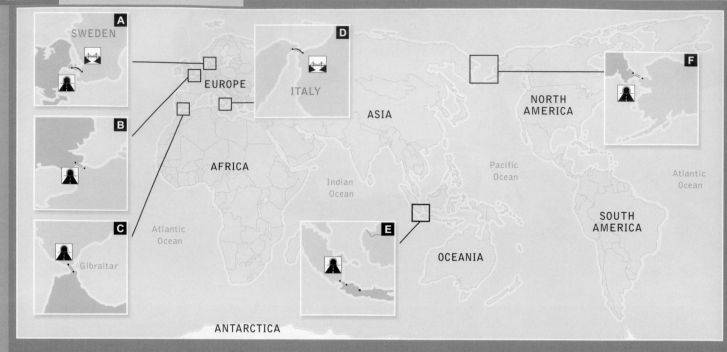

No more continents?

For centuries natural barriers such as rivers, mountains and seas have made travel difficult. Now, with modern technology, we are crossing these barriers and the world is becoming a much smaller place. Britain was an island for 8,000 years. But the Channel Tunnel opened in 1994 and connected Britain to mainland Europe. The Oresund Bridge and Tunnel opened in 2000 and connected Sweden to Denmark and the rest of Europe. Now there are more projects to link different parts of the world. The Italian government is going to build a 5km-long bridge between Sicily and the Italian mainland, and in Asia, Indonesia is going to build a tunnel between the islands of Java and Sumatra.

But there are bigger projects, to join continents! Spain and Morocco are going to build a tunnel connecting Europe to Africa. They are thinking of building a 38km tunnel between Punta Palomas on the south coast of Spain and Punta Malabata in northern Morocco, near Tangier. And the United States and Russia are discussing a project to connect Alaska to Siberia, joining the continents of North America and Asia.

Reading and vocabulary

1   Look at the map. Answer the questions.

   1 How many continents are there? What are they?

   2 How do we travel between continents?

2   **a** Read the text quickly. Is it about:

   1 the past and the present?

   2 the past, the present and the future?

   3 the present and the future?

b Read the text again and match the places. Then match the pairs to A–F on the map.

1	Java	a	the Italian mainland	☐
2	Sicily	b	Denmark	☐
3	Britain	c	Sumatra	*E*
4	Alaska	d	mainland Europe	☐
5	Sweden	e	Morocco	☐
6	Spain	f	Siberia	☐

3   **a** Look at the words in the box and <u>underline</u> them in the text. Then find:

   1 three verbs with the same meaning.

   2 three words connected with geography.

   3 three adjectives.

> continent   difficult   modern   island   connect   mainland   link   different   join

b Complete the questions about the text with words from the box in Ex. 3a, then write the answers.

   1 Which natural barriers make travel _____?

   2 When did a tunnel _____ Britain to mainland Europe?

   3 What is going to link Java with the _____ of Sumatra?

   4 Which _____ is Siberia part of?

Grammar | *be going to*

4 Look at these sentences and tick (✓) the correct explanation.

In the years to come the world is going to be a much smaller place.
Spain and Morocco are going to build a tunnel.

We use *going to* for:

1 intentions (things people plan to do in the future) ☐
2 things happening now ☐

5 Complete the Active grammar box.

Active grammar

	I	We/You/They	He/She/It
+	'm (am) going to + infinitive	____ going to + infinitive	____ going to + infinitive
−	'm (am) not going to + infinitive	aren't (are not) going to + infinitive	isn't (____) going to + infinitive
?	Am I going to + infinitive?	____ we, you, they going to + infinitive?	____ he, she, it going to + infinitive?

see Reference page 123

6 Write sentences and questions with *be going to* using the prompts.

Ford/build/a new electric car

Ford is going to build a new electric car.

your company/open/a new office/next year/?

Is your company going to open a new office next year?

1 Britain/not/build/any more airports
2 my parents/retire/next year
3 they/open/a new bridge/in 2020
4 the Americans/build/a space station/?
5 I/start/a new course/in September
6 we/not/have/a holiday/next summer

Pronunciation

7 a **12.2** Listen. What do you notice about the pronunciation of *to*?

I'm <u>go</u>ing to stop <u>smo</u>king

b **12.3** Listen and repeat these sentences, then mark the stress.

1 She's going to lose weight.
2 They're going to sell their car.
3 We're going to learn French.
4 I'm going to buy a laptop.

Vocabulary | future time

8 a Put the time expressions in the correct order.

next week   ~~today~~
in two years' time
next summer   ~~tomorrow~~
three years from now
later this year
the week after next

1 *today*   2 *tomorrow*

b In pairs, ask and answer about your intentions using the time expressions.

A: *What are you going to do tomorrow?*

Person to person

9 a Interview your partner about his/her intentions. Use the ideas below and some of the verbs in the box to make questions. Write down the answers.

1 health   4 holidays
2 work   5 friends/family
3 entertainment   6 sport

> do visit watch get
> start join meet change
> improve buy travel

A: *Are you going to improve your health?*

b Compare your information with other pairs.

Speaking

10 Work in groups of four.

Student A: turn to page 128.
Student B: turn to page 128.
Student C: turn to page 128.
Student D: Talk to the students in your group. Ask them questions and find someone who is going to:

1 change their job soon.
2 write a novel before they retire.
3 have more than three children.

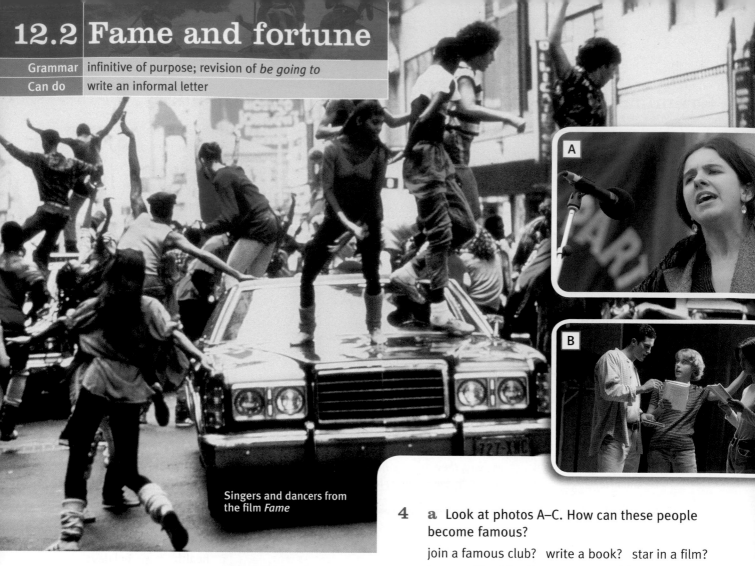

12.2 Fame and fortune

Grammar	infinitive of purpose; revision of *be going to*
Can do	write an informal letter

Singers and dancers from
the film *Fame*

Listening

1 How can people become famous? Make a list.

enter a 'pop star' competition

be on a reality TV show

2 **a** `12.4` Listen to the song *Fame!* and tick (✓)
the correct sentence.

1 The singer is famous. ☐
2 The singer wants to be famous in the future. ☐

b Look at the scene from the film *Fame!* and
answer the questions.

1 What is it about?
2 How are these people going to become famous?

3 Listen again and put the lines of the chorus in
the correct order.

I'm going to live forever	☐
I'm going to make it to heaven	☐
I feel it coming together	☐
People will see me and cry	☐
Fame!	1
Baby, remember my name!	☐
I'm going to learn how to fly	☐
Light up the sky like a flame	☐
I'm going to live forever	☐

4 **a** Look at photos A–C. How can these people
become famous?

join a famous club?   write a book?   star in a film?
become President?   win a competition?

b Use a dictionary. Match three phrases from
the box to photos A–C.

> politician   training session   acting   drama
> election   a play   politics   football team
> ball control skills

5 **a** `12.5` Listen to three interviews and match
them to photos A–C.

b Listen again and choose the correct answer.
1 Victoria is a) a university student or b) a TV
producer.
2 Helena is a) a politician or b) a student.
3 Lewis is in a) the first team or b) the reserve
team.

c Listen again and write sentences with *be
going to*. Then match your sentences with
reasons a–c.

Victoria _____

Helena _____

Lewis _____

a to get a place in a professional team
b to become a famous performer
c to learn more about elections

C

Grammar | infinitive of purpose

6 Look at what Lewis said and choose the correct answer.

I'm going to practise with them twice a week <u>to improve my physical fitness</u>.

I'm going to work really hard <u>to get into the first team</u>.

What does the <u>underlined</u> phrase do?

a It explains the purpose or reason for something.

b It gives more information about the verb.

see Reference page 123

7 Read the sentences. Are the reasons true for you? If not, change them so they are true for you.

I go on holiday to sunbathe and get tanned.

No, I go on holiday to visit new places.

1 I learn English to get a better job.

2 I go to nightclubs to meet new people.

3 I watch television to find out about other countries.

4 I go to work to have fun and relax.

5 I listen to pop music to improve my mind.

Reading and writing

8 **a** Read this letter from Victoria (from Ex. 5) to Josie and tick (✓) the correct sentence.

1 Josie is Victoria's sister.

2 Josie is Victoria's best friend.

Dear Josie

<u>Thank you very much for</u> your last letter. <u>It was great to hear about</u> your holiday in Cornwall. But <u>I was sorry to hear that</u> the weather was so bad.

<u>Everything is going well here.</u> My course is interesting and I've met a lot of nice people. The other students are very friendly. The most exciting thing is the drama group. I joined it last month and I'm really enjoying it. We're going to do a play at the end of term and I'm going to have one of the main parts! A TV company is making a film about the university and they are going to film the show. Yes, your little sister is going to be famous!

<u>Write soon and give my love to</u> Mum and Dad.

Love,
Victoria

b Read the letter again and discuss these questions in pairs.

1 How do we know that Victoria has had a letter from Josie?

2 How do we know this is a letter between relatives or close friends?

3 Why does Victoria use exclamation marks (!)?

9 Complete the How to box with the <u>underlined</u> expressions in the letter.

HOW TO... | organise an informal letter

Begin by mentioning the last letter you received	_____
Make a positive comment about it	_____
Describe your feelings	_____
Say something general about your life	_____
Make a request to end the letter	_____

10 Write a letter to a relative or close friend. Use Victoria's letter as a model. Follow these steps.

1 Make notes about your life now.

2 Make notes about your future plans.

3 Organise your notes into paragraphs.

4 Write the letter.

5 Check for grammar and spelling. Correct any mistakes.

6 Swap letters with a partner and check the spelling and grammar. Help your partner correct the mistakes.

12.3 | Charity challenge

Grammar	verbs + infinitive/-ing form (want, would like, like, etc.)
Can do	talk about likes, dislikes and ambitions

Reading

1 Look at the photo and answer the questions.

  1 Do you know this man? What is he doing?

  2 Why do you think he is doing it?

2 Look at the text. What is its connection with the photo above it?

3 **a** Match the words and phrases from the text to the correct meaning.

1	charity	a	something difficult for our bodies
2	raise money	b	happen
3	physical challenge	c	long, often difficult, journey
4	expedition	d	look for
5	take place	e	organisation that helps people
6	search	f	make money for someone/something

b Read the text. Mark the sentences true (T) or false (F).

  1 The text describes a few beach holidays.

  2 The expeditions are all very easy and relaxing.

  3 The expeditions take place all over the world.

  4 You can find information about the expeditions by searching the Internet.

4 Read some more information about Charity Challenge and tell your partner three important facts about it.

Student A: turn to page 129.

Student B: turn to page 130.

Listening

5 ▮12.6▮ David is phoning Charity Challenge. In pairs, listen and answer the questions he asks.

6 Listen again. Match the sentence halves.

1	David would like	a	horse-riding.
2	David enjoys	b	hiking.
3	He loves	c	sailing.
4	He hates	d	to think about it.
5	He doesn't like	e	to ask some questions.
6	He wouldn't like	f	to climb a mountain.
7	He can't stand	g	cycling.
8	He wants	h	going to the gym.

Mark Webber on his cycling, trekking and kayaking challenge round Tasmania. Sponsors of the challenge raised money for Mark's favourite charities.

Address: www.charitychallenge.com

Charity Challenge

Are you looking for a challenge?

Raise money for charity and take a physical challenge at the same time!

There are more than thirty different challenges to choose from including treks, mountain bike rides, mountain climbs, white-water rafting, sailing and horse-riding expeditions.

They are taking place in Africa, Latin America, the Caribbean, the Middle East, Asia and Europe, and there are three levels of difficulty to choose from, so there really is something for everyone.

They include trekking on the Inca Trail, along the Great Wall of China, or climbing Mount Kilimanjaro. You can search for an expedition by Location, Activity or within our Summary of Expeditions table.

Grammar | verbs + infinitive/-ing form

7 Complete the table in the Active grammar box with verbs from 1–8 in Ex. 6. Then complete the rule with *like/enjoy/hate*, etc. or *want/ would like*.

> ### Active grammar
>
> | | verb + infinitive (*to ...*) | verb + -*ing* form (*...ing*) |
> |---|---|---|
> | **Positive meaning** | *would like ('d like),* _____ | *likes,* _____, _____ |
> | **Negative meaning** | *doesn't want,* _____ | *doesn't like,* _____, _____ |
>
> We use _____ to express future desires and ambitions, and we use _____ to express present likes and dislikes.

see Reference page 123

8 Choose the correct form of the verb.

1 Angeles enjoys *to dance/dancing* and she would like *to be/being* a professional dancer.

2 Giorgio doesn't like *learn/learning* English. He wants *to leave/leaving* his classes.

3 Johann and Bettina would like *to travel/travelling* but Bettina can't stand *to fly/flying*.

4 My father hates *to live/living* in the city but he doesn't want *to leave/leaving* his house.

5 Susanna loves *stay/staying* at home with her children. She wouldn't like *to get/getting* a job.

9 Look at the table. Discuss the questions in groups.

1 Have you been to any of the places?

2 Do you do any of the activities? Do you enjoy them?

3 Which of the challenges would you like to do?/Which places would you like to visit?

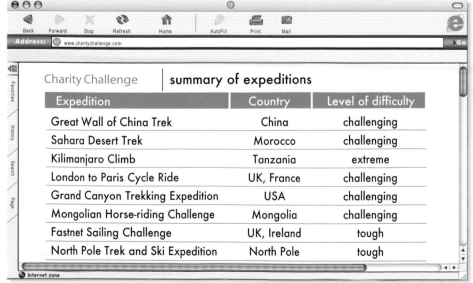

Charity Challenge | **summary of expeditions**

Expedition	Country	Level of difficulty
Great Wall of China Trek	China	challenging
Sahara Desert Trek	Morocco	challenging
Kilimanjaro Climb	Tanzania	extreme
London to Paris Cycle Ride	UK, France	challenging
Grand Canyon Trekking Expedition	USA	challenging
Mongolian Horse-riding Challenge	Mongolia	challenging
Fastnet Sailing Challenge	UK, Ireland	tough
North Pole Trek and Ski Expedition	North Pole	tough

Pronunciation

10 a [12.7] Listen and repeat this sentence. Do the <u>underlined</u> words have the same vowel sound?

I'd really <u>like</u> to <u>play</u> the classical guitar.

b [12.8] Listen and <u>underline</u> the word you hear in each pair. Then repeat.

1 a) wait b) white
2 a) Dave b) dive
3 a) late b) light
4 a) main b) mine
5 a) lake b) like

c [12.9] Listen to three sentences and write them. Then practise them.

Speaking

11 a Make a list of four or five ambitions.

Visit Machu Picchu.

b Compare your ambitions in groups, then as a class. Is there a top ambition in the class?

A: *I'd like to climb Machu Picchu.*

B: *Oh no. I don't like climbing.*

12 | Communication

Planning study objectives

1   In pairs, make a list of the ways of learning English in the photos. Do you do any of these?

2   a What do you like about learning English? Complete Part 1 of the questionnaire below.

   b In pairs, discuss your answers.

   A: *I like listening to English.*

   B: *I don't like that. I like ...*

Questionnaire
Part 1
Likes and dislikes about learning English

		I enjoy ...	I don't like ...
1	doing grammar exercises	☐	☐
2	learning new vocabulary	☐	☐
3	listening to English	☐	☐
4	listening to songs in English	☐	☐
5	reading texts in English	☐	☐
6	doing pronunciation exercises	☐	☐
7	having discussions in English	☐	☐
8	doing roleplays and speaking games	☐	☐
9	writing in English	☐	☐
10	doing tests in English	☐	☐

Part 2
Strengths and weaknesses

		I'm good at ...	I would like to be better at
1	using English grammar	☐	☐
2	remembering new vocabulary	☐	☐
3	understanding spoken English	☐	☐
4	understanding songs in English	☐	☐
5	understanding written English	☐	☐
6	pronouncing English	☐	☐
7	expressing my opinion in English	☐	☐
8	doing things in English (e.g. buy things)	☐	☐
9	writing English	☐	☐
10	doing tests in English	☐	☐

3   a What are you good at in English? Complete Part 2 of the questionnaire.

   b Discuss your answers in groups. Find other students who want to be better at the same things as you.

4   a Work with the same group as in Ex. 3b. Think of ways that you can improve your English.

Lifelong learning

Have clear study objectives

It's a good idea in any learning situation to know what your objectives are. Try to list them at different points in your studies.

   b Make a list of objectives for your group.

Our study objectives

We want to understand written English better, so ...

1 we are going to use a monolingual dictionary.

2 we are going to read the same graded reader.

3 we are going to discuss the reader together.

be going to

Form *be going to* with *to be* and the infinitive of a main verb.

I'm going to take *my driving test next week.*

	➕	➖	❓
I	'm (am) going to	'm (am) not going to	Am I going to ...?
We/ You/ They	're (are) going to	aren't (are not) going to	Are we/you/ they going to ...?
He/ She/It	's (is) going to	isn't (is not) going to	Is he/she/it going to ...?

***Are** you **going to have** a party for your birthday?*

*She **is going to become** the next president.*

We usually use the contracted forms in spoken English.

*It**'s** going to be a cold winter.*

*He **isn't** going to retire next year.*

Use *be going to* to express a personal or impersonal intention (a strong wish to do something in the future).

Impersonal intention

Spain and Morocco are going to build a tunnel.

They are going to close the factory next year.

Personal intention

I'm going to get thinner next year.

We're going to visit Poland next summer.

We use the Present Continuous for fixed plans and arrangements (see reference page 113).

They are closing the factory on February 24th.

Infinitive of purpose

Use *to* + infinitive to show the purpose or reason for an action.

*I'm learning English **to get a better job**.*

(= I want to get a better job. Learning English can help me do this.)

*I went to the shops **to buy some milk**.*

(= I went to the shops because I wanted to buy some milk.)

Verbs of liking/disliking

In English, a lot of verbs express likes and dislikes, e.g. *like, love, enjoy, hate, can't stand*. When another verb follows these verbs, we usually use the *-ing* form of the second verb.

*We really **enjoy** visit**ing** cities in other countries.*

*I **can't stand** gett**ing** up early in the morning.*

*They **love** watch**ing** motor racing.*

It is possible to use *to* + infinitive after *like, love* and *hate*. This is more common in American English.

*I **love to spend** time with my niece and nephew.*

would like to ...

Use *would(n't) like + to* + infinitive to express a desire for something in the future. It is similar to *want + to* + infinitive.

*Kev and Jane **would really like to go** to the opera, but they can't afford the tickets.*

We usually use the contracted forms.

*I**'d like to visit** the Caribbean next year.*

*Laura **wouldn't like to be** a housewife. She enjoys working in an office.*

Note the difference between *like + -ing* form and *would like + to* + infinitive.

Jessica likes playing the guitar. (She plays the guitar and she enjoys it.)

Jessica would like to play the guitar in a band. (She doesn't do this but she wants to.)

Key vocabulary

Geographical/landscape features

bridge canyon coast continent hill island mainland mountain river sea tunnel

Activities

cycling driving horse-riding kayaking mountain biking   mountain climbing sailing trekking white-water rafting

1 Here are some notes about your town's plans for next year. Use the notes to write five sentences with *be going to*. Begin sentences 1–2 with *They ...*, and sentences 3–5 with *Our town*.

||||||||||||||||||||||||||||||||||||||

- open a new bus station in Morton Road
- build an old people's home in the suburbs
- open a local history museum in the town centre
- close the swimming pool in Rectory Road
- introduce a 35 kph speed limit in the central area
- start a new 24-hour telephone information line

They are going to open a new bus station in Morton Road.

1 _____

2 _____

3 *Our town* _____

4 _____

5 _____

2 Use the prompts to write either a negative statement [✗] or a question [?] using *be going to*.

earth – get hotter [?]

Is the earth going to get hotter?

my sisters – visit us/next year [✗]

My sisters aren't going to visit us next year.

1 Toyota – build new factories/in Europe [✗]

2 the situation – get better or get worse [?]

3 all the students – pass the examination [?]

4 my parents – sell their house [✗]

5 your father – retire/next year [?]

6 your team – win/next swimming competition [✗]

3 Find and correct the mistakes.

Dana's going to ~~buying~~ a new car next month. *buy*

1 I going to visit my grandmother soon. _____

2 The children is going to stay with their uncle. _____

3 I think we're going go back to Turkey next summer. _____

4 Are you going to meeting your new girlfriend tonight? _____

5 She do not going to do her homework this evening. _____

4 Complete the sentences with a suitable phrase from the box.

> use the Internet   commute to work
> send text messages   ~~get healthy~~
> meet new people   see the Acropolis

I joined a gym *to get healthy*.

1 We went to Athens _____.

2 They bought a computer _____.

3 I'm going to join a club _____.

4 He uses his car _____.

5 Maria uses her mobile phone _____.

5 Complete the sentences with the correct form of the verbs in the box.

> ~~become~~ eat feel fly go live marry ~~play~~
> smoke study travel work

Mandy loves *playing* tennis. She would like *to become* a champion.

1 I don't like _____ so I don't want _____ to university.

2 Erica and Pietro like _____ and they would really like _____ around the world.

3 Josh enjoys _____ in restaurants, but he wouldn't like _____ in one.

4 Tanya can't stand _____ so she doesn't want _____ a smoker.

5 Harry hates _____ cold so he wouldn't like _____ in a cold country.

6 Use the text to complete the word puzzle with the activities on page 123. What is Activity X?

Activities 1, 5 and 8 take place on water – 1 and 5 on rivers and 8 usually on the sea. Activity 2 uses cars and activities 4 and 6 both use the same type of equipment, but activity 4 uses it on high ground. Activity 3 uses an animal but we do activity 7 on our own feet.

```
                                    X
                                    ↓
1               R _ _ _ _ _ _ _
2                           _ _ _ _ _ _ _ G
3               _ _ _ _ _ _ - _ _ _ _ _ G
4  M _ _ _ _ _ _ _ _ _  _ _ _ _ _ _
5                   K _ _ _ _ _ _ _
6                   C _ _ _ _ _ _
7       _ _ _ _ _ _ _ _  _ _ _ _ _ _ _ G
8               S _ _ _ _ _ _ _
```

Communication activities

Unit 1 Lesson 3 Exercise 10

Student B

Ask and answer questions about these forms:

A: *Ok. Let's start with Form A. Anne – what's her surname?*

B: *Simons – S-I-M-O-N-S.*

A: *What's her nationality?*

A

First name:	
Surname:	S I M O N S
Age:	
Place of origin:	
Nationality:	C A N A D I A N
Address:	
Email address:	a . s i m o n s @ t o t a l . c o m
Telephone number (home):	
Telephone number (mobile):	0 7 9 6 2 8 3 4 0 6 7
Occupation:	

B

First name:	D A V I D
Surname:	
Age:	2 7
Place of origin:	S Y D N E Y A U S T R A L I A
Nationality:	
Address:	8 4 W A L L S S T R E E T
	L O N D O N
Email address:	
Telephone number (home):	0 2 0 7 3 4 5 8 8 2 2
Telephone number (mobile):	
Occupation:	U N E M P L O Y E D

Unit 2 Lesson 2 Exercise 10

Student A

Read the text on the right. Answer Student B's questions, then ask questions to complete the diary.

Note: & = and, / = or

B: *What does Rob do at eight o'clock?*

A: *He gets up and he has breakfast. What does he do at nine o'clock?*

B: *He walks or takes the bus to work.*

Unit 3 Lesson 3 Exercise 4

Student A

Call 1 Answer the phone and start the conversation. (Jason isn't here today. Take a message for Jason.)

Call 2 Your name is Jack(ie). Phone your partner. You want to speak to Sylvia. Your number is 022 664 337.

Unit 4 Lesson 3 Exercise 4b

Student A

Answer your partner's questions. Use this information:

Burger $3.95
Chicken salad sandwich $5.50
Tuna and mayonnaise sandwich $4.95
Cheese sandwich $4.50
Vegetarian pizza $5.95
Chicken piece $5.25
Regular fries $2.50
Large fries $3.00
Small salad $3.45
Medium salad $4.00
Large salad $4.95
Regular coffee $1.95
Large coffee $2.95
Small mineral water $2.25
Large mineral water $3.60
Orange juice $3.85
Regular cola $2.50
Large cola $3.50

Rob Croft – Studio 2

8.00	get up & have breakfast
9.00	
9.15	open the studio
9.30	
10.00	meet clients & start recordings
1.00	
2.00	listen to the CDs from the morning & make changes
5.15	
5.30	finish work
5.45	
6.30	have dinner
7.00	
9.00	go to a bar/nightclub with friends
11.30	

Communication activities

Unit 5 Lesson 1 Exercise 9
Student B
Answer Student A's questions about this apartment.

For Sale

town house on three floors

- 150 square metres
- three bedrooms, two bathrooms
- two living rooms, dining room
- large kitchen
- garage at the back
- roof terrace
- near centre of town, close to schools, shops and restaurants

€395,000

You are interested in a country cottage. Student A has the details. Ask questions to find out these things about the cottage:

1 how big? 2 how many rooms? 3 what rooms?
4 garden/terrace? 5 where? 6 price?

Do you want to buy the cottage?

Unit 5 Communication Exercise 3
Student A
You have this information from the Internet.

www.Furnishyourapartment.com

Bookshelves	€50
Lamp	€45
Large sofa	€450
Dining table and four chairs	€395
Armchair	€125
Large bed	€250
Cupboard	€175
CD player	€100
Today's special bargains:	
Television	only €100!!
German washing machine	only €310

Unit 6 Lesson 2 Exercise 7a
Student A
Look at the pictures and prompts. Tell your partner what happened.

Robin stopped outside the phone shop in Shelton. A woman on the other side of the road called for help ...

Robin/stop   woman/call for help

Robin/try to help   woman/escape
man/push/Robin into car

that night/men/push Robin/out of car
old man/watch them

Unit 6 Communication Exercise 3
A pairs:
You work in a gift shop. Look at the categories below. Choose <u>two categories only</u>, and then make a list of <u>five different things</u> in each category. Give each item a price.

- travel guide books
- DVDs
- chocolates
- gifts (wallets, diaries, address books)
- stationery (pens, pencils, notebooks)

Let's sell DVDs and stationery.
OK. Which five DVDs?
How about a James Bond film for €15?

When students from B pairs come to your shop, you can answer their questions. But you can only sell them the things on your list!

Unit 7 Communication Exercise 4a

Report one of the men missing and answer your partner's questions to describe him.

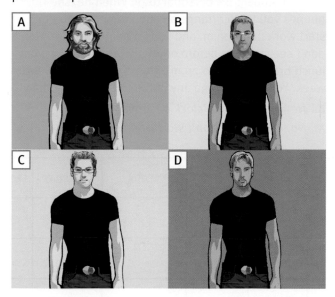

Unit 8 Lesson 1 Exercise 9b

Student A

It is November. Next month you begin a three-month job in your company's office in Toronto, Canada. You don't know what clothes to take. Write a letter to your colleague, explain your situation and ask for advice.

When you finish, give your letter to your colleague (a B student), and write an answer to B's letter. Remember it is very hot in Miami in the summer, but your offices have air conditioning and are quite cold!

Unit 8 Lesson 2 Exercise 9

Student A

Ask and answer questions about the picture. Write the missing names.

B: *Two girls are dancing. One of them is wearing a skirt. What's her name?*

A: *Is she looking at the boy in a black T-shirt?*

B: *Yes, she is.*

A: *OK. Her name is ...*

Unit 8 Communication Exercise 4

Student B

> ### Roleplay 1
> You are a shop assistant. You can't exchange the computer because you don't have another one in the shop, but you can give refunds.
>
> ### Roleplay 2
> You bought a wool jacket for €150 last Wednesday. It doesn't fit. You want a refund or another jacket in a larger size.

Unit 9 Lesson 2 Exercise 6b

Student B

> *Casablanca*   Hannibal Lecter   *The Cure for Insomnia*

Unit 9 Lesson 2 Exercise 6b

These are the answers to the quiz.

1   *Titanic* (1997) – it cost over $200 million.
2   *The Jazz Singer* (1928) – the first 'talking film'.
3   *The Cure for Insomnia* (1987) – it lasts 85 hours!
4   *Finding Nemo* (2003) – it made over $70 million in its first few months.
5   Harrison Ford – he has over $3,000 million (*Star Wars, Raiders of the Lost Ark, Witness*).
6   Tatum O'Neal – she was ten when she won an Oscar for *Paper Moon* (1974).
7   *Casablanca* (1942) – with Humphrey Bogart and Ingrid Bergman (American critics also voted Humphrey Bogart the best actor).
8   *Psycho* (1960) – with Anthony Perkins and Janet Leigh. Alfred Hitchcock was the director.
9   Hannibal Lecter – from *Silence of the Lambs* (1991). Anthony Hopkins played the character.

Antonio

Kostas

Julianne

Kristin

Ewa

Karina

Unit 10 Lesson 1 Exercise 7

A Students

Ask your partners questions with *Have you ever ...?*
If they answer *Yes,* find out when and where he/she
did the activity, and if he/she liked it. Check any
words you don't know in a dictionary before you
begin.

Have you ever been on ...

an adventure holiday?	a motorbike?
a cruise?	a motor boat?
a camel?	television?
a jet ski?	

Unit 10 Lesson 3 Exercise 9

Student A

You work for *Sunshine Travel*. Use this information.

Air France

Flights from Paris to Miami on Mondays, Fridays
and Saturdays only. Cost €400 return per person.
Flights are direct to Miami.

Lufthansa

Flights from Paris to Miami on Mondays,
Wednesdays and Sundays. Cost €760 return per
person for Business Class, €425 per person in
Economy. Flights stop in New York for one hour.

American Airlines

Flights from Paris to Miami every day. Cost €800
return per person for Business Class, €475 per
person in Economy. Flights are direct to Miami.

Unit 10 Communication Exercise 5b

Student B

Roleplay 1

You are the receptionist. The guest booked a
double room in the hotel but you have given him/
her a single room. Offer to find him/her a double
room (*I'll find ...*). You start the roleplay.

Roleplay 2

You are the guest. You asked for breakfast at
7.00a.m. in your room. It hasn't arrived and
it's now 7.30. You have a meeting at 8.00. Call
reception to complain.

Unit 11 Communication Exercise 3a

Student A

You are Student B's personal tutor. When he/she
phones you try to arrange an appointment. You don't
start work until 10a.m. and you go home at 5p.m. You
don't see students before or after work, or during your
lunch break (from 1 to 2p.m). This is your diary for next
week. You can't change any of the things in your diary!

B: *How about nine o'clock on Monday?*

A: *No, I'm afraid I don't start work until ten.*

	MONDAY	TUESDAY	WEDNESDAY	THURSDAY	FRIDAY
9am					
10am	meeting 10 –11.00				
11am		lecture from 10 – 12.30	staff meeting from 11 – 12.30		lecture 11 – 12.15
12pm					
1pm					
2pm	dentist 2.30	seminar 2 – 3.30		at academic conference all afternoon	
3pm	lecture 3 – 5				seminar 3 – 4.30
4pm					

Unit 12 Lesson 1 Exercise 10

Student A

Talk to the students in your group. Ask them
questions and find someone who is going to:

1 visit another country.   2 buy a new car.
3 start a diet.

Student B

Talk to the students in your group. Ask them
questions and find someone who is going to:

1 make lots of money.   2 get married.
3 join a club or team.

Student C

Talk to the students in your group. Ask them
questions and find someone who is going to:

1 join a gym.   2 learn to play a musical instrument.
3 move house or apartment soon.

Unit 12 Lesson 3 Exercise 4

Student A

Read the text below and answer your partner's questions. Ask your partner these questions:

1 Who pays for the expedition?
2 Who chooses the charity?
3 How can you raise more money?

Fitness

You have to be very fit to take part in one of our expeditions. Maybe you think you are generally very fit, but even if you are, you will have to do a lot of training in whatever activity you choose. It's a good idea to check your fitness with your doctor before you start training, then organise a training timetable. Start by training for half an hour three or four days a week, then every day, then an hour a day. We organise training weekends for people once a month, where we can give you lots of advice and help you with your training.

Unit 2 Lesson 2 Exercise 10

Student B

Read the text below. Ask questions to complete the diary, then answer Student A's questions.

Note: & = and, / = or

B: *What does Rob do at eight o'clock?*
A: *He gets up and he has breakfast. What does he do at nine o'clock?*
B: *He walks or takes the bus to work.*

Rob Croft – Studio 2

8.00	
9.00	walk/take bus to work
9.15	
9.30	make coffee & organise CDs for the day's work
10.00	
1.00	have a pizza/sandwich at his desk
2.00	
5.15	clean the studio
5.30	
5.45	get home
6.30	
7.00	watch the news on TV/read the newspaper
9.00	
11.30	go to bed

Unit 5 Communication Exercise 3

Student B

You have this information from the Ardent Catalogue.

Ardent Catalogue Store

Computer and printer	€400
Super vacuum cleaner	€99
American coffee machine	€60
Desk	€99
Large dining table and 6 chairs	€355
Small sofa with 2 armchairs	€325
Microwave	€60
Luxury bed	€500
Bookshelves	€750
Cupboard	€99
Video machine	€120

Unit 6 Lesson 2 Exercise 7a

Student B

Look at the pictures and prompts. Tell your partner what happened.

Robin finished at the phone shop and decided to go home. He started jogging ...

Robin/finish   decide/go home   start/jog home

Robin/halfway home   slip/knock head

After some time Robin/feel OK
decide/jog home   start/wrong direction

Communication activities

Unit 7 Communication Exercise 4b

Report one of the women missing and answer your partner's questions to describe her.

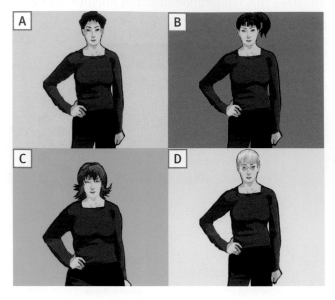

Unit 8 Lesson 1 Exercise 9b

Student B

It is May. Next month you begin a three-month job in your company's office in Miami, Florida, USA. You don't know what clothes to take. Write a letter to your colleague, explain your situation and ask for advice.

When you finish, give your letter to your colleague (an A student), and write an answer to A's letter. Remember it is very cold in Toronto in the winter, but it is quite warm in your offices!

Unit 8 Lesson 2 Exercise 9

Student B

Ask and answer questions about the picture. Write the missing names.

B: *Two girls are dancing. One of them is wearing a skirt. What's her name?*

A: *Is she looking at the boy in a black T-shirt?*

B: *Yes, she is.*

A: *OK. Her name is ...*

Unit 9 Lesson 2 Exercise 6b

Student C

The Jazz Singer   Harrison Ford   *Titanic*

Unit 10 Lesson 1 Exercise 7

B Students

Ask your partners questions with *Have you ever ...?* If they answer *Yes*, find out when and where he/she did the activity, and if he/she liked it. Check any words you don't know in a dictionary before you begin.

Have you ever been ...

mountain climbing?	windsurfing?
horse-riding?	rollerblading?
skiing?	ice-skating?
skateboarding?	

Unit 12 Lesson 3 Exercise 4

Student B

Read the text below and answer your partner's questions. Ask your partner these questions:

1 Do you have to be fit to do the expeditions?

2 How much training do you have to do at the start?

3 How can Charity Challenge help people?

Raising money

When you join one of our expeditions, we ask you to pay for the expedition and to raise money for charity. You can choose the charity and the amount of money you want to raise, but we ask you to raise as much money as you can. Of course, you will have to find people to sponsor your trip, but there are other ways of raising money to pay for your trip and to give to the charity. We can help you with ideas; for example, holding a car boot sale. You can sell your old things and give the money to your charity.

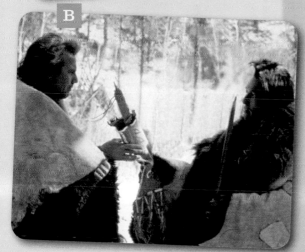

1 Discuss.

1 What is the situation in the photos?

2 Who are the people? Where are they?

3 Write a short dialogue for each photo.

    A: Hello, I'm ...

    B: Hello ...

2 Watch the film and match the names with the extracts (1–7.)

a Edward York ☐

b Julius Caesar ☐

c Mrs Wilberforce [1]

d Mr Robinson ☐

e Miss Wheeler ☐

f Miss Madderley ☐

g Captain ☐

3 Watch the film again and tick (✓) the expressions you hear in the extracts (1–7.)

	1	2	3	4	5	6	7
Hello.							
Good morning.	✓						
Good afternoon.							
Good evening.							
How do you do?							
May I introduce ...?							

4 Discuss.

1 Which extracts are good/funny? Why?

2 The extracts are from British comedy films of the 1950s and 1960s. Do you like them? What are your favourite comedy films?

1 Discuss.

1 Do you watch cartoons?

2 What are your favourite cartoons?

3 Do you know the cartoon characters in the photos? Do you like them?

4 Look at the man in photo B.
Do you think he is happy or sad? Why?

2 Match the words with the pictures. Use a dictionary.

1 break   2 dancer   3 daydream

4 music box   5 stamp   6 wake up

 A
 B
 C
 D
E
 F

3 These things happen in the cartoon *Unreal City*. Guess the order.

a He goes to sleep. ☐

b The man leaves work. 1

c He has a daydream. ☐

d He takes a box to the table. ☐

e He gets home. ☐

f He wakes up. ☐

g He breaks the music box. ☐

h He listens to the music and looks at his stamps. ☐

i He opens the box – it's a music box. ☐

j The girl in his daydream is real. ☐

4 Now watch the cartoon and check the order.

5 Discuss.

1 Do you like the cartoon *Unreal City*? Why/Why not?

2 In *Unreal City*, the man has a daydream. Do you daydream?

3 When do you daydream?

4 What do you daydream about?

3 Deborah's day

Uma Thurman

Morgan Freeman

Jude Law

Meryl Streep

1 Discuss.
  1 What do the people in the photos do?
  2 Who are your favourite actors?
  3 Is an actor's routine different from other people's? How?

2 Use a dictionary. Complete the sentences with words and phrases from the box.

| lines play personal stereo theatres |

  1 *Hamlet* is a famous _____ by William Shakespeare.
  2 There are about 100 _____ in London.
  3 _____ are the words actors speak.
  4 I listen to music on my _____ when I am on the train.

3 Deborah Manning is an actor. What do you think she does every day? Tick the *your ideas* boxes.

	your ideas	Deborah
get up early	☐	☐
do yoga	☐	☐
check emails and diary	☐	☐
send text messages	☐	☐
go to the theatre	☐	☐
run in the park	☐	☐
practise her lines	☐	☐
have meetings	☐	☐
go to bed late	☐	☐

4 Watch the film and tick the things you see her do. Tick the *Deborah* boxes

5 Discuss.
  1 Do you think Deborah has a nice life?
  2 What is your ideal daily routine?
  3 Which jobs have good daily routines?

1 Discuss.

1 What are your favourite comedy films/TV programmes? Why do you like them?

2 Look at the photos. Do you know any comedies about restaurants?

3 Think of three things that can go wrong in restaurants.

2 Match the words/expressions 1–5 with the explanations a–e. Use a dictionary.

1	waiter/waitress	a	we want/we'd like
2	soup	b	you can put soup or ice-cream in this
3	We'll have ...		
4	bowl	c	he/she brings food to your table in a restaurant
5	empty		
		d	there is nothing in it
		e	a hot liquid food; you can drink it

3 Watch the film. What goes wrong in <u>this</u> restaurant?

4 Answer the questions.

1 When is the woman's train?

2 How many people are there in the restaurant?

3 How many times does the waitress say 'Ready to order?'

4 How many times does the waitress come to the table?

5 How much soup is there in the bowl at the end?

5 Discuss.

1 Do you think the TV programme is funny?

2 What kind of people are usually waiters/waitresses?

3 What is good/bad about working in a restaurant?

1 Discuss.

1 What do you know about the ships/boats in the photos?

2 Do you like the idea of living on a ship/boat?

2 Match these places with the definitions. Use a dictionary.

1	an art gallery	a	actors perform plays here
2	a library	b	you can relax here
3	a theatre	c	you can look at paintings here
4	a spa	d	you can read books here, or take them away

3 You already know some facts about *The World of ResidenSea*. Do you think these statements are true (T) or false (F)? Watch the film and check your answers.

1 The ship sails round the world all year. ☐

2 It has got offices on it and people work in them. ☐

3 You can't have a holiday on *The World*. ☐

4 The apartments aren't expensive. ☐

5 There is a theatre on the ship. ☐

6 You can play golf and tennis on *The World*. ☐

4 Is there anything new or surprising about *The World* in the extract? Discuss your ideas with other students.

5 Work in pairs and discuss these questions.

1 Would you like an apartment on *The World*?

2 What are the good things about living on a ship, do you think?

3 What are the bad things about living on a ship?

A The Titanic

B The World of ResidenSea

C Kingfisher

1 Look at the photos and discuss the questions.

1 Can you match the photos with these cities: London, New York, Sydney, Paris, Bilbao?

2 Do you know these cities? What do you like/dislike about them?

3 Do you know any of the buildings in the photos?

4 Can you think of any other famous buildings in these cities?

2 Can you find an example of each of these words/phrases in the photos? Use your dictionary.

1 a skyscraper

2 an amazing shape

3 a roof

4 something made of stone

5 something made of glass

6 something made of metal

3 Look at some facts and figures about five buildings in these cities. Watch the film and tick (✓) the correct building in the table.

	The Flatiron Building	The Guggenheim Museum	The Eiffel Tower	The Gherkin	The Sydney Opera House
1 It opened in 1889.			✓		
2 It has 19 galleries.					
3 It opened over 30 years ago.					
4 It's made of stone and metal.					
5 It's only two metres wide.					
6 It opened in 2004.					
7 It's 300 metres high.					
8 Its roof comes from Sweden.					
9 It's 87 metres high.					
10 The architect was Danish.					

4 Discuss.

1 Which building from the film do you like most? Why?

2 Do you like old buildings or new buildings? Why?

3 Do you have a favourite building in your country? What is it, and why?

7 Great Expectations

1   Charles Dickens was a British writer from the 19th century. Do you know any of his books? Do you know the films in the photos?

2   Complete the sentences with words from the box. Use a dictionary.

| broken   scary   scared   come along   novel   wedding dress |

1   *Great Expectations* is a _____ by Charles Dickens.
2   When women get married they wear a _____.
3   I am _____ of water because I can't swim.
4   *Alien* and *The Exorcist* are very _____ films.
5   I can't use my DVD player now because it's _____.
6   Don't stand there! _____, we're late!

3   Now watch the film extract from *Great Expectations* and match the adjectives with the people and places.

	the boy (Pip)	the girl (Estella)	the woman (Miss Havisham)	the house
dark	☐	☐	☐	✓
large	☐	☐	☐	☐
old	☐	☐	☐	☐
pretty	☐	☐	☐	☐
rich	☐	☐	☐	☐
scared	☐	☐	☐	☐
scary	☐	☐	☐	☐
shy	☐	☐	☐	☐
strange	☐	☐	☐	☐
thin	☐	☐	☐	☐
young	☐	☐	☐	☐

4   Discuss.
1   Did you like the extract?
2   Do you like old films?
3   What is the relationship between Miss Havisham and Pip?
4   Why does the clock on the house show the wrong time?
5   What happens next, do you think?

A

B

C

D

1 Do you know any famous carnivals? When and where do they happen?

2 In pairs, describe the photos. Answer the questions.
   1 What are the people doing in the photos?
   2 What are they wearing? Describe the costumes.

3 Read this text about the Notting Hill Carnival. Then watch the film and find another seven mistakes.

> The Notting Hill Carnival is a huge London carnival – about a ~~thousand~~ *million* people come to be in the carnival or to watch it. It happens every July. There are about 17 bands with their own music, costumes and carnival queen. The costumes are very important for the carnival.
>
> Clary Salandy started designing costumes 50 years ago. Her carnival queen is a young woman called Tamiko, who doesn't have a lot of experience. She puts on her carnival costume – it's very uncomfortable because it's very heavy. When it comes to the carnival weekend, the bands parade through the streets – the costumes look amazing and it's a boring experience.

4 Discuss.
   1 Did you enjoy the film about the Notting Hill Carnival? Why/Why not?
   2 Do you have a big carnival in your town/country? What does it celebrate?
   3 What kind of things do people do at carnivals in your country?

1 Discuss.

1 Look at the painting by Richard Tate. Do you know which city it is? How do you know?

2 Do you like the painting?

3 How do you think Richard Tate made this painting?

    a He painted it from his head.

    b He sat in front of the buildings and painted it.

    c He painted it from a photo.

4 Why do you think Richard paints scenes from the city?

2 Look at the photos of buildings from London. Do you know any of these buildings?

3 Watch the film. Do you see the buildings from Exercise 2 in Richard's paintings (in the film), just in the film, or both? Tick the correct boxes. Watch carefully!

	photo	painting
a St Paul's Cathedral	☐	☐
b Battersea Power Station	☐	☐
c Tower Bridge	☐	☐
d The Dome	☐	☐
e The London Eye	☐	☐

4 Discuss.

1 Did you enjoy this film? Why/Why not?

2 Do you think that it gives a good impression of London?

3 Richard takes photos of London to do his paintings. Do you take photos? What kind of photos do you take?

1   Discuss.

    1   What are the people in the photos doing?
    2   How many ways of getting to work can you see in the photos? What are they?
    3   Can you think of any other ways of getting to work?

2   Match the words and phrases with the meanings.

    1   motorway   a   get up late
    2   pick up   b   not working
    3   space   c   collect someone or something from a place
    4   company   d   types of train
    5   oversleep   e   a big fast road
    6   cancelled   f   at the correct time
    7   tube/mainline   g   room to move around
    8   on time   h   somebody to talk to

3   Watch the film and tick (✓) the correct column(s).

	Penelope	Jonathan	Liz	Mike	Johnny and Rachel
1 walk to the station	☐	☐	☐	☐	☐
2 cycle to the office	☐	☐	☐	☐	☐
3 drive along the motorway	☐	☐	☐	☐	☐
4 have breakfast on the train	☐	☐	☐	☐	☐
5 read a book/a newspaper	☐	☐	☐	☐	☐
6 listen to the radio	☐	☐	☐	☐	☐
7 think public transport is noisy	☐	☐	☐	☐	☐
8 like short journeys	☐	☐	☐	☐	☐
9 usually on time	☐	☐	☐	☐	☐
10 never late	☐	☐	☐	☐	☐
11 sometimes late	☐	☐	☐	☐	☐

4   Discuss.

    1   Did you think the film was interesting?
    2   Who do you think has the easiest/most difficult journey to work?
    3   Is your journey to work the same or different from the ones in the extract? How?
    4   Do you agree with the opinions about the advantages and disadvantages of commuting?

A   B   C

1 Look at the activities in the photographs and discuss these questions.

   1 Have you learnt the skills in the photos?

   2 Have you learnt any other physical skills? Which one(s)?

   3 Is learning a physical skill different from learning academic subjects? Why?

   4 The film is about rock climbing. Have you ever been rock climbing? Did you enjoy it?

2 Match the words and phrases on the left with their meanings on the right.

1	a challenge	a	safe
2	take up (an activity)	b	when you want to try new things
3	spirit of adventure	c	a difficult task or activity
4	secure	d	go up or down very quickly, e.g. a hill
5	steep	e	when you haven't done a lot (of an activity)
6	inexperienced	f	start doing (an activity)

3 Match the pictures with the labels. Then watch the film extract and check.

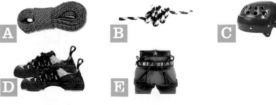

   1 rock boots   2 a helmet   3 a knot

   4 a rope   5 a harness

4 Are these statements true (T) or false (F)? Correct the false ones.

   1 Marian and Andy have done a lot of climbing. ☐

   2 Climbers don't have to use a lot of equipment. ☐

   3 Marian was scared at first when she started the climb. ☐

   4 Marian leads the way when they start climbing. ☐

   5 Stuart teaches Marian and Andy to make secure knots. ☐

   6 Andy says he doesn't want to climb again. ☐

5 Discuss.

   1 Did you enjoy the extract? Do you want to try rock climbing now? Why/Why not?

   2 Have you done any physical activities like rock climbing? What?

   3 Do you prefer physical or mental challenges? Why?

12 Ten great adventures

1 _____

2 _____

3 _____

4 _____

5 _____

6 _____

1 Discuss.

1 What do you usually do on holiday?

2 Do you think everyday holidays are interesting or not?

3 Would you like to do something different on holiday? What?

2 Write labels for photos 1–6. Use some of the activities a–j in the list in Exercise 3.

3 Look at this list of activities. With a partner write 1–10 in the YOU column. 1 is your favourite.

		YOU	GILL	
a	bungee jumping	☐	☐	It's _____.
b	swimming with dolphins	☐	☐	Dolphins are _____.
c	whale watching	☐	☐	Where? _____
d	an expedition to Antarctica	☐	☐	It's _____ to get there.
e	diving	☐	☐	It's _____.
f	skiing	☐	☐	Where? _____
g	dog sledging	☐	☐	Where? _____
h	sailing a ship	☐	☐	What type of ship? _____
i	parascending	☐	☐	It's the closest thing to _____.
j	riding the rapids	☐	☐	It's _____!

4 Now watch the film and complete the GILL column. 1 is Gills favourite. Answer the questions or complete the notes with one or two words.

5 Discuss.

1 Did you agree with Gill's list? Why/Why not?

2 Compare your own 'top 10 adventures' with other students.

Writing Bank

Part 1 | Types of writing

1 Emails

- *Email* means 'electronic mail'.
- Emails can be formal or informal.
- We don't include addresses or dates in the text of emails.
- Informal emails often begin with *Hi* + name, not *Dear* + name. (the greeting)
- In the opening sentence we usually thank the recipient (the person we are writing to) for their last email (or phone call/ letter, etc.).
- In the closing sentence we usually mention a future plan or wish (e.g. *I hope you can come./ Write soon.*).
- At the end of an email to a friend or colleague we write *Best wishes,* + name. For a close friend or family member we can write *Love,* + name.

greeting   opening sentence

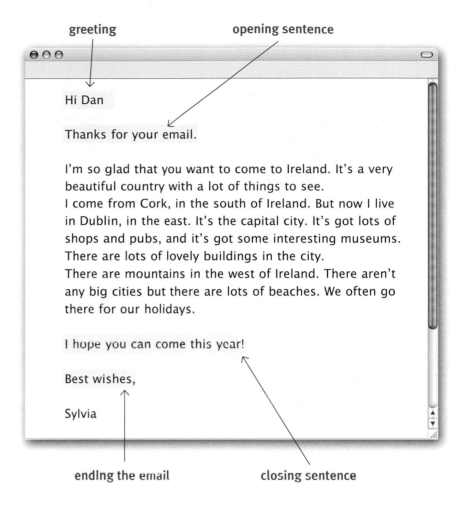

ending the email   closing sentence

2 Postcards

- Postcards are usually informal.
- We often send postcards when we are on holiday, or to thank people for invitations, parties, etc.
- We don't include our address in postcards.
- We begin postcards with *Dear* + name. (the greeting)
- In the closing sentence we usually mention a wish or a future plan (e.g. *See you soon*).
- We often write *Love,* + name at the end.

greeting   recipient's name and address

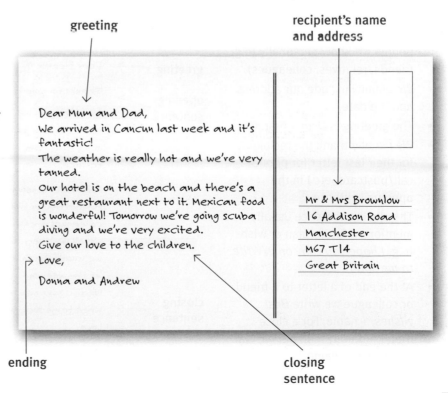

ending   closing sentence

③ **Formal letters**

- We write formal letters to people we don't know personally.
- We include the date.
- We usually include our address and the name and address of the recipient (the person we are writing to).
- When we know the name of the recipient the greeting is *Dear + title + surname* (e.g. *Dear Mr Brown, Mrs Jackson, Ms López, Dr Mahmud,* etc.) and the ending is *Yours sincerely,* + name.
- When we don't know the name of the recipient the greeting is *Dear Sir or Madam* and the ending is *Yours faithfully,* + name.
- We put our full name (or title + surname) at the end (e.g. *Jane Smith* or *Ms J Smith*)
- We can put a reference at the start of the letter (e.g. *Holiday Booking RJ1361*).
- We usually describe the purpose of the letter in the opening sentence.
- The closing sentence usually mentions a future plan or wish (e.g. *I look forward to your reply*).

④ **Informal letters**

- We write informal letters to people we know personally (e.g. friends, relatives, colleagues).
- We usually include our address and the date.
- The greeting is *Dear* + first name.
- We usually thank the recipient for their last letter (or phone call/postcard, etc.) in the opening sentence.
- The closing sentence usually mentions a future plan or wish (e.g. *I hope you can come/Write to me soon*).
- At the end of a letter to a friend or colleague we write *Best wishes,* + name. For a close friend or family member we can write *Love,* + name.

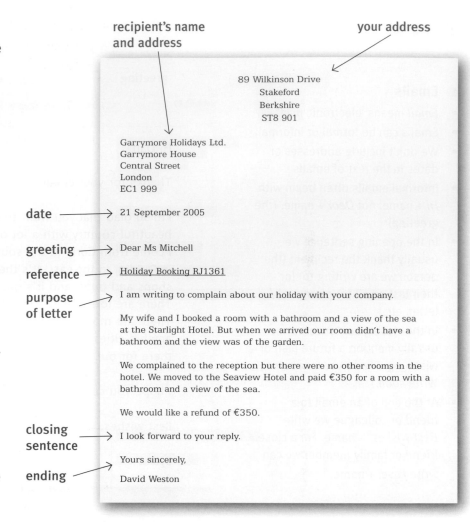

recipient's name and address   your address

89 Wilkinson Drive
Stakeford
Berkshire
ST8 901

Garrymore Holidays Ltd.
Garrymore House
Central Street
London
EC1 999

date → 21 September 2005

greeting → Dear Ms Mitchell

reference → Holiday Booking RJ1361

purpose of letter → I am writing to complain about our holiday with your company.

My wife and I booked a room with a bathroom and a view of the sea at the Starlight Hotel. But when we arrived our room didn't have a bathroom and the view was of the garden.

We complained to the reception but there were no other rooms in the hotel. We moved to the Seaview Hotel and paid €350 for a room with a bathroom and a view of the sea.

We would like a refund of €350.

closing sentence → I look forward to your reply.

Yours sincerely,

ending → David Weston

your address ↓

671 NW 81st Street # 226
New York
NY 89455

date → October 6, 2005

greeting → Dear Eleanor,

opening sentence → Thanks for your letter about my old friends in London!

Everything is fine here. I arrived in New York last month and I moved in to my new apartment. It's got one bedroom, a big living room, a kitchen and a bathroom. There's a small terrace.

I started my new job three weeks ago. The office is in Manhattan, on the thirtieth floor of a huge building! My new colleagues are very friendly and my work is really interesting. We all work very hard – we start at eight in the morning and we usually finish at seven in the evening. My only free time is at the weekend!

What is your new house like? Has it got a garden?

closing sentence → Write to me soon and tell me all your news.

Love,

ending → Damien

Part 2 | Skills of writing

Writing involves a number of skills, and these skills can be different in different languages. Here we look at some of the skills you need to write English.

1 Punctuation

Capital letters

We use capital letters (C, L) ...

- at the beginning of a sentence:
  He came into the room.
- at the beginning of names (of people, places, days, months, books, films):
  John Brown
  Paris, France
  Monday, Tuesday
  June, July
  War and Peace
  Independence Day
- for the pronoun *I*:
  What do I want?

Full stops

We use a full stop (.) at the end of a sentence:
Let's meet on Tuesday.

Commas

We use a comma (,) ...

- to separate parts of a sentence:
  I want to see you on Saturday, but I'm busy in the evening.
- to separate items in a list:
  I'd like some eggs, chicken, milk, cheese and a bottle of water.

Apostrophe

We use an apostrophe (') ...

- in short forms:
  I'm, haven't, can't
- to show possession:
  Give me John's ticket.
  Can you prepare the dog's dinner, please?

Speech marks

We use speech marks (' ') around the words a person says:
The doctor said, 'You have to do more exercise.'

Question mark

We use a question mark (?) at the end of a question:
Do you like coffee?
Where is she sitting?

Exclamation mark

We use an exclamation mark (!) at the end of a sentence to show that something is surprising, or exciting, or interesting:
Geoff gave me a new bike for Christmas!
We're going to India in the summer!

2 Spelling

It is not always easy to work out English spelling from the pronunciation (see Pronunciation Bank, page 147), but there are some helpful rules.

Noun plurals/Present Simple with *he/she/it*

These rules are the same for noun plurals and the Present Simple, third person:
words that end -*ch*, -*s*, -*sh*, -*x* and *z* – add -*es*:
watch → *watches, address* → *addresses*
most words that end -*f* – remove -*f* and add -*ves*:
scarf → *scarves, wife* → *wives*
words that end consonant + -*y* – remove -*y* and add -*ies*:
diary → *diaries, marry* → *marries*
Note: words that end vowel + -*y* are regular:
day → *days, play* → *plays*

Past tense endings

These rules are for the -*ed* endings in the Past Simple:
verbs that end in -*e* – add -*d*:
live → *lived, change* → *changed*
verbs that end in consonant + -*y* – remove -*y* and add -*ied*:
study → *studied, carry* → *carried*
Note: verbs that end in vowel + -*y* – add -*ed*:
stay → *stayed*
verbs of one syllable that end in one vowel + consonant – repeat the consonant and add -*ed*:
plan → *planned, jog* → *jogged*

Present Continuous endings

Some of the rules for the Present Continuous endings are the same as the rules for the past tense endings:
verbs that end in -*e* – remove -*e* and add -*ing*:
live → *living, change* → *changing*
verbs of one syllable that end in one vowel + consonant – repeat the consonant and add -*ing*:
plan → *planning, jog* → *jogging*

3 Linking words

In English, we don't write lots of very short sentences. We use linking words to join parts of sentences. Here are some common linking words.

- *and* – to link two affirmative sentences:
  *I got up early **and** I had breakfast.*
- *but* – to link two sentences that are different, or when the second is surprising:
  *I got up early **but** I was late for work.*
- *or* – to link two choices:
  *We can go to the museum **or** (we can go) to the park.*
- *after, before, when* – to link two sentences and show how the times in the sentences are related:
  *I spoke to my manager **after** he arrived at the office.*
  *I always drink coffee **when** I'm tired.*
- *because* – to give a reason for an action.
  *I arrived late at the office **because** I got up late.*

4 Paragraphs

When we write, we use sentences to separate ideas. If we use a lot of sentences, we need to use paragraphs to put similar ideas together.
For example, look at the information below about a person. It has four paragraphs, and each one is about a different part of Martin's life:

1 Martin's early life and education
2 His university years
3 His job at Oxford and life in England
4 His wife and family

1 Martin Robertson was born in 1974 in Washington. He lived with his family – his parents and two sisters – in a large town house near the centre of the city. He went to the local elementary school and junior high school.

—∞—

2 When Martin was 19, he went to Yale University. He studied American and British literature, and he got a very good degree. He stayed at the university to do some research, and he left in 1998.

—∞—

3 After a few months, Martin left the USA and took a job at Oxford University, England, as a lecturer in American literature. He has written three books and he is now very well-known. He is still at Oxford University and he plans to stay there.

—∞—

4 During Martin's years at Yale, he met Annabel. Annabel decided to come to England with Martin and they got married in 2000. They had their first child, a daughter, in 2003 and their second, a son, in 2005.

Pronunciation bank

Part 1 | English phonemes

Consonants

Symbol	Key word	Symbol	Key word
p	**p**ark	s	**s**ell
b	**b**ath	z	**z**oo
t	**t**ie	ʃ	fre**sh**
d	**d**ie	ʒ	mea**s**ure
k	**c**at	h	**h**ot
g	**g**ive	m	**m**ine
tʃ	**ch**urch	n	**n**ot
dʒ	**j**udge	ŋ	si**ng**
f	**f**ew	l	**l**ot
v	**v**isit	r	**r**oad
θ	**th**row	j	**y**ellow
ð	**th**ey	w	**w**arm

Vowels

Symbol	Key word	Symbol	Key word
iː	f**ee**t	əʊ	g**o**ld
ɪ	f**i**t	aɪ	b**y**
e	b**e**d	aʊ	br**ow**n
æ	b**a**d	ɔɪ	b**oy**
ɑː	b**a**th	eɪ	h**ere**
ɒ	b**o**ttle	eə	h**air**
ɔː	b**ough**t	ʊə	s**ure**
ʊ	b**oo**k	eɪə	pl**ayer**
uː	b**oo**t	əʊə	l**ower**
ʌ	b**u**t	aɪə	t**ire**d
ɜː	b**ir**d	aʊə	fl**ower**
ə	broth**er**	ɔɪə	empl**oyer**
eɪ	gr**ey**	i	happ**y**

Part 2 | Sound-spelling correspondences

In English, we can spell the same sound in different ways, for example, the sound /iː/ can be 'ee', as in *green*, 'ea' as in *read* or 'ey' as in *key*. Students of English sometimes find English spelling difficult, but there are rules and knowing the rules can help you. The chart below gives you the more common spellings of the English sounds you have studied in this book.

Sound	Spelling	Examples
/ɪ/	i	this listen
	y	gym typical
	ui	build guitar
	e	pretty
/iː/	ee	green sleep
	ie	niece believe
	ea	read teacher
	e	these complete
	ey	key money
	ei	receipt receive
	i	police
/æ/	a	can man pasta land
/ɑː/	a	can't dance*
	ar	scarf bargain
	al	half
	au	aunt laugh
	ea	heart
/ʌ/	u	fun sunny husband
	o	some mother month
	ou	cousin double young
/ɒ/	o	hot pocket top
	a	watch what want
/ɔː/	or	short sport store
	ou	your course bought
	au	daughter taught
	al	bald small always
	aw	draw jigsaw
	ar	warden warm
	oo	floor indoor
/aɪ/	i	like time island
	y	dry shy cycle
	ie	fries die tie
	igh	light high right
	ei	height
	ey	eyes
	uy	buy
/eɪ/	a	lake hate shave
	ai	wait train straight
	ay	play say stay
	ey	they grey obey
	ei	eight weight
	ea	break
/əʊ/	o	home phone open
	ow	show throw own
	oa	coat road coast
	ol	cold told

* In American English the sound in words like *can't* and *dance* is the shorter /æ/ sound, like *can* and *man*.

Part 3 | Weak forms

In English some words have two pronunciations – the strong form and the weak form, for example, *Can* (/kən/) *you dance*? *Yes, I can* (/kæn/). We usually use the weak form when the word is not stressed. Most of these words are 'grammar' words e.g. *a, an,* *than, have, been,* etc. Knowing weak forms helps you understand spoken English. The chart below shows some of the most common weak forms and examples of their use.

Word	Strong form	Weak form	Examples of weak forms in sentences
a, an	/æ/, /æn/	/ə/, /ən/	Did you bring **an** umbrella?
at	/æt/	/ət/	Let's meet **at** six o'clock.
and	/ænd/	/ən/	I'd like a burger **and** fries.
are	/ɑː/	/ə/, or /ər/ before vowels	What **are** your phone numbers?
been	/biːn/	/bɪn/	I've **been** to San Francisco.
can	/kæn/	/kən/	She **can** sing very well.
has	/hæz/	/əz/	Where **has** she been?
have	/hæv/	/əv/	What **have** you got?
than	/ðæn/	/ðən/	She's taller **than** Juan.
them	/ðem/	/ðəm/	Let's take **them** to the cinema.
to	/tuː/	/tə/ (before consonants)	I want **to** go home now.
was	/wɒz/	/wəz/	He **was** an architect.

Irregular verbs

Verb	Past Simple	Past Participle
be	was/were	been
become	became	become
begin	began	begun
break	broke	broken
bring	brought	brought
build	built	built
buy	bought	bought
can	could	been able
catch	caught	caught
choose	chose	chosen
come	came	come
cost	cost	cost
dig	dug	dug
do	did	done
draw	drew	drawn
drink	drank	drunk
drive	drove	driven
eat	ate	eaten
fall	fell	fallen
feed	fed	fed
feel	felt	felt
find	found	found
fly	flew	flown
forget	forgot	forgotten
get	got	got
give	gave	given
go	went	gone/been
grow	grew	grown
have	had	had
hear	heard	heard
hold	held	held
hurt	hurt	hurt
keep	kept	kept
know	knew	known
learn	learned/learnt	learned/learnt

Verb	Past Simple	Past Participle
leave	left	left
let	let	let
lose	lost	lost
make	made	made
mean	meant	meant
meet	met	met
pay	paid	paid
put	put	put
read/ri:d/	read/red/	read/red/
ride	rode	ridden
ring	rang	rung
run	ran	run
say	said	said
see	saw	seen
sell	sold	sold
send	sent	sent
shine	shone	shone
show	showed	shown
sing	sang	sung
sit	sat	sat
sleep	slept	slept
speak	spoke	spoken
spend	spent	spent
stand	stood	stood
steal	stole	stolen
swim	swam	swum
take	took	taken
teach	taught	taught
tell	told	told
think	thought	thought
throw	threw	thrown
understand	understood	understood
wear	wore	worn
win	won	won
write	wrote	written

Tapescripts

Do you know...?

Recording 0.1
a b c d e f g h i j k l m n o p q r s t u v w x y z

Recording 0.2
a h j k   b c d e g p t v   f l m n s x z   i y
o   q u w   r

Recording 0.3
oh/zero, one, two, three, four, five, six, seven, eight, nine, ten

Recording 0.4
eleven, twelve, thirteen, fourteen, fifteen, sixteen, seventeen, eighteen, nineteen, twenty, twenty-one, twenty-two, thirty, forty, fifty, sixty, seventy, eighty, ninety, a hundred

Recording 0.5
1 Look at page ... 2 Listen.
3 Ask and answer. 4 Read. 5 Write.
6 Complete. 7 Match. 8 Repeat.
9 Correct. 10 Check your answers.

Unit 1. Your Life

Recording 1.1
Woman: Hi I'm Jana. What's your name?
Man: Hi Jana. My name's Dominik.
Man: What's your name, please?
Woman: It's Patricia Pérez.
Man: Hello. My name 's David Cooper.
Woman: Hello. I'm Lisa Smith. Nice to meet you.

Recording 1.2
020 651 347

Recording 1.3
Example: 01452 946 713
1 02096 659 248 2 951 327 946
3 01542 984 731 4 951 372 964
5 02096 639 247

Recording 1.4
Male: Where is Paulo Coelho from?
Female: He's from Brazil. He's Brazilian.
Male: Where are Nokia phones from?
Female: They're from Finland. They're Finnish.
Male: Where are Catherine Deneuve and Gerard Depardieu from?
Female: They're from France. They're French.
Male: Where is Will Smith from?
Female: He's from the United States. He's American.
Male: Where is Penélope Cruz from?
Female: She's from Spain. She's Spanish.
Male: Where are Gucci handbags from?
Female: They're from Italy. They're Italian.
Male: Where are Ralf and Michael Schumacher from?
Female: They're from Germany. They're German.
Male: Where is Roman Polanski from?
Female: He's from Poland. He's Polish.
Male: Where is Gong Li from?
Female: She's from China. She's Chinese.
Male: Where are Jaguar cars from?
Female: They're from Britain. They're British.
Male: Where is Nicole Kidman from?
Female: She's from Australia. She's Australian.

Recording 1.5
Australian, American, Brazilian, Italian, German, Russian, Spanish, Polish, British, Finnish, Turkish, Chinese, Japanese, French, Greek

Recording 1.6
mother, brother

Recording 1.7
1 husband 2 father 3 grandmother
4 sister-in-law 5 daughter 6 cousin
7 uncle 8 nephew 9 grandson 10 niece

Recording 1.8
1
Male: She's nice. Is she your mother?
Female: No, she's my mother-in-law, Jack's mother.
2
Male: She's young! How old is she?
Female: Well, she's 48.
3
Male: And this man, is he your uncle?
Female: No, he's my sister's boyfriend.
4
Male: Where is he from?
Female: He's from Warsaw.
5
Male: The girls are beautiful. Are they your sisters?
Female: No. Clare's my sister and Liz is her best friend.
6
Male: How old are they?
Female: Clare is 18 and Liz is 22.

Recording 1.9
Jake: Hi Marta.
Marta: Oh, hello, Jake.
Jake: Are you OK?
Marta: No, I'm not ... this is difficult.
Jake: What is it? Oh, I see. Look, I can help you.
Marta: Thanks. What's 'surname'?
Jake: It's your family name – Nowak. And your first name is Marta.
Marta: OK. So, 'age', what's that?
Jake: How old are you?
Marta: Oh, OK. I'm 22.
Jake: Now, place of origin. Where are you from? Are you from Russia?
Marta: No, I'm not from Russia, I'm from Poland.
Jake: And the city?
Marta: Ah, yes, from Lublin.
Jake: OK, so write Lublin, Poland.
Marta: L-U-B-L-I-N, Poland. OK.
Jake: Right. The next question, what's your nationality? That's Polish. Right, and now, what's your address?
Marta: 36, Mill Lane, London.
Jake: And what's your email address?
Marta: It's marta.nowak@hotserve.com
Jake: And what about phones – what's your home phone number?
Marta: oh-2-oh-8-7-3-oh-6-5-8-9. This is easy.
Jake: And what's your mobile phone number?
Marta: oh-3-7-4-3-5-4-8-5-1-3-2. Oh, what's this? Occupation?
Jake: Yes, what's your job?
Marta: Ah, OK. I'm a student. Now ... oh, that's all. Thanks very much, Jake.
Jake: That's OK. See you in class.
Marta: Class? ... Oh, yes! See you there.

Recording 1.10
1
Female: Good morning.
Male: Hi.
Female: Are you a new student?
Male: Yes, I'm in the elementary class ...
Female: No, she's his girlfriend.
Male: OK. Well, see you later.
Female: Bye.
2
Female: Excuse me.
Male: Yes?
Female: Are you our teacher?
Male: No, I'm a student in the ...
Female: Great. Thanks for your help ...
Male: OK. Bye.
Female: Goodbye.

Recording 1.11
1
Maria: Hello, I'm Maria.
Clara: Hello Maria, I'm Clara.
Maria: Pleased to meet you.
2
Jordi: Excuse me, are you Silvio?
Silvio: Yes, I am. What's your name?
Jordi: My name's Jordi.
3
Maria: Where are you from?
Clara: I'm from Barcelona.
4
Jordi: What's your email address?
Silvio: It's silvio77@hotserve.com.
5
Maria: What's your job?
Clara: I'm a student at the university.
6
Jordi: Are you married?
Silvio: No, I'm not. I'm single.

Unit 2. Activities

Recording 2.1
1 What time is it? It's half past six.
2 What time is it? It's quarter to five.
3 What time is it? It's three o'clock.
4 What time is it? It's quarter past eight.

Recording 2.2
Interviewer: So, Jenny, you're a Fun Club holiday rep. Is it fun?
Jenny: Yes, of course.
Interviewer: Tell us about your typical day.
Jenny: OK. Well, I get up at about ten o'clock and go to the hotels at about eleven. I meet the clients at quarter past eleven and tell them about our parties and evening events, and I sell them tickets for excursions and day trips. Then I have lunch at about two o'clock.

Interviewer: Do you eat with the clients?
Jenny: No, I don't. I have lunch with the other reps.
Interviewer: And what do you do in the afternoon?
Jenny: At half past three I go to the hotel pool and help the other reps with games.
Interviewer: Games?
Jenny: Yes, we organise all kinds of games and competitions for the clients. It's great fun.
Interviewer: Do you play the games?
Jenny: Oh no, I don't. I'm the referee!
Interviewer: So, what do you do in the evening? Do you have dinner with the clients?
Jenny: Yes, I do.
Interviewer: Where do you go for dinner?
Jenny: I take the clients to a restaurant at quarter to eight and then I take them to a nightclub at about half past ten. Sometimes we have special parties and entertainment.
Interviewer: When do you finish work?
Jenny: Well, I leave the nightclub at about half past one in the morning. So I get home at about quarter to two.
Interviewer: What a busy life!
Jenny: Yes. But I love it!

Recording 2.3
Female: When do you get up?
Male: At ten in the evening.
Female: Do you work at night?
Male: Yes, I do.
Female: What do you do in the afternoon?
Male: I sleep.
Female: When do you have dinner?
Male: I have dinner at about eleven in the morning.
Female: Do you work in an office?
Male: No, I don't.
Female: Where do you work?
Male: I work in a hospital.
Female: So, what do you do?
Male: I'm a nurse.

Recording 2.4
walks, listens, organises

Recording 2.5
cleans, talks, washes, has, plays, watches, helps

Recording 2.6
Female: Does Jeanette like her work?
Male: Yes, she does. She loves it.
Female: Does she clean the tank every day?
Male: Yes, she does.
Female: Does she feed the sharks every day?
Male: No. She feeds them three times a week.
Female: Does she work every day?
Male: No. She works five days a week.

Recording 2.7
Man: Hello, Isabelle. You're here again, then?
Woman: Yes, that's right. I want to sell a lot of old things today.
Man: Do you come here every week?
Woman: No, not every week, only when I have a lot of things to sell.

Recording 2.8
Man: What do you want to sell today then?
Woman: Well, my old laptop computer – it works, but it's very old.
Man: Mmm. What about those watches?
Woman: Yes, they're my daughter's watches. She likes lots of different colours!
Man: I see.
Woman: And I want to sell these horrible shoes, and the lamps – they are just terrible!
Man: Yes, they are.
Woman: And I really want to sell this suitcase. Do you want to buy it?
Man: Er, no, I don't think so.

Recording 2.9
1
Female: What's this?
Male: It's a DVD player.
2
Female: What's that?
Male: It's a picture.
3
Female: What are these?
Male: They're mobile phones.
4
Female: What are those?
Male: They're dishes.

Recording 2.10
this, these

Recording 2.11
green, listen, niece, pink, read, sister, teacher, think

Recording 2.12
1
Security Officer: Excuse me, madam. Open your suitcase, please.
Female: Of course.
SO: What's this?
Female: It's a camera. It's for my son.
SO: And what are these?
Female: They're discs for the camera. It's a digital camera.

2
SO: Open your bag, please, sir.
Male: OK.
SO: What's this?
Male: It's a laptop computer, for my work.
SO: Mmm. And what are these?
Male: They're magazines – computer magazines.
SO: And this?
Male: It's a scarf, for my wife.

3
SO: Open your handbag, please.
Female: Oh, what's wrong?
SO: What's this?
Female: It's my wallet, of course!
SO: And what's this?
Female: It's a diary.
SO: Oh, what are these?
Female: They're scissors.
SO: No! No scissors!

Unit 3. Free time

Recording 3.1
Presenter: Traffic jams. We hate them, but what do we do in them? This is what some people say.
Melanie: Traffic jams are OK. I think about work and plan my day. I write my diary. My daughter doesn't like traffic jams – she calls her friends, but I don't make phone calls in the car. It's dangerous.
Nathan: Well, in the mornings I shave and listen to the radio. I listen to the news. I like music, but unfortunately my car doesn't have a CD player.
Simon: I don't do a lot, really. I hate traffic jams – they're so boring! I think about things or watch the people in the other cars. Sometimes I sing.
L: We play computer games or call friends on our mobiles.
E: Or we just talk. We don't like the radio.

Recording 3.2
1 Sunday 2 Monday 3 Tuesday
4 Wednesday 5 Thursday 6 Friday
7 Saturday

Recording 3.3
Journalist: Alistair, you're a very busy man, so I'm sure you use your lunch breaks. What do you do in your lunch break in the week?
Alistair: Well, you're right. I do a lot in my lunch breaks. I go for a walk or have a swim on Mondays and I go to the gym on Tuesdays. I sometimes meet friends on Wednesdays and we have lunch in a restaurant, and on Thursdays I sometimes listen to a lunchtime concert – when I don't have a lot of work to do. On Fridays I stay at my desk and work – I always have a lot of work to finish on Fridays.
Journalist: What about the weekend? What do you do on Saturday and Sunday?
Alistair: On Saturdays I go shopping – for food and also for other things, and on Sundays I relax. I sometimes watch football on TV and fall asleep!

Recording 3.4
Woman 1: Hello, Mrs Smith. How's your Susie?
Woman 2: She's fine, thank you, Mrs Jones. And how's Jonny?
Woman 1: He's OK, thanks. He can play the guitar now, you know.
Woman 2: Oh, Susie can play the guitar,

and she can play the piano too.

Woman 1: Well, Jonny can't play the piano but he can sing.

Woman 2: Oh, can he? Susie can sing, …

Woman 1: Can Susie dance?

Woman 2: Yes, she can. Can Jonny dance?

Woman 1: No, he can't. He doesn't have time to dance. He can play football – he's in the school team, and he can play tennis, and …

Woman 2: Susie can't play football – she doesn't like it. It's not a nice game for a girl. But she can play tennis, and she can ski, of course. Tell me, can Jonny ski?

Woman 1: No, but … he can speak French, you know …

Woman 2: Oh, of course Susie can speak French, and she can speak Spanish too, and she can …

Woman 1: Jonny can ride a bike and he …

Woman 2: Susie can't ride a bike but she can drive a car. Can Jonny drive?

Woman 1: Of course he can't drive. He's only ten!

Recording 3.5

Can you dance? Yes, I can. No, I can't.

Recording 3.6

1

Tony: This is 054 898 4567. Please leave a message after the tone.

Jane: Hi Tony, It's Jane. Let's meet outside the cinema at ten to eight. See you there, OK? Bye.

2

Mandy: Hello, this is Mandy and John's phone. We're not here right now so please leave a message with your name and number and the time of your call. Thank you.

Steve: Mandy, it's Steve Henshaw here. It's twenty past three on Wednesday. Can you call me? My number's 068 919 0752. Thanks.

3

Michael: This is Michael Brown's voicemail. Please leave a message now.

Carol: Good morning, Mr Brown. This is Carol at Benson Cameras. Your new camera is here. Can you come to the shop and get it this week? We are open from five to nine until half past six every day.

4

Judy: Hi, I'm not here right now so please leave a message after the beep. Thanks.

Damian: Judy, it's Damian. Why don't we meet for dinner this evening? How about the Italian restaurant in Green Street at twenty-five past eight? Give me a call. I'm in the office all afternoon.

5

Reception: Good morning. Brandon Travel Agency.

Mary: Hello. Can I speak to David Renton?

Reception: I'm afraid he isn't in this morning. Can I take a message?

Mary: Yes, can you ask him to call Mary Wilde?

Reception: Of course. What's your telephone number?

Mary: It's 713 391 8834.

Reception: Sorry? Can you repeat that?

Mary: 713 391 8834

Reception: Fine.

Mary: Thanks. Bye.

Recording 3.7

Female: Hello.

Male: Hello, can I speak to Laura, please?

Female: She isn't here right now. Can I take a message?

Male: Yes, please ask her to phone Jeffrey.

Female: OK. What's your number?

Male: It's 011 908 5561.

Female: OK. Bye.

Recording 3.8

(6) six, (16) sixteen, (60) sixty, (600) six hundred, (6,000) six thousand, (60,000) sixty thousand, (600,000) six hundred thousand, (6,000,000) six million, (6,000,000,000) six billion

Recording 3.9

six*teen*, *six*ty, four*teen*, *for*ty

Recording 3.10

1 *for*ty **2** *eigh*ty **3** seven*teen*
4 thir*teen* **5** *nine*ty **6** six*teen*

Recording 3.11

Interviewer: David, how old are you?

David: I'm 22.

Interviewer: Do you have any special abilities?

David: Well, I can play the piano and the guitar.

Interviewer: Can you speak any foreign languages?

David: No, I can't. Only English!

Interviewer: Can you use computers at all?

David: Oh yes. I can use a lot of different programs. And I really like computer games. In fact I have a certificate in computer programming.

Interviewer: Right. Well that's a useful qualification.

David: Yes, but I don't like computer programming – it's boring!

Interviewer: OK. Can you drive?

David: Yes, I can.

Interviewer: Lizzie, what about you? Do you have any special abilities?

Lizzie: I can play a lot of different sports.

Interviewer: Really?

Lizzie: Yes, football, basketball, tennis.

Interviewer: Do you do a lot of exercise?

Lizzie: Yes, I do aerobics classes, and dancing of course! I

really like dancing!

Interviewer: And do you speak any foreign languages?

Lizzie: Yes, my father is from Brazil, so I can speak Portuguese.

Interviewer: Do you have any qualifications?

Lizzie: Yes, a college diploma in sports medicine.

Interviewer: And you're 26?

Lizzie: Yes, 26.

Unit 4. Food

Recording 4.1

Male: How much rice do you buy each week?

Female: I usually buy two kilos of rice.

Male: And how many tomatoes do you eat?

Female: About six.

Male: How much coffee do you buy?

Female: I buy about 250 grammes of coffee.

Male: How many pineapples do you get?

Female: Oh, only one.

Recording 4.2

Female: How much water do you usually get each week?

Male: About six litres.

Female: What about milk?

Male: I get seven litres.

Female: And how much rice do you buy?

Male: One and a half kilos.

Female: How many bananas?

Male: Twelve.

Female: And coffee. How much do you buy?

Male: Two hundred and fifty grammes.

Female: How much cheese do you get each week?

Male: Four hundred and seventy-five grammes.

Recording 4.3

Laurence Redburn:

Hello and welcome to *In the rubbish bin*, the show where we look at people's lives by looking at their rubbish. I'm Laurence Redburn.

Today we look at the diets of two very different families. I have their rubbish bins in the studio, with a typical day's rubbish, so, let's start with rubbish bin A. What does this family eat and drink? We have some cans … cola cans – not very healthy. Mmm, instant coffee. Some boxes … cheese and tomato pizza, burgers. Some biscuits, and … crisp packets – all fast food, and not very healthy. Do they eat any vegetables or fruit? I don't think so. Oh dear, not a healthy diet. A lot of this food is bad for you, so this family is probably not very healthy.

Now let's look at rubbish bin B. This is very different – it's good. This family eats a lot of fruit and vegetables … some potatoes, carrots, … bananas and apples. What do they drink? We have some juice cartons, some milk bottles and we have a water bottle … two water bottles – very good, all very healthy so far. Tea bags …

well, OK. They eat some pasta, and fish – that's good. I can't see any fast food here. I think this is a very healthy family.

Recording 4.4
pasta, some

Recording 4.5
1 He has lunch on Sundays in his club.
2 My family travels by taxi, but my young cousin takes the bus.
3 Anne and Sally have butter on their pasta.

Recording 4.6
Waitress: Hi. What can I get you today?
Sam: Hi. I'd like a cheese sandwich, please.
Waitress: On white or brown bread?
Sam: On brown, please.
Waitress: Would you like fries?
Sam: Yes.
Waitress: Regular or large size?
Sam: Large.
Waitress: And your friend?
Sam: Jenny, what would you like?
Jenny: Do you have salads?
Waitress: Sure. Small, medium or large?
Jenny: Oh, I'd like a medium.
Waitress: OK. Anything to drink?
Jenny: Sam, do you want some juice?
Sam: No, thanks. Coffee for me.
Jenny: OK, a small cup of coffee for …
Sam: No, no, a large one.
Jenny: OK. A large cup of coffee for him and a small glass of mineral water for me.
Waitress: Fine. Coming right up!

Recording 4.7
Waitress: OK, here we are. Two vegetarian pizzas.
Sam: No, that's not for us. Our order is a sandwich with fries and a salad.
Waitress: Oh, excuse me, that's the wrong order. Just a moment.
Jenny: Two vegetarian pizzas? I really like them! Can we change our order?
Sam: Of course not.
Waitress: OK. I think this is your order. A medium salad for you, sir.
Sam: Oh no, the salad's for her.
Waitress: OK. Right. A medium salad and a small glass of mineral water for you, madam; and a cheese sandwich on brown bread with large fries and a large cup of coffee for you, sir.
Sam: Yes. Thanks. How much is that?
Waitress: That's sixteen dollars and seventy cents, please.
Sam: Can I pay by credit card?
Waitress: Of course.

Recording 4.8
1
Jenny: OK. A large cup of coffee for him and a small glass of mineral water for me.

2
Sam: No, that's not for us.

3
Jenny: Two vegetarian pizzas? I really like them!

4
Waitress: A medium salad for you, sir.

5
Sam: Oh no, the salad's for her.

Recording 4.9
Woman 1: Hello. I'd like three bananas, a kilo of apples and a melon, please.
Man: We don't have any melons today. Sorry.
Woman 1: OK, just the bananas and apples, then, please.
Man: A kilo of apples – that's two euros, and three bananas – that's one and a half euros. Here you are. That's three and a half euros, please.
Woman 1: Three and a half. Thank you. Bye.
Man: Bye.
Woman 1: Hello. I'd like 500g of minced beef, 200g of tuna and a chicken, please.
Woman 2: Um, we don't have any tuna, I'm afraid.
Woman 1: Oh dear. OK.
Woman 2: Right, so that's 500g of minced beef, one chicken … That's fifteen euros altogether. Thank you.

Recording 4.10
I'd like three bananas, a kilo of apples and a melon.
I'd like 500g of minced beef, 200g of tuna and a chicken.

Unit 5. Home

Recording 5.1
1 You can cook in the kitchen.
2 You can sleep in the bedroom.
3 You can have a shower in the bathroom.
4 You can put your car in the garage.
5 You can eat in the dining room or in the kitchen.
6 You can watch TV in the living room.

Recording 5.2
Woman: I just love this bedroom, don't you?
Man: Yes, I do, but the landscape outside the house is just fantastic. Those mountains are wonderful.
Woman: They are. And what do you think of the living room? I think it's from the same house.
Man: Yes, it has mountains outside too. It's great. This kitchen is from a different house, I think.
Woman: Mmm, you can see a forest from the window, so it is a different house. I don't like this room, really.
Man: Don't you? Oh, I do, but I don't like this bathroom. It's so …

Recording 5.3
Agent: The World of ResidenSea. Good afternoon. Can I help you?
Jon: Yes. I'm interested in an apartment on the World of ResidenSea. Can I ask you some questions?
Agent: Yes, of course.
Jon: Well, first of all. Are there any apartments for sale now?
Agent: Yes, there are, but we only have about three for sale right now. They're very popular.
Jon: Yes, I'm sure. OK. How many bedrooms are there in the apartments?
Agent: Well, we have apartments with two bedrooms and apartments with three bedrooms. At the moment, we only have the two-bedroom apartments for sale.
Jon: That's OK. I want two bedrooms, but how many bathrooms are there?
Agent: There are two bathrooms, one for each bedroom, and there's another toilet.
Jon: Great, but how big are the apartments? I mean, how much space is there?
Agent: Oh, they're quite big. Some are 100 square metres and some are 120 square metres. The apartments for sale now are 100 square metres.
Jon: That's good. OK, the big question … how much does the apartment cost?
Agent: The two-bedroom apartments for sale now cost around two million dollars.
Jon: Two million dollars? Oh, I don't know about that. It's very expensive. Let me think about it for a day or two.
Agent: Yes, that's fine. Thank you for your call, and please call again. Goodbye.

Recording 5.4
Amanda: So, where do you live, Pete? Have you got your own house?
Pete: No, I haven't. I've got a modern studio apartment in the centre of town.
Amanda: Has it got a garden?
Pete: No, it hasn't got a garden, but it's got a small terrace.
Amanda: Is there a kitchen in the apartment?
Pete: No, there isn't but there's a kitchen area with a fridge, a cooker and a sink. But I haven't got a microwave.
Amanda: What about furniture?
Pete: I've got a coffee table, and there are two chairs. And I've got a beautiful sofa – I love that sofa, I use it all the time – I eat my meals there because I haven't got a dining table!
Amanda: Is there a TV?
Pete: Yes, of course. And I've got a music system.
Amanda: Have you got a computer?
Pete: Yes, I've got a laptop computer – I use the Internet a lot.
Amanda: And have you got a mobile phone?
Pete: Yes, I have.

Recording 5.5

Amanda: Have you got your own house?
Pete: No, I haven't. I've got a modern studio apartment in the centre of town.
Amanda: Has it got a garden?
Pete: No, it hasn't got a garden, but it's got a small terrace.

Recording 5.6

He's got a laptop, a cat and a watch.

Recording 5.7

1 hot 2 an 3 top 4 pocket

Recording 5.8

1
Ana: I'm Ana. I'm from Spain and I love this country – in Spain there are so many places and things to see. There's even a famous desert in Spain – it's true – the Almeria Desert. It's in the south of Spain. They make a lot of films in this desert because it's really hot and dry. There are also a lot of beautiful beaches in Spain.

2
Gabriel: I'm Gabriel, from Argentina. People think Argentina is a hot country, but there are some very cold parts too. The south is very cold because it's very close to Antarctica and there are mountains there. Of course, there are very high mountains in all of Argentina – the Andes, but in the south the mountains meet the sea, and they're really lovely.

3
Monika: My name's Monika and my home is in Poland, in the east of the country. There are some beautiful lakes in the east of Poland – it's a lovely area. A lot of Polish people take their holidays here. In fact, it's quite popular now with people from other countries too.

4
Costas: I'm Costas. I live in Greece, on the island of Kefallonia. People don't think that Greece is a green country, with a lot of trees, but Kefallonia is a very green island. There's a lovely forest in the north of the island. Of course, there are also beaches on Kefallonia – it's a very popular holiday island.

5
Yumiko: My name's Yumiko. I come from Japan, from a city called Osaka. It's a huge city in the west of Japan, and it's very busy and noisy, and it's not very friendly. There are a lot of shops and offices in the city, and people are always in a hurry. I don't like it here – I like the mountains.

Recording 5.9

1
Ana: It's really hot and dry.
2
Gabriel: The south is very cold.

3
Monika: It's quite popular now with people from other countries.
4
Yumiko: It's very busy and noisy, and it's not very friendly.

Recording 5.10

river, desert

Recording 5.11

centre, island, Japan, Poland, China

Unit 6. City life

Recording 6.1

art gallery, bank, bar, bookshop, café, church, cinema, factory, hospital, library, museum, newsagent's, phone shop, police station, post office, restaurant, school, square, supermarket, train station

Recording 6.2

Example: Turn left at the bookshop.
1 Go straight on to the post office.
2 The bank is on the right.
3 Turn right at the church.
4 Go along the road next to the park.
5 The school is on the left.

Recording 6.3

1
Speaker 1: I live quite near the building. Some of my family worked in it – they produced electrical equipment, but that was a long time ago. It's funny to think that my family worked there and now I do my shopping in the same building.

2
Speaker 2: It's in a wonderful location, right in the centre. I like the fact that doctors and nurses lived and worked in the building; they looked after sick people and poor people, but now people come and look at the pictures and other works of art here. I visited it when I was in Madrid last month – it's got Picasso's *Guernica* in it – my favourite painting.

3
Speaker 3: This wonderful building started life as a school – rich young ladies lived and studied here – but in 1917 it changed into something quite different. Lenin decided to come to St Petersburg and he planned the Russian Revolution from this very building – amazing, eh? When the Revolution finished, he moved back to Moscow. The building is now offices – the offices of the city Governor – and we can't go into it.

4
Speaker 4: The station opened in 1900, and trains started from here on journeys to the west of France, but the station closed in 1937. The museum opened in 1986 and France's great collection of Impressionist painters moved here. Now millions of tourists come here every year to look at the collection.

Recording 6.4

work**ed**, open**ed**, decid**ed**

Recording 6.5

visited, finished, lived, changed, started, looked, produced, planned, studied

Recording 6.6

Interviewer: What exactly happened yesterday, Mr Andrews? Did you get lost?
Robin: I don't know. At about half past three, I walked to the village because I needed to get some money.
Interviewer: How far is the village from your home?
Robin: Not far ... two kilometres. It's an easy walk.
Interviewer: Did you get the money?
Robin: Yes, I did. I ... at the cashpoint in the bank, but I haven't got the money now. Then I called at the phone shop next to the bank ...
Interviewer: Where did you go then?
Robin: Well, I wanted to go to the Internet café but I don't remember ...
Interviewer: What do you remember after that?
Robin: Well, I was in front of a library. I was on the ground. An old man helped me to get up. I was very tired ... and I realised I was in Marbury.
Interviewer: Marbury is eight kilometres from Shelton. Did you walk there?
Robin: I don't know, I really don't know.
Interviewer: Do you know Marbury?
Robin: Not really. I was tired and lost. It was cold and dark. It was early morning, I think.
Interviewer: Did you have any money with you?
Robin: No, I didn't, not then.
Interviewer: So what did you do?
Robin: I asked the old man for directions to the police station. I walked there, but it was closed. I walked to the river and stayed under the bridge for an hour or two.
Interviewer: Did you go to sleep?
Robin: No, I didn't. I waited for the morning, then I walked back to the police station. They called my father, and he collected me in the car.
Interviewer: So how do you feel now, Mr Andrews?
Robin: I don't know ... confused ... it was all very strange.

Recording 6.7

in the bank   next to the supermarket
at the phone shop   to the Internet café
in front of a library   on the ground
behind the police station   at the bus station
under the bridge   between the trees

Recording 6.8

Listen ... I can remember now. I know what happened. I stopped outside the phone shop – there was a woman on the other side of the road. She called for help – there were two men there. I tried to help her and she escaped, but one of the men knocked me on the head with something and pushed me into a car. Then I don't remember anything – I was asleep, but I don't know how long, for how many hours. That night the men pushed me out of the car in Marbury, outside the library. There was an old man there. He watched and then he helped me.

Recording 6.9

Man: Are you OK?
Robin: Yes, I'm fine now, thanks. But where am I?
Man: You're in Marbury. This is the library.
Robin: Oh, OK. Listen, do you know the way to the police station?
Man: The police station. Yes, it's easy. You turn left at the next road, Mill Street ...
Robin: Turn left, OK ...
Man: Then go straight on for about 200 metres. Then you get to the post office.
Robin: The post office.
Man: Yes, it's on the right.
Robin: On the right, OK.
Man: Next to the post office, turn right into Beech Road.
Robin: Beech Road. OK.
Man: Go along the road, then turn left at the bookshop, into Lime Avenue.
Robin: Yes, OK.
Man: The police station is in Lime Avenue. It's at the end of the street, on the left.
Robin: OK, thanks very much.

Recording 6.10

Example:
Do you like buses?
No, I like trains.

1
Did you visit Venice?
No, we visited Rome.

2
Was it nice?
No, it was horrible.

Recording 6.11

1
Customer: Excuse me. Where can I find men's shoes?
Store guide: Men's shoes. That's on the first floor.
Customer: Where are the stairs?
Store guide: There are escalators on your right.
Customer: Right. And have you got maps of London?
Store guide: No, we haven't. Sorry.

Customer: OK. Thanks.

2
Store guide: Can I help you?
Customer: Yes. I'd like a laptop.
Store guide: You need the computer department.
Customer: Where's that?
Store guide: In the basement. There are stairs on your right.
Customer: Thanks very much. Oh, and I need a present for my son. Have you got any Christina Aguilera CDs?
Store guide: Yes, we've got a music department on the third floor.
Customer: Great.

3
Customer: Hello, is this the information point?
Store guide: Yes. How can I help you?
Customer: Where can I find dining tables and chairs?
Store guide: That's in the furniture department on the fourth floor.
Customer: Is there a lift?
Store guide: Yes. Go to the end of the beauty hall and turn left.
Customer: I need some other things. Have you got a store guide?
Store guide: Yes. They're just here.
Customer: Can I have a copy, please?
Store guide: Of course.
Customer: How much is that?
Store guide: It's free.
Customer: Right, thanks a lot.

Unit 7. People

Recording 7.1

1 C has got a pretty face.
2 G has got blue eyes.
3 A has got fair hair.
4 F has got dark skin.
5 D has got grey hair.
6 G has got a beard.
7 B is slim.
8 H is young.
9 F is bald.
10 A wears glasses.

Recording 7.2

Song: The girl from Ipanema

Tall and tanned and young and lovely
The girl from Ipanema goes walking
And when she passes, each one she
    passes goes – ah
When she walks, she's like a samba
That swings so cool and sways so gentle
That when she passes, each one she
    passes goes – ooh

(Ooh) But I watch her so sadly
How can I tell her I love her
Yes, I would give my heart gladly
But each day, when she walks to the sea
She looks straight ahead, not at me

Tall and tanned and young and lovely
The girl from Ipanema goes walking
And when she pauses, I smile – but she
    doesn't see (doesn't see)
She doesn't see, she never sees me ...

Recording 7.3

Mike: Hi Jane, it's me.
Jane: Oh, hello Mike. What's the problem?
Mike: You didn't write the names on those presents. Who are they for?
Jane: Sorry.
Mike: The electric drill. Is that for Gordon?
Jane: Yes, that's his.
Mike: And when's his birthday?
Jane: It's the third of next month.
Mike: What about the trainers ... are they Davy's?
Jane: Yes, the trainers are his. His birthday's on the twentieth of this month.
Mike: What about the clock? Who is that for?
Jane: That's for Mr and Mrs Clark.
Mike: OK, so the clock's theirs. And the handbag? Is that for Tara?
Jane: The handbag? Of course not. That's mine!
Mike: It's yours? Oh. So what did you get for Tara? I know it's her birthday on the first of next month.
Jane: The diary, that's hers.
Mike: Right. OK. Well, what about the umbrella?
Jane: The umbrella?
Mike: Yes, there's an umbrella on the table.
Jane: A black one?
Mike: Yes.
Jane: That belongs to us. It's ours!
Mike: Is it? Oh yes. Of course ...

Recording 7.4

birthday, brother, bathroom

Recording 7.5

1 thick   2 think   3 free   4 thirst   5 three

Recording 7.6

1 sixth   2 eighth   3 eat   4 hate   5 thin
6 three   7 lift   8 fifth

Recording 7.7

1 first   2 second   3 third   4 fourth
5 fifth   6 sixth   7 seventh   8 eighth
9 ninth   10 tenth   11 eleventh   12 twelfth
13 thirteenth   14 fourteenth   15 fifteenth
20 twentieth   22 twenty-second
30 thirtieth   31 thirty-first

Recording 7.8

1 What was in the rubbish bin?
2 Who did the girls tell about the money?
3 Where did they take the banknotes?
4 How long did the police keep the money?
5 Why did the police give it back to the girls?
6 How did the girls put together the notes?
7 Whose money was it?

Recording 7.9

Man: I want to report a missing person.
Officer: OK. Can I take your name first, sir?
Man: Yes, it's Kennedy. David Kennedy.
Officer: Right. Thank you Mr Kennedy. When did this person go missing?

Man:	Yesterday evening. She didn't come back to the hotel.
Officer:	When did you last see her?
Man:	Yesterday afternoon. We went to the museum together, then she went shopping.
Officer:	OK. Let me complete this form. You last saw her yesterday afternoon, right?
Man:	That's right.
Officer:	Your friend, what's her name ... how old is she?
Man:	Er, Gemma, that's G-E-M-M-A, Gemma Hunston – H-U-N-S-T-O-N. She's 24.
Officer:	Did you have an argument yesterday?
Man:	Oh no, you don't understand. She isn't my girlfriend. I met her a few days ago.
Officer:	Oh, right. Well, maybe she decided to leave the hotel ...
Man:	No ... no. All her things are in her room.
Officer:	OK. What does she look like?
Man:	Um ... she's tall, about 1.7 metres. She's got dark hair ... dark brown ...
Officer:	Wait a minute ... OK. How long is her hair?
Man:	Oh, quite long, but not very long, and ...
Officer:	Hold on ... What's her body type?
Man:	Pardon?
Officer:	Is she thin, fat ...?
Man:	Oh, slim, she's quite slim.
Officer:	And what colour eyes has she got?
Man:	She's got green eyes, I think ... yes, green.
Officer:	And what's her skin colour?
Man:	Dark ... well at the moment she's very tanned.
Officer:	Now, anything else. Are there any other features?
Man:	Oh, yes. She wears glasses. And she's got a big bag with her, but it isn't hers. It's mine.
Officer:	All right. And you last saw her yesterday afternoon. That's everything. Thank you, Mr Kennedy. Can we call you at your hotel when ...

Unit 8. Day to day

Recording 8.1

C a smart suit, a formal suit, a light shirt
D a loose pullover, a casual pullover
E a tight jacket, a smart suit

Recording 8.2

Jools:	Hello there, everyone, it's Jools and Anna here for today's round-up of the *We're watching you house!*
Anna:	Yes, it's Day 4 in the *We're watching you house*, and things are changing!
Jools:	That's right. Chloe left the house yesterday so now we've only got seven people here. Before we look at what happened today, let's see what they are doing now.

Anna:	OK. Screen 1, the kitchen. Greg's in the kitchen – he's preparing dinner. He's cooking pasta, I think.
Jools:	What's wrong with Greg? He's shouting about something.
Anna:	Mmm, yes. Let's look at Screen 2 – the girls' bedroom. Oh, that's Cara. Is she resting?
Jools:	No, she isn't. Listen. She's crying. Maybe she had an argument with Greg.
Anna:	Now, Screen 3, the garden. Jason's out there, but what's he doing? He's digging.
Jools:	Yes, he's digging up the flowers. Look at his face – he's angry. Let's go to Screen 4 – the gym.
Anna:	OK. Yes, that's Erica – she's riding the exercise bike. Wow, she's cycling fast. And she's shouting ...
Jools:	No, she isn't shouting; listen, she's singing.
Anna:	Well, I'm glad someone's happy! What's happening in the living room?
Jools:	Screen 5 ... Adam and Rosa ... what are they doing? Are they talking?
Anna:	Yes, they are, but they're talking very quietly. I can't hear them.
Jools:	No ... maybe they don't want the others to hear ...
Anna:	Or they don't want us to hear! Finally, Screen 6, the boys' bedroom. That's Gary ... what's he doing?
Jools:	He's looking for something ... he's looking very carefully. What does he want? Oh, well. We can't watch him now. Let's look back at Day 4 ...

Recording 8.3

1 They're talking quietly.
2 He's looking very carefully.
3 You're speaking loudly.
4 We're living healthily.

Recording 8.4

Forecaster:
Let's have a look at the weather map for Europe. Well, starting in the north, the weather isn't very good in Scandinavia – it's snowing in Sweden. It's foggy in the east of the UK, and at the moment it's raining heavily in the north of Germany. It's quite cold today in Poland – it's about five degrees in the east – and it's very cloudy in France. It's cloudy over the whole of France. The weather is looking good in the south of Europe, though. As usual, it's very sunny in the south of Spain and it's warm in Greece – up to about 20 degrees today. Finally, be careful if you're driving in northern Italy – it's very windy. The wind is coming down off the mountains and it's very strong. That's it for today's weather in Europe, so let's look at ...

Recording 8.5

cold, hot, foggy, snowing

Recording 8.6

1 old   2 clock   3 cost   4 note   5 hotel
6 not   7 on   8 wrote   9 own   10 bottle

Recording 8.7

1 It often snows a lot in Poland.
2 The doctor told me not to get cold.
3 She wears tops and coats in orange and gold.

Recording 8.8

1: Hello there, how are you today?
2: I'm fine. The weather's lovely, isn't it?
1: Well, I'm not sure. I always get headaches when it's very hot.
2: Really? Perhaps it's the sun.
1: No, I don't think so. I think that it's the temperature. My body doesn't like high temperatures.
2: Oh dear! That's a shame. I believe that the sun is good for us.
1: Yes, you're right, but sometimes I feel very slow and heavy when it's hot. It's the temperature, not the sun. It is nice to see the sun – we have so much cloud here.
2: Oh yes, I agree, we all like to see sunny weather.

Recording 8.9

1

Customer:	Excuse me. Can you help me?
Shop assistant:	Yes madam?
Customer:	I bought this jacket yesterday and it doesn't fit.
Shop assistant:	Do you want to try a different size?
Customer:	No, I'd like a refund.
Shop assistant:	Have you got your receipt?
Customer:	Yes. Here it is.
Shop assistant:	OK. So that's 150 euros. Here you are.

2

Shop assistant:	Can I help you?
Customer:	Yes. I bought this DVD player last week and it doesn't work.
Shop assistant:	I see. Have you got your receipt?
Customer:	Yes, I have. Can I exchange it for another one?
Shop assistant:	Of course. Just a moment. Here it is.
Customer:	Thanks very much.

Unit 9. Culture

Recording 9.1

Student 1:	So, we've got 'the arts' in the centre and five sections from it. I think the five sections are 'painting, film, music, literature and theatre'. OK?
Student 2:	Yes, that's right. I think we can put 'dance' and 'plays' under 'theatre'. And what about 'opera' and 'ballet' – they're 'theatre' too, I think.
Student 1:	Yes, I agree, but I also think that we can put 'ballet' and 'opera' under 'music'.
Student 2:	Oh, you're right. Well, let's put them under both 'theatre' and 'music'. So under 'music' we've got 'classical and rock music', and 'ballet' and 'opera'.

Student 1: And 'dance' can go under 'music' too, as well as under 'theatre'. Now, what about 'film'?

Student 2: I think film is 'cartoon, comedy and horror'.

Student 1: Yes, it's those three. Now, for 'literature' I think we put 'novels, plays and poetry'. Do you agree?

Student 2: Yes, I do. But 'plays' can also go under 'theatre', I think. And under 'painting' we can put 'modern art'.

Student 1: Yes, that's right, so it's only 'modern art' under 'painting'.

Student 2: Yes, so that's it.

Recording 9.2

1
I usually read newspapers because they're cheap. My newspaper costs about half a euro a day, but it costs over two euros to read the news on the Internet, so newspapers are cheaper than the Internet for me.

2
I use text messaging on my mobile phone to find out about sports results – I get the results about 15 minutes after they happen, but on the TV you need to wait for the next news programme. Text messaging is faster than TV.

3
I like immediate news so I use the Internet or teletext. You get complete news stories on the Internet, but with teletext you only get a few facts about the news story, so the Internet is more detailed than teletext.

4
I'm very busy and I don't have time to read newspapers, so I always watch the evening news on TV. Anyway, watching the news on the TV is more exciting than newspapers because it's visual.

5
I know it sounds old-fashioned, but I love the radio, and that's where I get my news. The radio is easier than newspapers or TV because you can listen when you're doing other things.

6
I don't like reading so I watch TV or listen to the radio to get the news. I think that TV is better than the radio because it's more interesting – you can understand things more when you have pictures.

Recording 9.3

Example: easier than
1 faster than   2 colder than
3 healthier than

Recording 9.4

Presenter: Good evening. Tonight we've got Mariela with us to talk about her favourite films from the last ten years. Mariela, what do you think is the best film of the last ten years?

Mariela: Hello, Neil. Well, there's no competition for me. I know a lot of people think it was *Gladiator*, but for me the best film in the last ten years was *American Beauty* – it was so different, very clever, and it had the best acting, I think. It was the most unusual film in the last ten years.

Presenter: So, no vote for *Gladiator* from you?

Mariela: Oh, I think *Gladiator* was really good. It was definitely the most exciting film, but it's not my favourite.

Presenter: Were there any surprises for you in the last ten years?

Mariela: Surprises … well, yes. I think the biggest surprise was *The Sixth Sense* – it was a fantastic film from an unknown director. No one expected it. I think it's also the scariest film in the last ten years.

Presenter: What about foreign language films? Any good ones there?

Mariela: Well, lots, of course, but the one that I think was best was *All about my mother*, by Almodovar. It was a lovely film, very sad, but the most interesting foreign language film of the ten years.

Presenter: Mmm, I liked that one too. You don't like violent films, do you?

Mariela: No, I don't, but there's one violent film that I want to talk about – *Pulp Fiction*. That was very violent, possibly the most violent film of the ten years, but it was so good – it was definitely the best mixture of action and comedy at the time. And John Travolta was really fantastic as a villain – it's not usually the kind of part he plays, but he played the bad guy so well in this.

Presenter: Well, I think that's all we have time for …

Mariela: No, wait a moment. There's one more film I want to mention, and that's *Chicago*. I don't usually like musicals at the cinema, but it really was the freshest musical for a long time – it was really good.

Presenter: OK. Thank you very much, Mariela, and now we turn to …

Recording 9.5

Jenny: Let's have a look in the shop.

Serge: There's a good selection of things here. Do you want to look at some posters of the paintings?

Jenny: I don't know. I like posters but they're quite expensive. I prefer buying postcards because they're cheaper.

Serge: Yes. You're right. There are some over there.

Jenny: What about this print of the *Wrapped Reichstag* by Christo?

Serge: It's OK, but I don't really like modern art very much. I prefer sculpture.

Jenny: There's a picture of that huge metal sculpture by Antony Gormley – *The Angel of the North*.

Serge: Oh yes, I like that, it's really nice. Oh, look at this lovely painting of a woman with an umbrella by Claude Monet. I really like it. I love Impressionist paintings – do you?

Jenny: Well, I like modern art more than traditional paintings really.

Serge: What about this abstract painting by Kazimir Malevich?

Jenny: Yes, I prefer Malevich to Monet. I really love abstract art. Those colours are beautiful. Oh, what on earth is this?

Serge: The shark?

Jenny: Yes.

Serge: That's by Damien Hirst. I love it. It's a tiger shark in a glass box.

Jenny: It's amazing! But I'm not sure if it's art!

Recording 9.6

Serge: There are so many things to do in London. What can we do tomorrow? Any ideas?

Jenny: I'm not sure. I'll get the guidebook. Um. What about the Tate Modern? It's got a lot of modern sculpture.

Serge: That sounds good.

Jenny: Right. Let's go to the Tate Modern in the morning. Now what about the afternoon?

Serge: I'd like to see the Hayward Gallery. Is that near?

Jenny: I'll look at the map. Oh yes, it's quite near.

Serge: Right. We'll go there after lunch then.

Recording 9.7

1 Any ideas?   2 Is it near?

Recording 9.8

1 Is it expensive?   2 It's expensive.
3 Is it interesting?   4 It's boring.
5 Are we late?   6 Does she know?

Recording 9.9

Male: So, Saturday. Any ideas?

Female 1: How about a film?

Male: During the day?

Female 1: Yes.

Female 2: I prefer watching films in the evening really.

Female 1: OK. Well, why don't we go to the sports centre? We can go swimming.

Male: There are always lots of children in the pool on Saturdays.

Female 2: And I don't like swimming very much.

Female 1: Well, how about shopping then?

Female 2: Yes, I like shopping more than swimming!

Male: There's that new shopping centre in Bath …

Female 2: That sounds like fun.

Male: What about the shops in Clifton?

Female 1: No, the shops are more expensive there.

Female 2: Yes, and Clifton's very crowded at the weekend.

Male: All right, we'll go to Bath then.

Female 2: I think the new shopping centre in Bath's got a good restaurant.

Female 1: Well, let's go to the shopping centre in the morning and then we can have lunch there.

Female 2: OK, that sounds good.

Male: Let's meet at eleven and we can get the bus.

Female 1: OK. We'll meet at eleven outside the bus station.

Unit 10. Journeys

Recording 10.1

Jason: I'm here at Heathrow Airport with the Garfield family: Derek and Moira and their children Todd and Alicia. Today's the start of an amazing adventure for them. In half an hour they get on a plane to begin the holiday of a lifetime. Derek, how are you feeling right now?

Derek: To be honest, Jason, I'm feeling quite nervous ... nervous but excited.

Jason: Why are you nervous?

Derek: Well, this is my first long plane journey. I've never been on a long-haul flight before so it's my first time ... and Australia is a long way away.

Jason: Are the rest of you experienced travellers?

Alicia: We've been to America!

Moira: Yes, the three of us have been on a long-haul flight before. I took Todd and Alicia to Florida last year.

Jason: Have you ever been to Australia?

Moira: No, we haven't.

Derek, Alicia, Todd: No, we've never been to Australia.

Jason: So I guess you are all very excited about those activities in Australia? Have you ever been horse-riding, hiking or bungee jumping before?

Todd: Alicia and I have been horse-riding. We went horse-riding when we were in Scotland two years ago. But mum and dad stayed in the hotel! They've never been on a horse!

Moira: It was cold!

Derek: But we've all been hiking. We went last year.

Jason: And have you ever been bungee jumping?

Derek: Oh no. We haven't been bungee jumping. It's the first time for all of us.

Moira: I'm very nervous about it!

Recording 10.2

1 But have you ever <u>been</u> to Australia?
2 No, we've never <u>been</u> there.

Recording 10.3

1 Have you been to the cinema in Italy?
2 I've never been on a ship with him.
3 Has she ever been to dinner in Finland?
4 We've never been to Paris in spring.

Recording 10.4

parked, seen, bought, had, written, got

Recording 10.5

1 have 2 fit 3 short 4 park 5 bald
6 sleep

Recording 10.6

Julia: The way I commute to work is probably quite unusual! I rollerblade! I live in Surfside, a suburb in the north of Miami and I work at a hotel on Miami beach. It takes about twenty-five minutes to get to work. And of course it costs nothing. It's usually warm and sunny in Miami and rollerblading is very healthy – I really enjoy it. But rollerblading is a bit dangerous when you cross busy roads. And it's tiring!

Billy: Commuting is really difficult in London. It's a huge city and there's a lot of traffic. You can't really commute by car because it's impossible to park in the centre of London. There's a good underground system but there aren't any stations near my house so I get the bus to work. It isn't expensive but it's sometimes quite slow because of all the traffic. And I hate waiting at the bus stop in the winter, it's very boring!

Recording 10.7

Agent: Good morning. Distant Dreams Travel.

Billy: Oh, hello. Do you sell airline tickets for New Zealand?

Agent: Yes.

Billy: Right. I'd like four tickets from London Heathrow to New Zealand.

Agent: What's your exact destination?

Billy: Auckland.

Agent: And when do you want to go?

Billy: I'd like to go on Friday the fifth of next month.

Agent: Return or one-way?

Billy: I'd like return tickets, please. We want to come back one month later.

Agent: OK. I'll just check on the computer. OK, do you want economy or business class?

Billy: Oh, business class is expensive. I prefer economy. How much is that?

Agent: Let me see. Four return tickets in economy, and your departure date is the fifth. OK. We've got Air New Zealand and Qantas for those dates. On Air New Zealand it's six thousand New Zealand dollars, about two thousand pounds. Qantas is more expensive – about two thousand, three hundred pounds, but it's a shorter flight. Which do you prefer?

Billy: The cheaper one, Air New Zealand, I think. What time does the flight leave London?

Agent: At ten thirty in the morning.

Billy: Is it a direct flight?

Agent: No, there's a short stop in Bangkok.

Billy: Fine. I'd like four tickets then, please.

Recording 10.8

Reception: Hello. Hotel Europa. Can I help you?

Woman: Yes. I'd like to book a room, please.

Reception: OK. For how many nights?

Woman: For two nights.

Reception: Which dates, please.

Woman: For the 15th and 16th of May, please.

Reception: OK, that's fine. Would you like a single or double room?

Woman: Do you have twin rooms?

Reception: Yes, we do.

Woman: I'd like to book a twin room, then. Does it have a private bathroom?

Reception: All our rooms have private bathrooms, madam.

Woman: Oh, OK. How much is that, please?

Reception: That's 240 euros, 120 a night.

Woman: Is breakfast included?

Reception: No, it isn't. Breakfast is ten euros.

Woman: OK. Oh, just one thing. Can I book a beauty treatment before we come?

Reception: Yes, madam. I can transfer you to the beauty salon, but can I take your name and credit card details first, please?

Recording 10.9

1

Reception: Can I help you, madam?

Woman: Yes. I asked for a twin room.

Reception: Yes, madam.

Woman: Well, you've given me a double room.

Reception: Oh, I am sorry, madam.

Woman: Can we have a twin room, please?

Reception: I'll just have a look ... yes, we have one on the second floor.

2

Reception: Reception. Can I help you?

Man: Yes, I asked for tea with my breakfast.

Reception: Yes?

Man: And you've given me coffee.

Reception: I'm sorry, sir. I'll call the kitchen and get you some tea.

Man: OK. Thank you.

3

Reception: Yes, sir, can I help you?

Man: Yes, I booked golf for this morning.

Reception: Yes, sir?

Man: The golf club has just told me that there isn't a booking for me.

Reception: Oh, that's strange. I'm sure the golf club can fit you in later. I'll call them and sort it out for you.

Unit 11. Learning

Recording 11.1

Biology, Chemistry, college, Geography, History, kindergarten, Languages,

Mathematics, Physics, polytechnic, primary school, Science, secondary school, university

Recording 11.2

Part 1

Welcome to the free Tourist Information Line for visitors to Great Britain. For information on visas and immigration, please press one. For information on driving in Britain, please press two. For information on hotels, please press three. For information on public transport in Britain, please press four. To return to this menu at any time press the star key. You have chosen option two: driving in Britain.

Part 2

If you have a valid driving licence from your own country, you can drive in Britain without a British licence for six months. After six months, you have to get a British driving licence. To get a British licence you have to take a driving test. You can find information about the British driving test on our website.

To rent a car in Britain you have to have a valid driving licence from your country and a credit card. Drivers under the age of 18 can't rent cars in Britain.

When you are driving in Britain, you don't have to keep your documents with you. The British drive on the left side of the road and, unlike the United States, you can't turn right at a red traffic light. For more information on British driving regulations, please look at our website. That is the end of the driving section. To return to the main menu press the star key.

Recording 11.3

You don't have to be a British citizen to take a British driving test but you have to have a valid British visa.

Recording 11.4

1 leaf 2 few 3 fan 4 v

Recording 11.5

1 Philip finds French films very violent.
2 Very few fines feel fair.
3 Fiona Philips never gives fitness advice to fresh fruit fanatics.

Recording 11.6

Steve:
We don't have a lot of rules in the United States really. I mean we don't have to do military service and we don't have to have identity cards. You can drive when you're 16 and you can even buy a gun when you're 21!

But some things aren't so easy. You have to be 21 to go into a bar or a nightclub, and smoking is difficult – you can't smoke in offices, shops or restaurants. And of course we have to pay when we see a doctor or go to hospital.

Recording 11.7

Interviewer: Nicole, tell us about the educational system in New Zealand. For example, how long do students spend in the system?

Nicole: Oh, … a long time! Usually about 17 or 18 years if they go to university.

Interviewer: When did you start school?

Nicole: At the age of five. Compulsory education is twelve years – from five to about sixteen, but a lot of children in New Zealand go to pre-school classes, you know, kindergartens. I went to a kindergarten when I was four and after a year I went to primary school.

Interviewer: How many years were you at primary school?

Nicole: Five years – from five to ten.

Interviewer: Where did you go after primary school?

Nicole: Well, then I went to an intermediate school, from ten to twelve. Then at twelve we start at secondary school.

Interviewer: Mmm. When can students leave secondary school?

Nicole: Well, we can leave secondary school at sixteen, but most students stay till they're eighteen.

Interviewer: Do a lot of students go on to higher education?

Nicole: Yes, I think about fifty per cent of students go into higher education – that's universities, polytechnics, colleges of education …

Interviewer: Which type of institution did you go to?

Nicole: I went to a college of education because I wanted to be a teacher. I became a primary teacher, so I studied for three years and finished when I was twenty-two.

Interviewer: Do you have to pay for your higher education studies in New Zealand?

Nicole: Yes, we have to pay some of the costs, but not all.

Interviewer: How much does a student have to pay?

Nicole: Oh, it depends. It can be 2,000 dollars or it can be 20,000.

Interviewer: Well, thank you, Nicole. That was very interesting …

Recording 11.8

1 What did you do there?
2 Was it interesting?
3 Who did you see? 4 Did you like it?

Recording 11.9

1 How does the educational system work?
2 How long do students spend in the system?
3 When did you start school?
4 How many years were you at primary school?
5 What subjects did you take?
6 Where did you go after primary school?
7 Which type of institution did you go to?
8 How much does a student have to pay?

Recording 11.10

Host: Good afternoon. Welcome to Live to Learn. People today often want to continue learning through their lives, but what are their choices? First, let's talk to Aileen Murphy, head of Haresfield Adult College.

Local College: Good afternoon. Well, at Haresfield College, we organise classes in local schools and in our centre. The classes are usually in the evening, but we do have some day classes. Most of our classes are once a week, for about three hours.

H: What can you study at your college?

LC: Well, we have classes in academic subjects, such as History. We offer five foreign languages and we also offer courses in vocational subjects like Computing.

H: How much do the courses cost?

LC: An average course costs about £100 for an academic year.

H: Thank you, Aileen. Now we have Graham Knight, from the Open University.

OU: Well, the Open University is a distance-learning university – that is, you study at home. There are a few classes during the year, and there are often summer schools. Our students have to study for about 12 hours a week.

H: Thank you, Graham. Oh, what about cost?

OU: Most of our courses are about £500 a year, at the moment.

H: Thanks. Now, Beth Anderson works for a professional training company, MicroMatters Ltd.

MM: Right. We offer training courses in computer skills for people who are actually working with computers.

H: Do you offer courses to people who aren't working?

MM: Oh, yes. Most of our courses last two or three days, for people in work, but we also have week-long courses and evening courses.

H: And the cost?

MM: A week's course costs about £900. Of course, we provide everything – the trainers, the training room, the computers – the trainees don't have to pay for any extras, so we aren't cheap.

H: Thank you. Now, finally, James Beecham, to tell us about the University of the Third Age.

U3A: Good afternoon. The University of the Third Age is for retired people, so it is mostly older people. We have groups across the country, and each group organises its own courses. Usually, the group uses a hall in its town, or a local school, and lecturers come to speak to the group. We try to make our type of learning very cheap. Members have to pay £2.50 to join, and then a small part of the costs – so it is very cheap.

H: Yes, I see. And what kind of courses or subjects do you offer?

U3A: Well, the speakers talk about their special subjects or their interests, so we have a lot of different topics, but it's not usually very academic.

H: Right. Thank you, everyone, for coming. Now, let's move on to …

Recording 11.11

Man: Hello. Staff room.

Carlos: Hello. Can I speak to Mrs Alders, please?

Man: Just a moment. I'll get her. Jill, it's for you.

Alders: Hello. Jill Alders.

Carlos: Mrs Alders? It's Carlos Brent. My son, Karl, is in your class.

Alders: Oh yes, Mr Brent. How can I help you?

Carlos: I'd like to meet you next week to talk about Karl's examinations.

Alders: Fine. Can you come on Thursday? I'm teaching in the morning but I'm free in the afternoon.

Carlos: I'm afraid I can't come then because I'm working. What about Wednesday?

Alders: No, I'm afraid I'm teaching all day on Wednesday.

Carlos: Well, I can come on Tuesday.

Alders: Er, Tuesday. Well, I'm teaching a class at ten thirty and I'm taking the children swimming in the afternoon.

Carlos: How about earlier in the morning?

Alders: Let me see … OK. Let's meet at nine o'clock.

Carlos: Nine o'clock on Tuesday morning. Thank you very much.

Alders: I'll see you next week then. You can come to the staff room …

Unit 12. Ambitions

Recording 12.1

Dario: Look, here's the photo of us rafting on the Colorado River last summer.

Mia: Oh yes. That was so frightening. I didn't really enjoy that – the raft went so fast! It was really dangerous.

Dario: Well, I thought it was fantastic.

Mia: I preferred trekking in the Grand Canyon really.

Dario: Yes, that was fun. But a bit slow. And do you remember when we went on those bikes in the hills behind San Francisco?

Mia: Yes. I remember cycling up the hills and through all those tunnels!

Dario: Yes, that was great.

Mia: Mm, I really enjoyed that. Do you think that was the best part of our trip?

Dario: No, horse-riding was the best. That was really exciting.

Mia: Yeah, You're right. I think horse-riding was my favourite too. It was a lot of fun.

Recording 12.2

I'm going to stop smoking.

Recording 12.3

1 She's going to lose weight.
2 They're going to sell their car.
3 We're going to learn French.
4 I'm going to buy a laptop.

Recording 12.4

Song: Fame!

Baby look at me
And tell me what you see
You ain't seen the best of me yet
Give me time and I'll make you forget the rest
I've got more in me
And you can set it free
I can catch the moon in my hand
Don't you know who I am?
Remember my name

Chorus
Fame!
I'm gonna live forever
I'm gonna learn how to fly
Fame! I feel it coming together
People will see me and cry
Fame! I'm gonna make it to heaven
Light up the sky like a flame
Fame! I'm gonna live forever
Baby, remember my name!

Recording 12.5

1 Victoria

I've joined the drama group at university because I really love performing. I'm going to learn how to sing and dance. I want to act in plays and musicals and of course I'd like to be famous one day. Sometimes TV producers watch our student shows so anything is possible!

2 Helena

My ambition is to become a famous politician, perhaps a minister in the government. At the moment I'm just a student – I'm studying politics at college. But I'm going to work for a politician next summer. I want to learn more about elections and voting. I'm really excited about it.

3 Lewis

I've just had my first training session with the team, so I'm a bit tired. It's only the reserve team but I'm going to practise with them twice a week to improve my physical fitness and ball control skills. I'm going to work really hard to get into the first team. I know I'm a good footballer and I'm sure I'm good enough to get a place in a professional team. These days footballers are the biggest stars in the world, and I'd really like to be rich and famous.

Recording 12.6

Andi: Good morning. Charity Challenge, Andi speaking. How can I help you?

David: Oh, hello. My name's David MacMahon. I'm interested in doing one of your challenges and I'd like to ask some questions.

Andi: That's fine, David. Please, go ahead.

David: Well, first, where exactly do the challenges take place?

Andi: All over the world, in Africa, Latin America, and the Caribbean, Asia, the Middle East and Europe.

David: Oh, I see. And what kind of challenges are they? I mean, what kind of activities are they?

Andi: Well, we have hiking, cycling, sailing, rafting, mountain climbing and horse-riding.

David: Oh good. I enjoy hiking and I love cycling – I use my bike every day – but I hate horse-riding and I don't like sailing.

Andi: What about rafting and mountain climbing?

David: I wouldn't like to climb a mountain, and I've never done any rafting, but I'd like to try. Do you have to be very fit?

Andi: Yes, you do. Our expeditions are difficult and you have to have a good level of fitness. Choose an activity you know you can do, start training very early and join a gym.

David: Oh, I can't stand going to the gym … it's so boring, but I can train in other ways.

Andi: Yes, and we have training weekends. People find them very useful.

David: Yes, I think I'd like to do a training weekend. How often do you have them?

Andi: About once a month.

David: OK. Who pays for the expedition?

Andi: Well, you pay for the expedition. We also ask you to raise money for your charity.

David: Oh, yes, of course. Who chooses the charity?

Andi: You choose the charity. Do you have any other questions, David?

David: Yes, just one. How do I raise the money?

Andi: We can help you with ideas. For example, you could do a car boot sale to get money.

David: Oh, I'd like to do that. I love going to car boot sales, but I've never done one.

Andi: OK. So do you want to join one of our expeditions, David?

David: I want to think about it for a few days. I'd like to find out more. Can you send me some information?

Andi: Certainly. I can send you a brochure and …

Recording 12.7

I'd really like to play the classical guitar.

Recording 12.8

1 white 2 Dave 3 late 4 mine 5 lake

Recording 12.9

1 I hate waiting for bus rides in the rain.
2 Mike likes riding his bike but he hates playing games.
3 We prefer safe day trains to late night flights.